Born Out of Place

Born Out of Place

MIGRANT MOTHERS AND THE POLITICS
OF INTERNATIONAL LABOR

Nicole Constable

UNIVERSITY OF CALIFORNIA PRESS
Berkeley   Los Angeles   London

University of California Press, one of the most distinguished university presses in the United States, enriches lives around the world by advancing scholarship in the humanities, social sciences, and natural sciences. Its activities are supported by the UC Press Foundation and by philanthropic contributions from individuals and institutions. For more information, visit www.ucpress.edu.

University of California Press
Berkeley and Los Angeles, California

University of California Press, Ltd.
London, England

Library of Congress Cataloging-in-Publication Data

Constable, Nicole.
    Born out of place : migrant mothers and the politics of international labor / Nicole Constable.
        pages cm
    Includes bibliographical references and index.
    ISBN 978-0-520-28201-8 (hardback)—
    ISBN 978-0-520-28202-5 (paper)—
    ISBN 978-0-520-95777-0 (ebook)
    1. Women immigrants—China—Hong Kong—Social conditions.
    2. Hong Kong (China)—Emigration and immigration. 3. Women foreign workers—China—Hong Kong—Social conditions.
    4. Emigration and immigration—Social aspects. I. Title.
    JV6347.C65 2014
    306.874′308864095125—dc23

                                                2013036683

Manufactured in the United States of America

23 22 21 20 19 18 17 16 15 14
10 9 8 7 6 5 4 3 2 1

In keeping with a commitment to support environmentally responsible and sustainable printing practices, UC Press has printed this book on Natures Natural, a fiber that contains 30% post-consumer waste and meets the minimum requirements of ANSI/NISO Z39.48–1992 (R 1997) (*Permanence of Paper*).

In honor of my mother
In memory of my father

Contents

Illustrations

Preface

The most striking migratory pattern of the late twentieth and early twenty-first centuries is of young women from poorer parts of the so-called Global South or Third World who provide intimate labor—as caregivers, cleaners, cooks, nurses, sex workers, entertainers—for those in and from the wealthier parts of the Global North or First World. Much has been written about this gendered migration: about labor import and export schemes; the parasitic relationships created by the policies of sending and receiving governments; the capitalist and neoliberal institutions that broker and profit from labor migration and intimate labor; and the precarious, cheap, disposable, exploitable, and replaceable nature of such workers.

Governments in poorer, migrant-sending regions of the world, such as Indonesia and the Philippines, facing unemployment, underemployment, poverty, and debt, promote female labor exportation as a solution to their economic and development problems. At the same time, these governments face their citizens' popular concern about the shame of exporting young women, the harm and violence they might experience far from home, and the possible damage that female migration does to families. Meanwhile, neoliberal governments of wealthier, migrant-receiving regions like Hong Kong, Taiwan, Singapore, and the Gulf States welcome the importation of women workers as a cheap, market-driven solution to their own shortage of local labor available to look after the children, elderly, sick, and disabled and to do the household work of the growing middle classes. The citizens of receiving countries mainly want easy access to inexpensive, reliable, and disciplined workers who know their place, work hard, and then go home. These temporary workers and outsiders provide the "good life" for local citizens while they seek to improve their own lives as well.

The impacts of migration on migrant workers' home countries, including the value of their remittances and the detrimental effects of women's absence on the marriages and children they leave behind, have received significant attention. Migrant workers have been the subject of academic, government, and nongovernmental organization surveys and research. Yet one critical subject that has been largely overlooked, perhaps because it is invisible or because it is linked with notions of national or personal failure, dishonor, and shame, is that of babies born of migrant workers abroad.

Born out of Place focuses on the largely invisible and often overlooked topic of babies born of migrant worker mothers. Such a focus brings to light the flaws and unintended consequences of migration laws and labor policies, the often poignant and painful experiences of migrant mothers, and the ambivalent roles of fathers. Within the context of contemporary global capitalism, this research yields a deeper understanding of the practical problems and the cruel disappointments faced by those who take part in "guest worker" programs. New insights about the problem—some would say the crisis—of temporary migration, which all too often is not temporary, are revealed through ethnographic research that attends to the everyday lives and stories of migrant mothers and their Hong Kong–born babies.

My first argument in this book is simple: temporary migrant workers are expected to enter the destination country as *workers*, setting aside other aspects of their lives. But they are not and never can be *only* workers. As in the quip attributed to Swiss writer Max Frisch following the post–World War II guest-worker program in Germany, "We asked for workers; we got people." It is "people" who are often seen as the antithesis of good migrant workers. It is people who dare to become mothers and lovers—by accident or by design. Their humanity unveiled, they are often deemed not only bad workers but also ungrateful or even immoral women who have failed their families and their nation.

Migrant workers with babies in Hong Kong are an anomaly and a surprise. To some locals, a pregnant domestic worker is the epitome of the bad—immoral, undisciplined, undedicated, ungrateful—"helper." She should have an abortion or go home. Yet, as this book describes, there are other options and many other routes she can follow. Thousands of babies are born of former domestic workers who marry locals and become permanent residents. There are also thousands more Hong Kong–born children of current or former domestic workers, some of whom remain there with mothers who overstay their visas or who file asylum or torture claims in an effort to delay or avoid returning to their home countries. Migrant mothers strive for fuller lives, with children and partners, but their "good life" fantasies often prove fragile and fleeting.

My second main argument is that the laws and policies meant to create a revolving door—intended to ensure that domestic workers leave the region when their contracts expire, to prevent overstaying and illegal work, and to ensure that they are *only* workers—often have precisely the opposite effect. Some women become pregnant after they overstay, and many overstay because they are pregnant.

My third argument is that women who return home as "single mothers" often face severe stigma and economic pressures that propel them to continue in what I call a *migratory cycle of atonement*: a self-perpetuating, precarious pattern of migration that is often the only route to escape the shame that single motherhood brings to them and their families. Remitting money is one means of absolving themselves of the stigma of single parenthood and "failed" migration. The everyday experiences and challenges faced by these mothers and their babies provide a unique angle on the precarity of temporary migration and the underlying inequalities of citizenship and belonging.

Acknowledgments

My work among Filipino and Indonesian migrant workers, mothers and children, asylum seekers and torture claimants, advocates and service providers, lawyers, activists, and volunteers has been immensely humbling and gratifying. Despite the pain and tears—witnessed and shed—it was a privilege to share the lives of migrant women and their children. I am deeply grateful to the children for their unforgettable hugs, shrieks, and greetings; to the migrant women for their kindness, honesty, and generosity; and to those who welcomed, trusted, challenged me and offered sustenance over the years.

PathFinders and its dedicated directors and staff helped make this project possible. Corazon Cañete first introduced me to PathFinders, Kylie Uebergang welcomed me and gave me a key to the office, and Lia Ngatini opened doors for me to meet people, see things, and go places I never imagined. Nancy Lee, Ada Yip, Luna Chan, Jennifer Lee-Shoy, and many others shared expert knowledge, valuable insights, and friendship, and they kindly tolerated my interruptions and questions.

The community of migrant workers and activists in Hong Kong is phenomenal. I am forever thankful to Cynthia Abdon Tellez and the Mission for Migrant Workers for introducing me to migrant workers almost twenty years ago; to Ramon Bultron and Rey Asis, Asia-Pacific Mission for Migrants; Edwina Antonio Santoyo, Bethune House; Eni Lestari, International Migrants Alliance; Rendy Wasiarting, Association of Indonesian Migrant Workers; Dolores Balladares and Eman Villanueva, United Filipinos in Hong Kong; Sr. Madeenah Molina, Helpers of Islam; Sringatin, Indonesian Migrant Workers Union; Holly Allen, Helpers for Domestic Helpers; and Doris Lee, OpenDoor. The following organizations helped in many ways: African Community, Christian Action, the Hong Kong Labour and Immigration Departments, Mother's Choice, Philippine Consulate General, Seeking Refuge Hong Kong, St. John's Cathedral HIV Education Centre, United Nations High Commissioner for Refugees, and Vision First, as did the following extremely obliging individuals: Peter Barnes, Cosmo Beatson, Jonnet Bernal, Richard Butt, Janet and Norman Carnay, Michele Chan, Richard Clement, Mark Daly, Irene Domingo, Elija Fung, Sithi Hawwa, Chandrika Kularatne, Lisa Lee, Charles Macaspac, Daisy Mandap, Devi Novianti, Sol Pillar, Mohammad Sunnah, Revd. Dwight dela Torre, Michael Vidler, and Jan Yumul.

Friends and colleagues at the Chinese University of Hong Kong, Hong Kong University, Hong Kong Baptist University, and National University of Singapore, including Joe Bosco, Sidney Cheung, Sikying Ho, Shirlena Huang, Hans Ladergaard, Maria Tam, and Brenda Yeoh, provided input and vital opportunities to talk about my research in progress. Gordon Mathews generously commented on the manuscript and introduced me to great people in Chungking Mansions. Sealing Cheng, Tsz-Wah Tse, Eliot and Ariel, and Tess provided friendship, inspiration, and intellectual and other forms of nourishment.

Nancy Abelmann, Joe Alter, Gabriella Lukacs, Kevin Ming, Melody Ornellas, and Carol Chan offered intellectual insights and comments, and they helped fuel my interests in gendered migration, citizenship, precarity, and hope. Thanks to Naomi Schneider for her support over many years, to the anonymous reviewers, to Julia Zafferano for copyediting, and to Michael Duckworth for opening doors for copublication with Hong Kong University Press. Dean N. John Cooper and the Dietrich School of Arts and Sciences provided essential research time and funding.

My deepest gratitude is to the many migrant women and children—my global daughters and grandchildren—in Hong Kong, Indonesia, the

Philippines, and beyond who captured my heart, and I am grateful to the men and fathers too. To protect their confidentiality, I cannot list their many names and give them the proper recognition they deserve. I hope they understand my reasons. This book is my tribute to them.

Last but not least, words cannot express my love and thanks to Joe Alter and to Peter and Nathaniel Constable Alter, who make my life much fuller and less precarious than it would otherwise be.

Nicole Constable
Pittsburgh, Pennsylvania, USA

1 A Very Tiny Problem

> Regardless of her own subjective intention or purposes, a
> foreign domestic helper's stay in Hong Kong is for a very
> special, limited purpose from society's point of view—to
> meet society's acute demand for domestic helpers which
> cannot be satisfactorily met by the local labour market.
> Hence, their stays in Hong Kong are highly regulated so as
> to ensure that they are here to fulfil the special, limited
> purpose for which they have been allowed to come here in
> the first place, and no more.
>
> — High Court Chief Justice Andrew Cheung (2012, 50)

MIGRANTS AND THEIR BABIES

Babies of migrant workers are "just a very tiny problem" in relation to
the "much bigger issues migrant workers face," said a staff member
from a Hong Kong migrant advocacy nongovernmental organization
dismissively, after I described my research topic. His comment stuck
with me as I pondered how best to explain the critical situation of
migrant workers' pregnancies and babies. Babies born of migrant workers are indeed tiny, and the number born in Hong Kong is probably
several hundred each year, with the cumulative total in the thousands.[1]
The number of pregnancies is, of course, much higher than the number
of babies born in Hong Kong, since some women opt for abortions and
many return home to give birth in their own country. But despite the
innocuous image of thousands of very small, innocent babies and young
children, the topic and the issues surrounding them are of critical
importance.

1

Born within the wider context of colonial and post-colonial global inequalities that help fuel labor migration, migrants' babies cut right to the heart of many problems surrounding temporary labor migration in the world today. They serve as a barometer of wider structural problems, social meanings, and migratory policies. A window into understanding changing cultural values and the more subtle and symbolic meanings of mobility, they raise critical questions about citizenship and belonging. They serve as a focal point for understanding differences and inequalities of gender, class, race, religion, family, and sexuality. Babies are indeed a very tiny problem, but they are central to what it means to be human and to how we understand and practice humanism and humanitarianism.

Stories of migrant mothers, their babies, and the fathers are increasingly relevant to the many regions of the world in which temporary workers or "guest workers"—among the most precarious of workers—are imported to fill local labor needs for cheap, docile, and flexible workers who work for lower wages and without the social benefits of locals and citizens. Little thought is given to the issue of children or to the stigma that mothers and children might carry to their home countries. Propelled by poverty and lack of opportunities at home, which are part of the colonial legacy as well as further fueled by post-colonial, neoliberal economic policies that benefit the wealthy and privileged, migrants seek out opportunities to work abroad. Increasingly, global labor migrants are young women in the prime of their child-bearing years who leave their families behind or delay childbirth for the sake of employment. Inevitably—by choice or by accident—some become pregnant and have babies.

The question of what to do about migrants' babies is echoed in many regions of the world, including North America, Europe, and Asia, where heated debates are waged regarding migration, birthrights, citizenship, and belonging. Cheap flexible workers are desired but not their children. In the United States in 2010, Congress debated repeal of the Fourteenth Amendment granting citizenship as a birthright, raised vehement criticisms of so-called "anchor babies," and voted down the DREAM Act (Development, Relief, and Education for Alien Minors) amid growing anti-immigrant hostility.[2] In 2013, such debates continued in the United States, fueled by new, controversial guest-worker schemes. In Israel in 2009, 1,200 children of migrant workers were due for deportation, which raised public outcry and global media attention, protest marches in Tel Aviv, and a vehement debate that largely pitted humanitarian values and the Jewish history of migration against the preservation of Jewish identity and the promotion of the Jewish state. The following year, a "compromise" was reached, and 800 children were permitted to remain.[3] In Japan in 2008, after many years of legal battles, the presiding judge of Japan's Supreme Court announced the decision to grant Japanese nationality to ten Japanese Filipino children (colloquially known as "Japinos") "born to unmarried Filipino women and Japanese men, and who were legally acknowledged by the men after birth" (Suzuki 2010, 31). Later that year, another law was changed so that parental marriage was no longer required for a child to become a Japanese national. Public reactions to these changes revealed "fear and concern about Japanese national sovereignty" (Suzuki 2010, 44–45). As similar issues are raised in Ireland (Luibhéid 2004a; Bhabha 2009), parts of Europe (Van Walsum 2009; Soysal 1994), and other regions of the world, we begin to see the political, nationalistic, legalistic, global, transnational, and ideological issues that come to play around a baby *born out of place* (Benhabib and Resnick 2009).

In Hong Kong, babies often make headlines—not so much the babies of migrant workers, who mostly stay out of the limelight, but the wider shortage of babies and stories having to do with mainland women's babies. Hong Kong, like Singapore, Japan, South Korea, and other wealthy areas of Asia, has a strikingly low fertility rate and an anticipated future labor shortage (Watson 2010; Bowring 2011; Ngo 2012). The babies of mainland Chinese mothers who flock to Hong Kong to give birth are subject to vehement public hostility (Newendorp 2008; Ornellas 2012). As Chinese citizens, Hong Kong–born babies of mainlanders are entitled to Hong Kong permanent residence, known locally as "right of abode," but they are widely viewed as a threat to local identity and to locals' material well-being. Fervent opposition to mainland Chinese mothers giving birth in Hong Kong hospitals, even those married to Hong Kong men, reached a hysterical climax in 2011–12 when they were blamed for causing a critical shortage of hospital beds and of pre- and post-natal medical care facilities for Hong Kong citizens. Mainlanders were popularly depicted as locusts or leeches, spawning out of control, devouring everything, leaving only waste in their wake.[4] Following anti-mainlander protests and public expressions of hostility, the Hong Kong government effectively banned most mainland mothers from giving birth in the city starting in January 2013. Hong Kong—which has one of the largest gaps between rich and poor in the world—relies economically on its mainland neighbors, but it also fears an influx of poor and "other" migrants. Against this backdrop, babies of migrant workers are unwanted and unwelcome but to a large extent unknown.

INDAH, TIKA, AND BABY NINA

My first memory of Indah is of her sitting on a tiny couch, crying, being comforted by Liana, who spoke to her gently but firmly in Javanese. Indah was gaunt, with protruding cheek bones and deep circles under her eyes. Tika, five years old then, seemed more curious than upset as she studied me and Liana, the two strange women her mother had invited into their home, from a distance. Tika repeatedly ran up the metal spiral stairs to see her sleeping father, then back down. We did not see or hear him. Baby Nina, who was less than a year old and could crawl, tried to follow Tika. I was on edge, afraid Nina would fall between the steps. As Tika watched, I laid out the board game we had brought. It was not the Barbie game she had longed for, but it had Mickey Mouse, Pooh Bear, and other characters she liked. Liana had brought Tika a pencil sharpener and colored pencils, knowing she loved to draw. At first Tika was shy about showing us her drawings, but, at her mother's urging, she displayed skilled sketches of her parents.

To get to Indah's place from the Kam Sheung Road Mass-Transit Railway (MTR) station, a region of the New Territories that is home to many of Hong Kong's "ethnic minorities"—including Pakistani, Sri Lankan, Indian, Bangladeshi, and Nepalese asylum seekers, residents, and undocumented workers—Liana and I had headed to a village with many new, attractive three-story homes, a world away from the crowded urban Kowloon neighborhood where I lived. The sun set as we walked along the unpaved path behind the village. The house we sought was near some neglected vegetable fields, next to a shallow stagnant pond and piles of construction debris. It was dilapidated. Dogs belonging to an old disabled

Chinese man who rented the downstairs apartment barked angrily. The place reeked of dog urine; mosquitoes buzzed overhead. The upstairs windows and balcony were hidden by striped plastic sheets and plywood boards. We carried a heavy bag of rice and other supplies up three flights of stairs to the top floor where Indah and her family lived. They rented a corner room that served as the living area and kitchen, and they slept in a makeshift space on the roof, despite the recent government crackdown against such illegal structures. Tika was rollerblading on the narrow balcony when we arrived.

Indah had seen PathFinders, the charity organization where Liana worked, advertised in a copy of *Suara*, the local Indonesian free newspaper that her sister, a domestic worker, left when they last met. The ad offered free assistance to migrant women with children who want to find a safe path home. Indah was desperate to leave her self-imposed prison in Hong Kong. A few years earlier, she had tried to leave. She went to the Indonesian Consulate for help but was turned away by a staff member because she had no passport. Like many foreign domestic workers whose passports are confiscated or "taken for safekeeping" by an employer or an employment agency, or are lost or sold out of desperation, Indah had no passport. When Indah saw the ad in *Suara*, it brought her to tears, and she felt hope "for the first time in years." She phoned the hotline. Liana answered, immediately grasped the gravity of the situation, and arranged our visit.

Between tears, Indah poured out her worries: her severely drug-addicted Nepalese husband no longer provided money for subsistence; they were behind on their rent and could be evicted at any moment; she could not ask her sister for money because she had her own debts and children to support; her Hong Kong–born children lacked birth certificates; and Tika should already be attending school. Indah had recently seen police or immigration officers searching the village, which reinforced her fear and self-imposed isolation. She stayed indoors and was low on food. The winter temperature on the roof had been close to freezing. Even though the children were dressed warmly and looked healthy, they could not afford to be sick, and they had not received childhood inoculations.

Liana assured Indah that PathFinders could help. She told her about a shelter where she could stay with the children, but—due to their regulations—only after she surrendered to the Hong Kong Immigration Department. It was dark by the time we left. By then, Nina had fallen asleep at her mother's breast, and Tika had warmed to us. We promised to return the next day with more food. Tika energetically waved good-bye from behind the plastic sheeting, shouting "see you tomorrow" and flashing her winning smile as we walked down the village path into the dark. It was a greeting that I became used to and then missed deeply once I left Hong Kong. The distant "talk to you soon" over Skype and then later on a muffled telephone line when they returned to Central Java were a poor substitute.

On our way home, Liana and I talked about Indah's dire circumstances. Only later would I began to think of her vulnerable, stripped-down existence in relation to concepts of "bare life" (Agamben 1998), "precarity" (Puar 2012; Butler 2004), "cruel optimism" (Berlant 2011), and "zones of social abandonment" (Biehl 2005), all of which contribute to my analysis of the lives of migrant mothers and children in relation to the inequalities of temporary migration. At that time, I knew that Indah had overstayed longer than most of the women I met and had two undocumented children. Most women surrendered to the authorities when their children were younger than Tika, and they wanted to stay in Hong Kong as long as possible, whereas Indah had been worn down over time and was desperate to leave.

At the time, Liana and I wondered if Indah would leave her husband. She was deeply attached to him and worried sick about separating Tika from her father. But she was also concerned about the children's physical well-being. She agonized about what would happen to them if she surrendered and had to serve time in prison for "overstaying." Women we knew with babies who had not been caught working illegally, and who surrendered after overstaying less than two years, typically received suspended sentences (no custodial time), but those who overstayed more than two years or were caught working illegally had mostly served time. Nina, who was still nursing, might be allowed to stay with Indah in prison, but Tika was too old. Indah dreaded the thought of Tika going to a welfare institution and being separated from both parents. These worries consumed her for the next several months.

Liana and I made plans to visit Indah the next afternoon, but that night Indah phoned Liana, resolved to leave as soon as possible. The next morning, while I spoke at a local university, Liana accompanied Indah, Tika, and Nina to the Immigration Department in Kowloon Bay to sur- render. That began the next chapter of their lives and the many emotion- ally fraught and bureaucratically complicated months along their path back to a dirt-poor region of Central Java, a "home" that Nina and Tika did not know and that Indah had left behind a decade earlier.

MIGRANT MOTHERS, MARGINAL BABIES

In Hong Kong, the primary and—some would say—exclusive government- regulated role of "foreign domestic helpers" is to provide the "good life" for their employers (Agamben 1998; Ong 2009). They are prohibited from bringing family members, including children and spouses, with them. Nonetheless, despite many obstacles, some domestic workers like Indah manage to give birth and to create small and usually temporary families in Hong Kong. A lucky few manage to obtain Hong Kong residency for their children if not for themselves.

"Helpers," as they are commonly called, must leave their own families behind and make the Hong Kong employer's household their first priority. They are denied permanent residency or citizenship in Hong Kong and are allowed there "to fulfil the special, limited purpose [of their employ- ment] . . . and no more," as bluntly stated by Justice Andrew Cheung, the presiding magistrate in the 2012 High Court ruling that sided with the Hong Kong government in opposition to the rights of foreign domestic workers to apply for permanent residency. As this book illustrates, how- ever, migrant workers are never *only* workers. Although their lives are highly regulated by employers, agencies, and the sending and receiving states, they nonetheless manage to have personal lives, relationships, and sometimes babies abroad.

Migrant mothers and their Hong Kong–born babies—like Indah, Tika, and Nina—are at the heart of this book. The mothers are mostly in their twenties or thirties and mostly from Indonesia (Central and East Java) and the Philippines. Motivated by a desire for a better life for themselves and their families, they originally came to Hong Kong as "foreign domes- tic helpers" (FDHs), in official parlance, or as "foreign domestic workers"

(FDWs), the term preferred by politically active domestic workers because it highlights the significance of their labor (as opposed to minimizing it as "help"). Unlike previous studies (my own included) that aimed to understand them primarily by virtue of their roles as workers and migrants, my aim here is to understand their wider experiences becoming mothers in Hong Kong and how policies and practices shape their choices as well as their own and their children's lives. The children in this research, who range from newborns to a few like Tika who are a bit older, could not speak for themselves, but they nonetheless constantly reminded me, and their mothers, that they were there. Born "overseas" to migrant mothers, they are in a much different situation than that described in studies of children who are "left behind" in the migrant mother's home country (Parreñas 2001, 2005; Silvey 2006) or who go overseas to join their migrant mothers years later (Pratt 2012). Mothers, babies, and children at the heart of this study show us how multiple policies, laws, practices, conflicting desires and assumptions, social values, and expectations of morality affect their everyday lives.

Whereas much of this book draws on the experiences and words of mothers, their children are always there, laughing or crying, playing or sleeping, hungry, sick, or needing attention. Fathers are also part of this study. A few fathers were deeply attached to their children, but most played only a temporary, secondary, or tangential role in their lives. Some men provided nothing more than the sperm that led to conception. In a few cases, the fathers were spouses living in Indonesia or the Philippines, where the child was conceived, or they were Filipino men who worked in Hong Kong as domestic workers alongside their wives. In most of the cases I followed, the babies were conceived in Hong Kong and the fathers were men of many different nationalities, including local or mainland Chinese, South Asians (from India, Pakistan, Nepal, Bangladesh, and Sri Lanka), Africans (from Congo, Ghana, Mali, Niger, Nigeria, and elsewhere), or Westerners (from North America, Europe, and the United Kingdom). Many of the African and South Asian fathers are asylum seekers. Some women were legally married to local resident men, whereas others had long-term relationships (like Indah and her partner) or took part in a religious or informal marriage. In some cases, the men disappeared at the first sign of pregnancy or were unaware of it after a one-night stand, a brief relationship, or, in the worst cases, rape. Sometimes, men only learned about the pregnancy later when they faced paternity claims in family court.

In her study of "illegal" migrants in Israel, Sarah Willen (2007a, 2007b) promotes a "tripartite approach" to understanding the connections between juridical status, sociopolitical conditions, and lived experiences. Similarly, the stories and lived experiences of mothers and babies described in this book are shaped by Hong Kong laws and policies in which FDWs are defined as temporary workers and noncitizens who cannot qualify for residency, even after working there for decades. Mothers' experiences are colored by the sociocultural, historical, and political-economic conditions of Hong Kong as well as those of their countries of origin and sometimes also by international laws and conventions. Mothers' experiences point to global patterns of inequality that perpetuate and naturalize migration as the best or only solution to poverty paired with single motherhood.

As I argue, gender is an integral part of why migrant mothers choose to overstay and work illegally in Hong Kong. They do so not because of their shortcomings or moral failings but because of the shortcomings of laws and policies in Hong Kong and abroad that make it virtually impossible to be a good worker as well as a good wife, mother, and daughter. In other words, the migrant mothers in this book confound Hong Kong's attempt to fashion them as *just workers*, and they also confound their home country's view of them as immoral or bad women. Women who overstay with their children and take up illegal work often do so precisely to *be* good mothers *and* workers, something they find impossible to do "legally" in Hong Kong or if they return home.

Women who return home with their children often resort to migrating again. They do not leave because they lack commitment to their children or out of selfishness and consumer desires but in order to be good mothers and daughters. Many women have little choice but to reenter what I call the *migratory cycle of atonement* so as to spare their children and their immediate families the shame and stigma associated with what is called, in Indonesia, *wanita jalang* or *wanita tuna susila* (bad girls or women of loose morals), terms that include prostitutes and single mothers. Not only is ongoing migration a way for single mothers to escape criticism, condemnation, and stigma, but it is also a way to spare her family shame by association. Other than remarriage, which was very rare among returned mothers I knew, migration offers a way to absolve herself in the eyes of her family and neighbors. It is a way to atone for her failings, to be recast as a good daughter and mother who sends remittances home for her family to build a house or install concrete floors or walls, buy land, or start a business. Only by entering the migratory cycle of atonement can her failings be temporarily overlooked or forgotten, at least until her remittances stop or the impact of her investments are no longer felt. In other words, gender inequalities and social stigma—specifically as attached to single mothers, adulterers, prostitutes, and "bad girls"—further fuel and perpetuate migration, complicating simple assumptions about family, mobility, citizenship, and belonging, and contributing to the supply of women workers for the global market.

CITIZENSHIP AND THE GOOD LIFE

As temporary migrants, FDWs are excluded from becoming permanent residents or citizens of Hong Kong. "Citizenship" may be a strange word to use in relation to Hong Kong, since it is not a nation-state but a global city with a population that is 95 percent Chinese, and it has been a Special Administrative Region (SAR) of China since the end of the British colonial period on July 1, 1997, when the "One country, Two systems" policy went into effect and Hong Kong was to function with its own economic and political system for fifty years, as spelled out in the Basic Law (Hong Kong's mini-constitution). Although some people hold an HKSAR passport, most non-Chinese permanent residents must maintain a passport from elsewhere. Permanent residence, or right of abode in Hong Kong, is like political citizenship. It entitles a person to vote and to all local political rights. Permanent residents are not subject to special "conditions of stay" and cannot be deported, in contrast to an array of others, including FDWs.

Hong Kong's process for obtaining "citizenship" (that is, permanent residence or right of abode), in the sense of political belonging, is spelled out in the Basic Law and Immigration Ordinance (CAP 115), although both were subject to legal debate at the time of this research. Normal practices by the government are that babies who are born in Hong Kong of Chinese nationals (including Chinese mainlanders) or Hong Kong permanent residents automatically obtain right of abode (assuming the parent acknowledges the child).[5] As in many parts of Asia, this system represents a combination of *jus soli* (birthright based on birth in a territory) and *jus sanguinis* (blood right, whereby citizenship is inherited from one or both parents) (Shipper 2010).

A citizen of another country, according to the Immigration Ordinance (CAP 115, paragraph 2d), can obtain permanent residence if he or she "entered Hong Kong with a valid travel document, has ordinarily resided in Hong Kong for a continuous period of not less than 7 years and has taken Hong Kong as his or her place of permanent residence." Non-Chinese under 21 qualify for permanent residence (2e), if they are "born in Hong Kong to a parent who is a permanent resident of the HKSAR in category (d) . . . if at the time of his or her birth, or at any later time before he or she attains 21 years of age, one parent has the right of abode in Hong Kong." For the babies in this book, permanent residency rights are fairly unambiguous if the father is a Hong Kong permanent resident who recognizes the child, but this does not automatically give the mother the right to remain in Hong Kong, even if she is the sole caregiver (see chapter 6). In cases where the parents are only temporary migrants, such as domestic workers, asylum seekers, or refugees, the baby is assumed to belong elsewhere. The question of where such a child can go and what claims the child's mother can make to remain in Hong Kong are the subject of this book. "Returning home" to a place they have never been, and in which their mothers may be unwelcome and have no way to support them, is a challenge, especially with regard to the *wider* concept of citizenship.

"Citizenship" can be understood to refer to legal status and political citizenship, but it can be used more broadly and provocatively to include variations in social rights and privileges, thus raising questions about the "*substance* of citizenship" and meanings of belonging (Bosniak 2009, 127; Rosaldo 1994).[6] Men and women or majority and minority groups may share the same stated political rights, but there may be differences based on gender, ethnicity, religion, class, sexuality, generation, and so forth. Children and, in some times and places, women cannot vote; nationality may be determined by the gender or marital status of the parent; and people are excluded from "belonging" by virtue of being gay or a member of a religious or other minority group. Others, such as migrant workers, are excluded from citizenship in the host country in both the political and the wider social sense.

Hannah Arendt and Giorgio Agamben have drawn attention to distinctions in early states between noncitizen women household workers and citizens whose good life depends on the exclusion of others. These distinctions are remarkably fitting in Hong Kong today. Exclusion from citizenship divides those who belong to the nation-state and are entitled to its rights and privileges from those who generally are not. Those who belong are entitled to a "good life," which refers not only to the vernacular idea of living well but to the distinction between *zoe* (natural life), which is associated with *zen* (simple or bare life), and *bios* (formal life), which is associated with *eu zen* (the good life) (Agamben 1998, 2). Good life is made possible by the role of the state in transforming bare life (or basic existence) into good life. Arendt argues (1958, 144, 28) that, in early states, life-sustaining reproductive labor was located in the private sphere (*oikos*) and done by women and slaves so that free men or citizens were spared from the repetitive chores of household life to participate in the *polis* or public sphere. Agamben expanded this dichotomy to apply to "states of exception" where bare life exists outside the polity (9–13).

The dichotomy between bare life and good life has been aptly criticized as too static and dichotomous, and Judith Butler and Gayatri Chakravorty Spivak argue (2007, 37–38) that bare life cannot be outside of the political field of power. Nonetheless, the term "bare life" in the sense of a life that it is slowly, through time, stripped of its hope, affect, and social relations, that is precarious, as Laurent Berlant describes, in the desperation and violence that take place "when the capitalist 'good life' fantasy no longer has anything to which to attach its promises of flourishing, coasting, and resting" and when hope and optimism erode away (in Puar 2012, 171; see also Berlant 2011), and that exists within "zones of social abandonment" (Biehl 2005) aptly describe Indah's circumstances and that of many other migrant parents and children I knew.

Despite growing demand and a recent shortage of domestic workers in Hong Kong, mainland Chinese are not considered a viable alternative.

Given their nationality and race, they would be much harder to regulate than Southeast Asian workers to ensure that they remained temporarily. FDWs are more identifiable and thus more easily regulated and excluded. With temporary visas and contracts, they are imported by agencies to Hong Kong and other parts of the world as "guest workers," a term that highlights their impermanence. They are welcomed to do the dirty work and to care for locals as long as they are docile and able-bodied. Without them, local women could not go out to work or lead lives of leisure. The state would be forced to come up with more costly solutions or perhaps admit problematic mainland workers. Neoliberal governmentality ensures the availability and precarity of cheap, flexible migrant workers for privileged citizens.

PRECARITY AND NOT QUITE "BARE LIFE"

Domestic workers sometimes face excruciating violence, debilitating mental and physical abuse, or, in the worst case, returning home in a coffin (Guevarra 2006; Rafael 2000; Torrevillas 1996). But, for the most part, except for those migrants in the worst slave-like conditions, describing their lives as a state of "terror" would be an overstatement. Most of them are not in the dire circumstances of concentration camp prisoners that epitomize Agamben's discussion of bare life. Most domestic workers who are employed are better off than asylum seekers and refugees, who have no legal right to work in Hong Kong. Domestic workers' lives appear fortunate from the perspective of those less fortunate: they are permitted to work, and their work legally entitles them to certain rights and protections. Yet, their lives overlap and intertwine in important ways with those of refugees and asylum seekers.

Life for domestic workers who have lost their jobs, been terminated with or without reason, and who remain in Hong Kong as overstayers or torture claimants—who then feel obliged to hide or work illegally—resembles bare life. They are, in a sense, "outlaws," but since "no exclusionary field can be set up between life and politics" they are never outside of politics (Butler and Spivak 2007, 38). Domestic workers are welcomed to Hong Kong as workers and not as people or citizens. They are not

welcome as women with families of their own or with sexual lives and relationships. They are stripped of these. One domestic worker was fired by
her employers when they discovered that she had a husband and children.
Despite their satisfaction with her work, they said they would not have
hired her had they known about her family. Another was terminated
because she washed a pair of men's brief with her laundry, which suggested
to her employers that she was sexually active. Many domestic workers cannot fathom combining domestic work and pregnancy and terminate their
own contracts when they become pregnant. They may experience terror
resembling bare life when they are out on the street with no job, no home,
mounting debts, and expired papers. A very young Indonesian woman
described how she slept near the Star Ferry or at McDonalds in Tsim Sha
Tsui after her employer kicked her out, then out of naivete and desperation
became the target of an African trader who befriended her, invited her to
his flat, seduced her, and later abused her. Another woman slept several
nights, terrified, in Kowloon Park until someone told her about a shelter.
Another was invited with her friends to a party; she awoke the next day
naked, in pain, remembering nothing, only later to learn that she was
pregnant.

When I first asked a nongovernmental-organization (NGO) director in
2010 about whether many fathers are in the picture, she replied, cynically
I thought at the time, that when the men are still around, the women are
often worse off. Later, I would hear this from some women firsthand,
including several who remained with physically abusive partners but who
feared single motherhood as a worse alternative. I watched and listened as
several women with cuts, bruises, and black eyes experienced the repeated
cycle of abuse and were gradually stripped of confidence, pride, and hope.
In other cases, like Indah's, where love and kindness were once clearly
present in the relationship, the emotional abuse was more subtle but all-
pervasive. She waited for years as her partner deteriorated and succumbed
to his addiction, recovered briefly, and relapsed again. He would give her
money for food and then take it back to buy drugs. Even though he was a
Hong Kong resident (or a dependent of one), Indah was unwilling to put
him on the children's birth certificates, because she knew staying in Hong
Kong would be her ruin. She hoped desperately that her leaving might
motivate him to change. Suicide crossed her mind, as it had a few women

I knew who weighed the option of returning home with "out of wedlock" children, as single mothers.

Tika voiced her five-year-old dreams in colored-pencil drawings. Her father would no longer be "sick"; he would come to Indonesia and marry her mother; then they would all go to Nepal and wait with her grandmother until her grandfather could sponsor them to come to the United States where they would see Aunty Nicole again. The wedding dress Tika drew for Indah was long with large flowers all over; she wore "Barbie shoes." She asked her mother, "Do you want a white dress or a pink one?" "You decide," Indah said wearily. Tika chose white. Her father had a beard (she called it "a moustache"), and she drew a talking bubble near his mouth and explained with a giggle that he was saying "I love you." Indah no longer believed in fairytales. She survived on nerves and just did what the NGO, the Immigration Department, the Birth Registry, the Consulate, and others said. Tika had more energy and curiosity than her mother could handle. For months, Indah, Tika, and Nina shared a room at the shelter. Several other migrant women and babies came and went. Despite exhaustion and depression, Indah could not sleep, anxious the children would disturb the other residents and worried about expenses, serving prison time, and being separated from Tika. She agonized about her husband and paid him illicit visits after curfew, bringing him food and the children to hug, despite NGO staff advice to "let him go."

The day Liana accompanied Indah, Tika, and Nina to surrender at the Immigration Department was the day before the Chinese New Year holiday. The officer behind the glass window complained that they had arrived "too late in the day" and urged Liana to come back another time. Liana politely but insistently told him that she was trying to do her job and that she knew he was, too. He replied that the office staff just wanted to go home for the holiday so "please come back another time." Partly because Indah could not stay in the shelter otherwise, Liana persisted, and he finally agreed to accept Indah's "surrender." There is a sad humor to a situation in which a desperate overstayer—at risk of arrest and detention if she is caught—is told by an immigration officer to "come back another day." Indah's experience was not unique. Several mothers were told to come back and surrender when they got passports or when there was more time. Liana's own papers were periodically checked, and she was asked why she kept bringing people to surrender. For several months, Indah jumped through bureaucratic hoops. The staff at the Birth Registry would not create birth certificates without Immigration Department documentation, but the Immigration Department insisted that Indah bring birth certificates first. All she wanted was to go home. This strange form of ambivalent governmentality turns away undocumented migrant women and children on the pretext that they are paperless, in contrast to others who are rounded up during searches and crackdowns of immigrant neighborhoods and subsequently imprisoned. Such inconsistencies contributed to Indah's purgatory-like situation.

HUMANITARIAN REASON AND WORK-AS-AID

Humanitarian aid, according to Didier Fassin, focuses "mainly on the poorest, most unfortunate, most vulnerable individuals: the politics of compassion is a politics of inequality" (2012, 3). Inequality is at the center of the tension that exists between domination and assistance. This tension explains both the "compassion fatigue" of donors and those who provide assistance that can turn to indifference or aggressiveness "toward the victims of misfortune" and also the shame, "resentment and even hostility sometimes expressed by the disadvantaged and the dominated toward those who think of themselves as their benefactors" (3). Recipients of humanitarian assistance "are expected to show the humility of the beholden rather than express demands for rights" (4).

Hong Kong's pregnant FDWs are not, strictly speaking, recipients of humanitarian aid, nor are former FDWs who become overstayers or file torture or asylum claims judged to be among the "neediest." When former FDWs file torture or asylum claims and receive aid, they are often regarded with skepticism and criticism. Some African asylum seekers I knew resented domestic worker asylum seekers, whom they did not consider "legitimate" and who, they said, "slowed the process" and took resources from "real" refugees. Staff at NGOs and aid organizations widely regard former FDWs as "less deserving" than claimants from parts of Africa and South Asia; they are considered a time-consuming nuisance at best, or undeserving and immoral at worst, taking resources to which they are not entitled. One former staff person at a government-funded agency described to me how the Chinese staff looked down on domestic worker clients; they could not understand why those clients should receive support. She recounted how the staff pointed to the sexy style of some Indonesians and Filipinas who came for their required meetings with social workers, and they openly questioned the morals of women who flaunted their sexuality rather than act with humility, gratitude, modesty, or shame. Ironically, former domestic workers were often considered less aggressive and easier to deal with than many South Asian and African claimants, who were sometimes described as rude, demanding, or emotionally unstable, provoking fear among the staff. But, unlike "deserving" asylum seekers and torture claimants, domestic workers were viewed as taking advantage of the system in order to stay in Hong Kong when they had been allowed in to work.

In his discussion of humanitarian aid in relation to the body, Fassin points to a time in France before border closures in 1974 when migrant labor was needed and welcomed on condition that the worker had a healthy body. He quotes Franco-Algerian sociologist Adelmalek Sayad, who wrote, "The immigrant has no meaning, either in his own eyes or those of others, and because ultimately he has no existence except through his work, illness, perhaps even more than the idleness it brings, is experienced as the negation of the immigrant" (cited in Fassin 2012, 85). The migrant's body is an instrument of production, valued only for his labor power, so when its performance is interrupted "because of illness or an accident" as in the case of pregnant domestic workers in Hong Kong, it becomes a problem and a source of suspicion, and they are considered socially illegitimate (Fassin 2012, 86).

FDWs from the Philippines and Indonesia are brought to Hong Kong as "helpers" who receive lesser rights and benefits than local service workers, even those doing the same type of work. Like post–World War II guest workers in Europe, domestic helpers' bodies, if too old, sick, or physically impaired by pregnancy, are deemed unfit for work and socially illegitimate. Although, narrowly speaking, the importation of women workers from poorer countries is not the same as "humanitarian aid," I argue that their employment and the attitudes toward them in Hong Kong are part of a wider pattern of humanitarian governance, whose agents range from government officials, employees of NGOs, and international organizations to employment agencies and employers. The employment of women from Indonesia and the Philippines (a country sometimes referred to as the "sick man of Asia") points to assumptions about their poverty, despera-tion, and unemployment that presume gratitude from those who are for-tunate enough to "be given" or "receive" the opportunity to be "helpers" in Hong Kong. As recipients of "assistance" or charity in the form of the low-est paid jobs, as the following chapters illustrate, they are often seen and treated as unappreciative recipients of "gifts" that create an obligation in the form of obedience and gratitude to the benefactor, as opposed to expectations of labor rights, fair wages for their work, and the right of abode.

Fassin does not write of employment as a form of assistance, but humanitarian reason clearly underpins attitudes toward the employment of migrant workers from regions of the world that are considered poor, "backward," or "basket cases" by wealthier labor-importing regions. Humanitarian aid following Southeast Asian earthquakes, tsunamis, and volcanic eruptions translate directly into Fassin's analysis; the fact that Indonesia and the Philippines receive those forms of assistance contrib-utes to the impression of desperate need and dysfunction in the Global South.

As I have written elsewhere, domestic workers express a spectrum of perspectives concerning work and political activism, with, on one end, the most passive "helpers" who avoid activism, do their work, and do not com-plain (Constable 2007). From many employers' perspectives, they are ideal helpers. Such workers may be well treated and satisfied with their jobs, or they may be maltreated, abused, and underpaid, but they aim to be toler-ant and grateful "helpers." On the opposite end are workers who are highly active in advocating for labor rights, involved in home country politics, and concerned with local and global issues of justice and equity. In some cases, their employers are also political activists or advocates for humanitarian causes who approve of, encourage, or even select activist domestic workers. Many such migrant workers become involved in activism after experienc-ing work abuse, seeking help, and receiving assistance from domestic worker organizations. Later, they volunteer at the shelter or one of its spon-soring organizations, or they join the struggle for workers' rights and social justice (Constable 2009, 2010). Whether a domestic worker goes to the

Labour Tribunal in an effort to require the employer to pay her legal wages, or whether she marches with local labor unions to raise the minimum wage, many employers and the Hong Kong public criticize the FDW as having no business doing so. It is as though the laws do not apply to her and as though asking for contractual rights displays an inappropriate, presumptuous, and misplaced sense of entitlement.

Like recipients of humanitarian aid who are deemed ungrateful, FDWs are routinely criticized as spoiled, demanding, unappreciative, impolite guests and are told to go home if they are unhappy. Some workers are afraid to join or even watch rallies for fear that, if they are seen on the evening news, their contracts will be terminated. "Good helpers" are those who are willing to be *only workers* and who treat the work as their life, whereas "bad workers" are those who demand recognition of their rights as workers while expressing political subjectivities that go well beyond that of worker. The "problem" with "helpers" who want to be treated like deserving workers is that they are from "poor countries" and should thus "be happy with what they get." This work-as-aid attitude—a variant of humanitarian reason—is encountered among employers as well as staff in government offices.

One NGO staff member who assists domestic workers with their cases against employers described to me her long-term frustration with her work. She was concerned about maltreated domestic workers and certain Labour Tribunal officers. As she explained, most domestic workers "are very timid and not good at representing themselves." When they meet tribunal officers, "they cower and act as though the person is the boss," not someone who is there to assist them. The tribunal officer's job, she explained, is "not to take sides" in domestic worker/employer disputes but to mediate and help reach a mutually agreeable solution that avoids the time and expense of a tribunal hearing. Yet one Chinese tribunal officer she dealt with routinely displayed favoritism toward the Chinese employer. Despite evidence of alleged abuses, including underpayment, failure to provide an air ticket home, or illegal termination, the tribunal officer insisted time after time that the worker should settle amicably with her employer or drop the complaint, often remarking on the impossibility or unlikelihood that the worker would win at a hearing for lack of "good evidence." The tribunal officer chatted in Cantonese and laughed with the women employers as though they were friends, and she spoke to the domestic workers in a condescending and intimidating fashion that, the NGO worker added, "is the way I'm sure she talks to her own maid." The unspoken "alliance" that many advocates and service providers describe, in which many Chinese judges and civil servants seem to automatically and perhaps unconsciously "take the side" of the Chinese employer, is one that I have witnessed in courtrooms where lower-level magistrates speak in respectful tones to the employer and in angry, condescending, and impatient tones to domestic workers. As this staff member described, the boss's tone of voice that demands a "Yes sir, yes ma'am" reply is often enough to intimidate domestic workers so that they give up their cases.

That migrant workers are considered charity cases helps to explain why their official rights as workers often seem more theoretical than real and why migrant workers are often presumed guilty and their employers (seen as good citizens who struggle to help undeserving domestic workers) assumed innocent. An unspoken alliance exists between government bureaucrats who share similar class identities and experiences (or lower-level staff who aspire to them) and who feel sympathy toward Hong Kong employers because they personally understand the "challenges" involved with employing domestic workers. Literally and figuratively, bureaucrats and employers often speak the same language. Employers are often professionally dressed Chinese women who are accompanied by Chinese employment agency staff who readily corroborate their stories; employers express resentment at missing valuable work time. Meanwhile, as one domestic worker described, "I felt very, very small and frightened and just wanted to go home."

THE ORDER OF THINGS

Like a colorful woven scarf, this book can be seen in many ways. Some readers may be drawn more to the weft—the one long thread that literally ties the whole thing together with argument, theory, analysis, structure, and interpretation. Others may prefer to follow the repeated warp threads—the different textures, colors, and thicknesses of individual life stories and experiences of mothers, their babies, and some fathers.

The weft of this book is fashioned from theories of gender, citizenship, mobility, and precarity. Juridical modes of belonging are key elements that shape individuals' socioeconomic well-being. Legal status runs a continuum from the most privileged citizens, on one end, to the most precarious undocumented overstayers, on the other. Between these extremes are dependents and residents (who might one day become citizens), temporary workers, tourists or visitors, asylum seekers, and refugees who have visas or papers that afford or deny them rights, such as the right to work or to settle permanently. All of the women and men in this book are located somewhere along this continuum of privilege and precarity, and their positions often shift through time, shaping their lives, life chances, and those of their children.

The overall arrangement of this book is thematic and argumentative, but the weft is intended to be subtle enough so as not to excessively confine the warp of the stories. Individual stories of mothers, children, and men illustrate key points of each chapter but also overflow beyond them. They are not reduced to small, neat topical bits. Instead, I have tried to maintain some sense of wholeness and individual integrity, such that some stories could be read alone as portraits that reveal the arbitrariness of sociological categories. Certain idiosyncrasies stand out when the weft fades into the background; at other times, intersections of warp and weft reveal new patterns. All of the stories illustrate the interweaving of hope and vulnerability, optimism and precarity in migrant workers' lives.

My approach to ethnographic research and writing, described in chapter 2, emphasizes the importance of stories and my evolving relationships with mothers and babies. It also points to the challenges of research that combines public anthropology—with its critical policy implications—with concerns that I call micro-feminist-ethnographer-activism. Chapters 3, 4, and 5 focus in turn on women, men, sex, and babies, though these topics clearly overlap. Chapter 3 highlights the position of women migrants *as workers* in relation to what Rachel Silvey aptly calls the "gendered tensions of modernity" (2009, 54). Serious tensions exist between women's roles overseas as migrant workers and their expected roles at home as wives, mothers, and daughters. The vulnerabilities of FDWs in Hong Kong that are compounded by employment policies and practices, overcharging by employment agencies, the two-week rule, and the live-in requirement are all forms of governmentality that serve to discipline and regulate worker's (particularly women's) bodies. Chapter 4 turns to the vast diversity of nationalities, histories, and juridical status of men who become fathers. Against the historical backdrop of Hong Kong, and based on interviews and conversations, I explore men's perspectives on relationships with FDWs and their cultural and gendered misunderstandings and miscommunications. Chapter 5 focuses on sex and babies. Why do domestic workers get pregnant and have babies, and how do they make sense of options regarding abortion, adoption, or keeping the baby? Sex and babies are linked in complex and contradictory ways to ideas about good and bad women. Babies paradoxically anchor women down and offer hope of family and security in a precarious world, an apt example of "cruel optimism" (Berlant 2011).

Chapters 6 and 7 present stories of current and former domestic worker mothers along the spectrum of privilege and precarity, from secure citizens to undocumented overstayers. Chapter 6 focuses on the more privileged: women who are officially married to local men and whose children are citizens, and women who have managed to maintain their domestic worker contracts during and after the birth of a child. The controversy over granting domestic workers right of abode and legal tactics for obtaining children's residency are also discussed. Chapter 7 tells the stories of the most precarious former domestic worker mothers who are overstayers (sometimes referred to as "illegal" or "undocumented" migrants) and those who file asylum or torture claims to extend their time in Hong Kong. In both chapters I consider the "tactics" that mothers use, in Michel de Certeau's sense of the arts of the unempowered (1984), and both chapters illustrate the importance of remaining in Hong Kong after a baby is born, the value of "time," and the means by which women manage to stay and to subsist. Chapter 8 concludes with stories of leaving Hong Kong, returning home, and the almost inevitable draw for single mothers to reenter the migratory cycle of atonement.

2 Ethnography and Everyday Life

I have a story to tell and maybe it helps you to understand
the situation.

— Hope, a Filipino migrant mother, in 2011

Academic studies of migrant domestic workers tend to lean in one of two
directions. Some studies focus primarily on the exploitation and abuse of
migrant workers, providing analysis of structural constraints, inequality,
and oppression within global capitalism. In the other direction are those
studies that pay more attention to migration as a resource—a source of
agency, pleasure, desire, and new subjectivities for migrants. Geraldine
Pratt's *Families Apart* (2012) is a powerful example of the former. She
writes about the Canadian Live-In Caregiver Program (which allows
migrant caregivers to apply for permanent residency after a minimum of
two years and to sponsor family members to join them) as a "catastro-
phe" because of the "violence of separation" it creates, the failures of
immigrant children in Canadian schools, and the loss, sacrifice, loneliness, and suffering of migrant women and their family members during
the long separation (4, 44). Pratt argues, following the Philippine
Women Center of British Columbia, that the program should be scrapped
entirely and replaced by a normal immigration scheme (like for skilled

workers), and she criticizes "a language of migrant choice and freedom" that "obscures processes of forced economic migration . . . " (163).

The other approach is illustrated by a collection of essays edited by Mark Johnson and Pnina Werbner, who write:

> Whereas the dominant scholarly narrative construes these female migrants as hyperexploited and compliant workers, we focus on the way migrants challenge their abjection in the alternative spaces they create and in which they live richly complex religious and social lives. Although shaped and constrained by the migration context, we argue that overseas female migrants nevertheless create alternative worlds of fun, piety and rights activism. . . . [I]n their diasporic encounters, migrants creatively engage with the places and landscapes in which they live and labour, sharing conviviality with others like themselves through ritual performance, pilgrimage journeys, mobilisation for rights, religious worship and new intimate relationships. (2010, 205–6)

Despite their seemingly opposed approaches—one highlighting labor exploitation, political structures, and calling for activism and change, and the other attending more to the ways that migrants respond to conditions of migration and create meaningful lives *despite* structures of inequality and oppression—I see these as two sides of the same coin. Many scholars, including Pratt and Johnson and Werbner's contributors (myself included), consider both perspectives. Which side is highlighted depends on scholarly and activist goals and priorities. For primarily activist purposes, it is best to highlight the former, but the latter can also serve political purposes.

As a politically engaged humanist, anthropologist, and feminist, deeply sympathetic to migrant workers and the struggle for justice, I think it does migrant workers a disservice to deny the depth and richness, pathos as well as the pleasure, of their lives. This is meant not to romanticize them or to deny the exploitation and discrimination they face but to see them as people, not just as workers. As Stephen Castles wrote of guest workers in Western Europe, the cause of marginalization and problems facing new ethnic minorities "is not the employment of migrants in itself, but rather the attempt to treat migrants as pure economic men and women, and to separate between labor power and other human attributes" (1986, 776).

My writing about domestic workers has faced criticism from both sides. I have been taken to task for paying too much attention to exploitation and not enough to good relations that can (of course) exist between Hong Kong employers and domestic workers (Yu 2011).[1] I have also been criticized for attending to forms of power and resistance that are deemed irrelevant or trite from a particular activist perspective. Yet each researcher must define the parameters of her study and consider the implications.

Inequities, denigration, and exploitation in Hong Kong and in their home countries are central to the experiences of the mothers and children about whom I write. In the face of severe challenges, migrants face the "trauma of dislocation" (Pratt 2012, 70), but they also express humanity, desires, and an ability to survive as well as generosity and selfishness, kindness and sometimes sheer desperation when hope has been pared away. The effort to render meaningful the poetics and politics of the everyday lives of migrant mothers and their babies is the main goal of this book. I seek to convey the policies and laws as well as the social structures and cultural constructs they are up against and the unintended violence of those structures; I also highlight the women's creativity, bravery, and sheer resilience and the sense in which they often simply react in the only way possible, with little forethought except to continue to live as best they can. I hope to contribute to the struggle for social justice for migrant workers by offering insight and increasing awareness into how structures of oppression work in predictable and unintended ways and how individuals function within, submit to, or aim to transform or utilize those structures. As such, this is a type of critical public anthropology that reveals practical ways in which troubled policies create worse problems or defeat their stated purposes and thus should be abandoned or changed (Bourgois and Schonberg 2009, 23).

In the pages below, I describe my approach to the ethnography of everyday life, my first encounter with migrant mothers and babies, my research methods, and my relationships with these women and children. In closing, I introduce Melinda and Hope and their children. Hope's vulnerability illustrates many of the themes of this book. It also provides examples of feminist-ethnographer-activism: small, everyday examples of human involvement that preclude the option of being a dispassionate, detached observer.

MULTIPLE TRUTHS

Interviews and conversations with migrant mothers and people who know them or work with them, various documents, records, and written materials, and my observations and interpretations of what I saw and heard are all part of this study, but at its core are women's words and stories. Stories are not fixed. Like migratory status, they change through time. They look and sound different depending on the teller's and listener's positions. Some of the stories I heard and interviews I conducted seemed to serve as a sort of "rehearsal"—especially those told early on by women I did not know well. These included stories designed to support torture or asylum claims, like practice sessions for upcoming interviews with the Immigration Department or the United Nations High Commissioner for Refugees (UNHCR; see chapter 7). Other stories were like dress rehearsals for breaking the news to parents (trying on explanations or justifications for their circumstances) or confessions or therapy sessions (the listener provides a secure environment, and the speaker expresses fear, guilt, depression, or loneliness). Some stories or story fragments felt like fundraising or sponsorship drives. Many stories shifted through time and key elements changed, circling seemingly closer to truth.

Women's own stories sometimes conflicted with what other mothers, acquaintances, or service providers said about them. Rumors and gossip, official files and records (viewed with consent), and conversations all constituted "partial truths."[2] By that I do not mean that they are untrue—although some are—but that, like all stories, they are incomplete intersubjective productions. Stories were often messy, with knotted warps, not told in linear fashion, sometimes internally contradictory. Unlike social workers, immigration officers, lawyers, or UNHCR or Hong Kong government staff, my job was, thankfully, not to verify claims or to determine some essential truth. Whether a worker actually signed a termination letter willingly, as her employer asserted, or whether she was pressured into doing so was not for me to judge, but it is an example of an issue which demands that I raise questions and contextualize the subtle and complex power relations between employer and worker. In some cases, women's stories were explicitly told for a purpose, such as fabricating a marriage to fend off gossip and criticism. One mother told her parents she had married the

Englishman with whom she had been involved for several years. She did not tell them when they broke up. Suspicious, they asked to speak to him and questioned why he was never home. She said, "He works late, and only speaks English, so you can't speak to him." Her cousin who had worked in Hong Kong cast doubt on her story, but her parents were more critical of the cousin than of her. She speculated that one day she might tell them he had died. We joked that she would "kill him off" and join the many migrant "widows" whose stories are often coproduced with their parents, in an effort to save face.

During fieldwork, I listened to women's stories, responded, and asked questions. At the writing stage, other issues came into play. Which stories should I include? How do I link them to deeper meanings, patterns, and what Clifford Geertz (1973) famously called "thick descriptions"? In my earlier work, I often used only parts of women's narratives thematically, to illustrate a particular topic or category of experience. Here, I keep individual mothers and their stories more intact, allowing their voices, personalities, and experiences to emerge more cohesively. Whereas the first approach better protects individual identities, it fails to depict the complexity and integrity of those individuals. The second approach raises confidentiality issues but renders more complex, multidimensional, nuanced human beings. As feminist ethnographers have argued, quantitative survey research protects "informants" but does violence by turning them into numbers, generalizations, or abstract sociological patterns (Stacey 1988; Visweswaran 1994; Abu-Lughod 1990). Ethnography and qualitative methods may do less violence to individuals' complex subjectivities but risks their exposure, vulnerability, and betrayal.

Although I am committed to identifying sociological patterns, I especially value the richness and complexity of individual lives, yet I do not take confidentiality lightly. In some cases in this book, I have altered or omitted identifying characteristics and split or merged people or events. Following anthropological convention, I have used pseudonyms and disguised geographic and demographic details. For example, given the relatively small number of African fathers, I have erred on the side of overgeneralization, referring to them as "African," not by their specific nationalities. I have left out potentially incriminating details about illegal work and ongoing legal cases. The names of NGOs and charity organizations or government offices have sometimes been omitted to protect the identity of employees, clients, or claimants.

THE BEGINNING: JULY 2010

In July 2010, during a short, hot summer visit to Hong Kong, a Filipino friend I knew from my earlier research in the 1990s invited me to join her for a meeting organized by PathFinders, a charity organization for migrant women, specifically migrant women who are mothers or are pregnant. The meeting took place in a rented classroom space in a community center on a small back street in Yaumatei, an old Kowloon neighborhood. Unbeknownst to me at the time, that meeting marked the beginning of my new project. It was the first of many PathFinders meetings and discussion groups I attended over the next two years.

At that first eye-opening meeting, two or three dozen chairs were arranged in a circle, and colorful, square foam interlocking alphabet tiles were arranged on the ground for children and babies to play on. Gradually, in addition to the meeting organizers, a few staff members from other migrant NGOs, and two well-known human rights lawyers who had been invited to speak, dozens of women—predominantly Indonesians and a few Filipinas, all in their twenties and early thirties—entered the room. Some were visibly pregnant; others led small children by the hand or had sleeping babies swaddled tightly over their chests with sarongs; a few steered strollers into the corner of the room. Many of the children looked as though they might be African or South Asian; some were more Chinese or East Asian in appearance. They ranged in age from newborn to three years old. More than thirty women and around twenty-five children attended in all. In some cases, it was difficult to tell whose child was whose, since a few of the children were clearly comfortable with several women who picked them up, offered treats, or comforted them. The children remained remarkably quiet during that meeting (in contrast to the chaos and liveliness of others I attended). They nursed from bottles or discreetly from breasts, getting restless only toward the end of the ninety minutes.

My first meeting with migrant mothers and their children was moving, surprising, and haunting. All of the women had originally come to Hong

Kong as domestic workers, but those at the meeting no longer had employment contracts. Many were either overstayers or had "immigration" or
"recognizance" papers.[3] Many had overstayed their visas at one point, but
to my surprise, as became evident as the two lawyers posed and answered
the women's questions, more than half of them had over the past few years
filed "torture claims" under the United Nations International Convention
Against Torture or asylum claims through the UNHCR. Occasionally,
women had filed claims on the advice of their African or South Asian boyfriends who were claimants, but they also learned of this option from
other women they met in detention or in prison, or they learned about
torture claims from sympathetic or impatient government officers who
informed them they could then qualify for medical care and aid through
the International Social Service (ISS) and remain in Hong Kong while
their claims were processed. The lawyers at the meeting discouraged the
women from filing such claims, patiently explaining that it is essentially
impossible for a former FDW to win a torture claim. However, as I later
learned, few harbored the fantasy of a successful claim. The main goal was
to get recognizance papers to allow them time in Hong Kong, sometimes
several years, while their claims were in process.

The migrant women I met that day were mothers: not the mothers I
had met, knew in person, and had read and written about who were com-
pelled to leave their children behind in Indonesia or the Philippines in
order to earn money abroad to help support their families, but women
who had become pregnant or had borne children in Hong Kong. Pushing
a stroller, carrying a baby, or holding a child's hand on the street, these
women would not stand out. One might assume they were caretakers, the
children their charges. But these were their own Hong Kong–born children, and it surprised me to see a room full of women and babies, many of
whom had overstayed, and to begin to learn about these women's painful
struggles to remain in Hong Kong or to plan their futures elsewhere, and
about the limited choices and the complex decisions they faced that would
affect their lives and their children's futures.

Before the meeting began, by way of an unsolicited explanation, an
Indonesian woman sitting next to me said that women, like her, "are too
trusting of men" who pay them attention and flatter them, and that they
"give their hearts" without "thinking of the future." In Java, she said, her

father and brothers would have pressured the man to take responsibility. Here, she said, men often leave their girlfriends when they become pregnant. Another Indonesian woman, whose boyfriend had left Hong Kong, had put her son up for adoption a year earlier, but she was adamant that she would not do so again; the next time she would keep her baby. When I met her again in 2011, she brought birthday cake to celebrate her son's second birthday, and she introduced me to her new baby daughter; she and her friends wondered where in Hong Kong's upscale neighborhoods or elsewhere in the world her son might be with his expatriate adoptive family.

Although some of these women were married back home and left children behind, many were single; others were separated, divorced, or estranged from their husbands.[4] In some cases, failed marriages contributed to their motivation to work abroad. As Lilik, a young Indonesian woman from East Java described, she began her married life at twenty. The marriage was approved but not arranged by her parents. As we sat on her bed at the shelter where she was staying, she said she had never told this to anyone but that, soon after they married, she became pregnant and he began beating her. Bruised and swollen, she claimed to be ill so as to stay home and avoid family and coworkers. She did not want to worry her parents and was ashamed of the beatings and the failure of her marriage. "After my marriage ended I could not face my family. I was so depressed when my husband left and took my son and started living with his new wife. So I ran away. . . . Then I told my parents I was going to work in Jakarta, but really I went to a training camp and then left for work in Hong Kong." It was during her first day off from her new job in Hong Kong that she met Rashid, a young Pakistani man who is described in chapter 4.

According to Hong Kong, Philippine, and Indonesian law, most of the children at the meeting were born "out of wedlock" because the parents were not officially married to each other in a civil ceremony. Most fathers did not maintain a relationship with the mother or child. With the exception of two Chinese fathers and a Vietnamese one, most of the fathers of the children at the meeting were South Asian or African and were in Hong Kong, I was told, as asylum seekers, illegal workers, or both. Some were traders or businessmen who pass through Hong Kong on visitor visas en route to China. A few were white tourists or Hong Kong permanent residents.

Later, I would hear about men who were proud of fathering a child but who provided no support; men who claimed to be single but already had a wife, multiple girlfriends, and children; a few men and women who married in the mosque and lived together as a family; and men who were physically or emotionally abusive. Later, I would also learn about women's views regarding abortion and contraceptives; anxiety about returning home with a child born out of wedlock; fear of telling their parents because of the shame it would cause them; concerns about the difficulties faced by "mixed race" fatherless children; challenges of having a child and no legal work in Hong Kong; the pain and hardship of deciding whether to keep or give a child for adoption; and sometimes glimmers of hope for the future as they weighed the options for themselves and their children.

Prima, a Filipina I met at the 2010 meeting, had recently told her mother about her child. Her mother gradually adjusted to the news and urged her to bring the child home. She offered to care for her so that Prima could return to work and resume sending remittances. Eighteen months later, Prima and her child (by then four years old) were still in Hong Kong, living under the official radar. Eager to stay that way, Prima did not respond to my invitation to meet. A year later, in late 2012, an NGO caseworker told me that Prima had "finally resurfaced," was given some financial assistance, and had returned home with her child. But when I met Bethany, who attended the same church and knew Prima well, she said "Huh? That's not true. I just saw her at church!" My brief acquaintance with Prima and the conflicting stories of her coming, going, and disappearing are not unusual. They illustrate both the caution and the resourcefulness of mothers who want to stay in Hong Kong with their children as well as the difficulty, sometimes, of knowing the "truth" of the matter—and whether, ultimately, the truth is as important as attempts to create the unknowable. For that reason, instead of seeking the "fact" of the matter, or weighing evidence and making judgments, I often simply identify contradictions and loose ends within stories. Unlike officials and caseworkers with whom the mothers dealt in their daily lives, my role was mostly as a sympathetic listener, often friend and sometimes advisor, but never judge or interrogator.

My first meeting with migrant mothers and their babies raised many questions: What are the legal and practical options for pregnant migrant workers? What are the everyday lives of mothers and children like? Where do they go, how do they survive day-to-day? Who are the fathers and what role do they play? What resources, laws, or policies exist to protect the children, and how are their legal rights understood by parents, NGO workers, activists, and state officials? Where do the children ultimately obtain citizenship, and where do they belong? What happens when they go to Indonesia, the Philippines, or are adopted in Hong Kong? How do these cases force us to rethink the meaning of "family" in relation to international migration?

BEING IN THE WORLD

Years ago, when I conducted dissertation research on a very different topic, I learned that field research requires putting yourself out there and talking to people who are often—in Hong Kong at least—very busy. Anthropologists can expend a lot of effort with little result, seeking out individuals who are both willing and able to answer questions and engage meaningfully with our research interests. There is little room for shyness or introversion in the field, and I quickly learned that my future projects would need a better entrée and subject matter that people would *want to* talk about, not something that made me feel I was trying to sell them unwanted wares. I wanted my future research to place me within a public sphere of readily accessible fieldwork. My ideal—hoped for but not always accomplished—was for life and fieldwork to become seamless, for research to take on a momentum of its own and to become pleasurable and relatively effortless, and for research to become part of everyday life.

With the exception of the first week or so of jetlagged entry or reentry into the field in 2011 and 2012, the main period of this project mostly felt like life. Each day I immersed myself in the pleasures and sorrows of mothers and babies. My early routine involved going to PathFinders meetings, classes, and discussion groups; reconnecting with old contacts and migrant NGOs; and asking mothers and others who worked with migrant workers for interviews. Very quickly, my routine built momentum, and women were readily available for interviews. I learned that all I had to do was ask the questions I thought might be too personal, sensitive, or invasive—about their legal status, their relationship with the child's father, or their attitudes toward contraception—and they usually provided direct answers. Some of the topics that I considered sensitive did not seem that way to them. Once I got to know them, many of the women were forthright in talking about illegal abortions and illegal work, though others avoided those subjects or spoke only in generalities. Especially painful topics, such as rape, sex work, or giving a child for adoption, were spoken of indirectly, cryptically, or briefly, if at all. Most women were open to discussing their past and present in Hong Kong but reluctant to speculate about the future.

As time passed, I often felt more like a friend, older sister, mother, or even grandmother—more of a person than a researcher. This project brought me back to the place where, in my mid-thirties in 1993–94, as the young mother of a one- and a three-year-old, I began to learn from migrant domestic workers. At that time, I asked migrant workers not to call me "ma'am" (as they did their employers and others in a position of authority); I became known as Nicole or "ate" (sister in Tagalog). To my surprise, in 2011 and 2012, I became known as Sister, Mom, Tita, or Auntie, and some women told their children to call me "grandma." The latter began with Rose, whose child's absent father was American, so we joked that onlookers might imagine, as I carried him or held his hand as he learned to walk, that I was her mother-in-law, "the grandmother," and in that case the label stuck. (Part of the humor was that the baby's father was around my age.) Many migrant mothers' mothers were my age; some were older and had raised a dozen children; a few were younger, having given birth in their teens or early twenties. Casting me in the role of surrogate mother, mother-in-law, or their child's grandmother was in some cases influenced by the fact that their own mothers (or in-laws) were painfully absent at times when mothers "should" (in their words) be there to offer comfort, such as during the birth of a child. Several women I visited in the hospital after they gave birth cried and said how happy they were to see me, especially since their own mothers were so far away. Others recounted how lonely and sad it was to give birth all alone and with no visitors in the maternity ward, in contrast to local women. In 2012, I visited one of the women who had returned to Indonesia, and she happily encouraged the rumor that I was the mother-in-law; why else would I have come so far to see her?[5]

At the peak of my research in 2011 and 2012, I spent all my waking hours with mothers and babies, and when I returned to my room at night I kept in touch by phone, through SMS (text) messages, and on Facebook. At night I dreamed of them. In the morning, before they were awake, I wrote about them in my fieldnotes and interview transcriptions. I did not draw a rigid line between work and research and life, nor did I attempt to circumscribe my work and myself. When I left the field, I felt disoriented for months, only somewhat reassured by Facebook messages and Skype calls that offered tidbits of news that made me feel more connected. Because I am an ethnographer of "migrant workers" who contends that they are never just workers, perhaps it was inevitable that, for a time, my research and my own position embodied the lack of clear separation between work (research) and life or personhood. Despite my initial introduction to people as a researcher, giving a description of my research and my plans to write a book (reiterated each time I conducted an interview and used my digital recorder), several women nonetheless seemed to forget. Some assumed I must be a volunteer at PathFinders or an odd freelance social worker who was in no rush to end the meeting.

One day, I was visiting Hope and Melinda, two Filipino mothers, and their babies near Yuen Long. Having just returned from her appointment with the Immigration Department, Hope complained, "Questions, questions! All the time more questions!" Melinda vigorously concurred, describing the constant barrage of questions from immigration officials and others. "I am so tired of all the questions," Melinda sighed. Imitating their tone, I said emphatically, "and *all* Nicole's questions too!" They both laughed reassuringly, insisting that my questions were completely different. "The main difference," they said, is who I am and that my questions "cannot get you into trouble." That day they had invited me to come to meet and interview their friend April, who had recently gotten out of prison, saying "she really needs to talk to you about her situation."

After the first few months, when my interview style became more fluid and conversational, I would thank women for their time, and they in turn thanked me for listening, for coming to their homes, for spending time with them and their babies, for my "help" accompanying them on appointments, and for writing what they hoped would be a book that might "help" women in similar situations. Some, like Hope and Melinda, introduced me to friends with babies who they encouraged to talk to me because I could "help." When I asked what help I could give since I was a researcher, not a social worker or a counselor, they reminded me that I had offered advice, such as referring them to PathFinders or to various service providers, depending on their problems. Although such interventions seemed minimal to me, they made it clear that talking helped. Some expressed a need to "tell someone my problems and let them go," and some stressed that there was "no one else" they could trust to tell. Their "trust" of other mothers, especially compatriots, was sometimes a major issue. One Filipina told me that she no longer had friends—except for me and one other— since she had rejected their repeated advice to leave her abusive boyfriend. As she put it, we were the only ones who stuck with her and whom she trusted.

Mistrust and jealousy are common among those who work illegally and fear the outcome of revealing too much and making themselves vulnerable. This mistrust among those who I naively assumed were friends—because they all had children and attended the same meetings and sometimes babysat each other's children—was brought home to me when Mia, an Indonesian mother whom I had interviewed earlier, spoke of her isolation and intentional avoidance of other mothers. She was afraid of petty jealousies and gossip. She reminded me that, in the interview, I had asked if she has friends in Hong Kong with babies. She had answered "no," she said, because although "I *know* a lot of mothers and babies, they are not friends." I had taken for granted that the mothers who knew each other through an NGO, church, or classes were friends, but she explained otherwise. Several women stressed that they could trust me with their stories. It was an advantage to be older and from outside the community. They did not have to worry that what they said to me would give me fodder to grant or deny them aid, resources, or assistance, unlike NGO staff members, case workers, and government employees. If they told other women about their part-time jobs, creative sources of support, or boyfriends and partners, it opened them up to criticism, gossip, competition, envy, pity, or, at worst, arrest, detention, or prison. I did not compete for boyfriends or resources and did not judge them; I could offer advice, refer them to migrant advocates, and help in small ways; I was generally safe to talk to.

Later, when I knew many more women and had paid them repeated visits, and when many women thought they knew who my friends were, the issue of "gossip" became more sensitive. Women who had fallen out with others I visited would subtly ask for news or would say that they had not heard from so-and-so for a while. My answers were usually vague or I feigned ignorance, but the latest conflicts were often central topics of conversation. Women who were considered too distant, snobby, happy, wealthy, successful, self-righteous, or stingy were often targeted for gossip. One woman said she had no money, but others claimed she worked and had substantial savings. Some children, it was rumored, shared the same father but different mothers. Some women acted happy and pretended all was well but were abused or their partners cheated. Some women claimed to be single but were married and had children at home, as was revealed to others in one case by the woman's own vindictive sister. Some mothers pretended to be married to locals, but others claimed the man was an asylum seeker or that he had already sponsored a wife. One woman said she was pregnant as a result of rape, but others claimed she freelanced at bars. Mostly, I listened and made mental notes.

Although some women thought I would be a good source of money or material resources, I had been urged by NGO staff not to give out money. At first, with the exception of chipping in or giving "red envelopes" at birthday parties, I rarely gave money.[6] Normally I gave small gifts, treated people to meals, chipped in for social events, or brought the birthday cake. When I went to their homes, I brought food and sometimes diapers, a valuable commodity rarely distributed by NGOs and charity organizations. Netty, an Indonesian mother of two Hong Kong–born children, was less subtle than most about getting resources. I invited her for an interview over lunch at a small restaurant and treated her and gave her my usual gifts of baby clothes and books. In the course of our conversation and on numerous subsequent occasions, she told me about the cash, gifts, and diapers that another Western woman had given her. She often compared herself to others and had alienated herself from some mothers who criticized her for her stinginess and lack of reciprocity. Despite their relative poverty, sharing was necessary to maintain social relationships. Netty was known to be resourceful at finding work. When she had money, she went to restaurants and was seen taking taxis, but she rarely shared or reciprocated. Mia, by contrast, kept to herself and spent very little on herself or her daughter and saved every penny for her inevitable return to Indonesia.

Another way I tried to give back to the women I knew, not only those whom I interviewed, was to take photographs of them and their children. Each week I had dozens of photographs I had taken the week before printed and gave them to the mothers. Besides rent and food, photo printing was my largest expense. Although most women took pictures on their mobile phones, few could afford the luxury of printing them. As a local photographer, I had a role that helped me to break the ice, introduce myself, learn people's names, and observe. Another way that I assisted was by accompanying women on appointments to doctors, hospitals, government offices, and sometimes lawyers. I spent countless hours with women and babies in waiting areas for appointments at the Birth Registry, the Immigration Department, the Labor Tribunal, courtrooms, consular offices, numerous hospitals and social welfare counters, Food for All, the ISS, and other service providers. Sometimes I helped pacify or entertain children while their mothers took care of business; at other times, I stood next to them to face the staff person at the counter. For women with babies or toddlers, another adult can alleviate the tedium, help distract children, hold their place in line while they go to the toilet, carry things, or babysit while waiting in long lines or in waiting rooms to speak to the staff person behind the glass window. I was never as good as PathFinders staff at navigating the situation at the Birth Registry, the Immigration Department, the consulate, or the social welfare office at the hospital, and I often called for instructions.[7] But I provided moral support, especially for those who felt intimidated by the bureaucracy. As some said pointedly, just having a white woman (or an NGO staff member) accompany you might mean that you are harder to ignore, less likely to be shunted to the end of the line or treated rudely by the official behind the counter. Sometimes my presence seemed to make little difference; I witnessed various forms of rudeness and disrespect on several occasions, one of the worst at the Indonesian Consulate.

THIRTY PAIRS OF TINY SHOES

After several months of research in 2011, I returned home to spend December in Pittsburgh with my family before returning to Hong Kong in January. At home, I carefully considered what gifts to bring back with me. During my earlier stint of research, I had bought a few dozen pairs of baby pajamas in an array of sizes and had given them to the women I interviewed, leaving additional pairs for future newborns with PathFinders. Pajamas were a bit like bringing coals to Newcastle, since PathFinders had shelves of donated clothing to give to clients, but the fact that these pajamas were new and brought from the United States seemed to render them special. This time, however, I wanted to do something different.

I had noticed that the shoes at PathFinders were usually worn out, and the good ones quickly disappeared. I heard several women ask whether more shoes had come in and complain about how expensive new ones are. So I bought thirty pairs of shoes of different sizes that were on clearance at two discount department stores, and I filled one suitcase with them to give as gifts. Given the women's insistence on gender-specific clothing, I bought some little boy's shoes and some in girl colors. They were in an array of styles: sneakers, dress shoes, boots. I was thrilled with how they looked and did not mind that many of them were "made in China" and might have cost less in Hong Kong.

I intended to give the shoes to the children I knew, but reality was more complicated. I relearned the importance of the classic anthropological topic of "the gift." The first problem was practical: How could I distribute the shoes without knowing the children's sizes? Pajamas are simple, because their size corresponds roughly to the child's age and they can be discreetly given to someone without attracting the attention or envy of others. But shoes require a proper fit and are more difficult to distribute unobtrusively. Plus, I should have bought larger sizes. Mothers prefer shoes that are too big, requiring two or three pairs of socks, but that allow the child to grow into them. Shoes also draw on wider notions of "taste" than pajamas, so I thought women might enjoy some input into selecting the shoes for their children.

My first attempt to give away the shoes was after attending a January birthday party for a one-year-old. I invited the birthday girl and her mother and four other women and their children, all of whom had seemed to be friends before I had left, to stop by my place in the afternoon to choose their shoes. This revealed not only a recent social rift between one woman and the rest of the group but also a competitiveness for resources that, until then, I had witnessed hints of but had not fully appreciated. It came as a shock in the context of what I assumed was simple gift giving.

Mia and her daughter Annie, a two-year-old and one of the largest children, arrived first. Annie had fun arranging the shoes in parallel rows along the wall of my tiny studio. She had to pick the largest pair of girl's shoes because they were the only ones that fit. The next to arrive was Endri and her child, who was too young to care. Endri spent a lot of time inspecting all the shoes and eventually said that she could not pick just one, could she not have two and also an additional pair for her older child in Indonesia? I explained that none of them would fit her five-year-old and that there would not be enough for everyone if I let her have two pairs. She persisted, and eventually Mia came to my aid and firmly told Endri to just pick one pair. Eventually the birthday girl and her mother, Eka, and two other mothers arrived, and Mia and Annie left. Eka asked for three pairs, which she quickly put next to her bag. Eventually I crumbled under pressure and let her have two, saying that one pair was her gift for the New Year, like for everyone else, and the other was her daughter's "birthday present." Endri, who had until then seemed relatively happy with her pair, began removing the tags and trying several other pairs on her child. She then asked again for two pairs, but I stood my ground. Shortly after, loaded with boxes of crayons and little cardboard children's books, they left. I was relieved to see them go, as much to have the crowded place to myself again as to puzzle over what had just happened.

As I was catching my breath and wiping crayon marks off the wall, Mia called to tell me that Endri phoned her to complain that Eka got two pairs of shoes and she only got one. Mia said, "I told her she didn't have to pay for the pair, but still she wasn't happy." I wondered why Mia felt a need to report this to me, and also about the response I had expected. A few days later, another mother told me that she thought Eka was treating her daughter's birthday "like a business." As she reported, Eka had hosted three birthday parties but put minimal expense and effort into them (the normal practice is to treat guests to food and children to gift bags) so that she could reap more than she gave.

Since I had been away during the December holiday party at PathFinders, my intent had been to give a gift to demonstrate my appreciation and affection for the mothers and children. But I had not wrapped the shoes and had not given them out individually as gifts. Instead, the rows of shoes, beautifully arranged by Annie, were treated like—and probably resembled—either a shop where one is entitled to select, inspect, and criticize, or the charity organization's end-of-season clothing giveaway. For that giveaway event, I had witnessed several large piles of clothing, placed on a cloth on the floor and given away to make way for the next season's supplies. Bethany, whose small son often looked like a fashion model, was ever on the lookout for particular items to augment his impressive wardrobe, and she dove right in. Wati, who was quiet, shy, and less aggressive, seemed rarely to get what her son needed. Others, like Eka and Mia, went through the piles methodically and tossed items across the room to others whose children they thought it might fit or who might need it. Others simply grabbed everything they could fit in their bags, planning to use them, send them home, give them away, or sell them.

Some of my visitors had approached the shoes like the free clothing giveaways. And, like the humanitarian reasoning of the charity worker who expects grateful recipients but is faced with people who resemble disgruntled customers, I was surprised and taken aback. Their reactions were not appreciation or pleasure for the gift but a sort of bargaining and taking measure of how many they could get and which were best. For a long time afterward, I thought about how a gift can appear as charity. It also struck me—as would become even clearer after my trip to Java—that some women viewed me explicitly as a resource, whereas others, if they saw me that way, were more subtle in their requests and expectations of friends or benefactors. All of them were desperately poor.

After the shoe mart in my room, I made a point of studying the size of children's feet, used my best judgment, and gave the pair of shoes to the child's mother in a gift bag, usually when no one else was around. One mother told me her son liked the light-up shoes so much he would not take them off at bedtime. Another two mothers seemed thrilled with the shoes, explaining that these were "truly the best gifts for the mother."

Distributed more like gifts, the responses were more the sort I had expected. My initial awkward attempt at gift-giving and expectations of appreciation must be understood within the wider context of inequalities that are reinforced by humanitarian reason (Fassin 2012).

FIELD METHODS

My ethnographic approach is similar to what Sarah Willen (2007a, 2007b; building on Desjarlais 2003) calls a "critical phenomenological approach." In her study of "migrant illegality" in Israel, Willen considers juridical status, sociopolitical conditions, and lived experiences, and she highlights both the juridical and sociopolitical dimensions of how adult migrants in Israel are transformed from "benign 'Others'" into "illegals" and "wanted criminals." She stresses the importance of examining "migrants' modes of being in the world" and linking these with intended and unintended consequences of laws and policies (2007a, 9). This approach, with a key focus on everyday life, articulates well with public anthropology and ethnographic approaches that illuminate the subtle and complex processes through which policies not only affect everyday lives but are also approached or grappled with by migrants as they struggle to find logic, meaning, and humanity in what often appear to be heartless bureaucratic procedures and policies. As Willen argues, "Not only can a three-dimensional, critical, phenomenological perspective help social scientists better understand the form, contours, texture, and dynamics of illegal migrants' everyday lives in diverse host settings, but it can also help ethnographers sensitize policymakers, politicians, and potentially even broader public audiences to the challenging, and often deeply anxiety-producing, at times terrifying consequences that laws and policies frequently generate" (2007a, 28).[8] My aim is for this study to do the same.

My research—on the everyday lives of migrant mothers and babies and how they are shaped by laws, policies, and juridical status as well as by the wider socioeconomic and cultural contexts of migration—began in July 2010 but built on earlier research and relationships I had developed working with domestic workers and their advocates and service providers since the early 1990s. The 2010 PathFinders meeting—indeed, PathFinders itself—served as a key entrée. I was permitted to attend their meetings and discussion groups with migrant mothers. At the first few meetings in September 2011, I introduced myself and my research. Thereafter, I was introduced to more mothers and children and met some through my older contacts and domestic worker networks. I conducted structured "life history" interviews with over fifty-five migrant mothers that lasted typically about an hour but occasionally lasted over three hours. I got to know many of these women outside of the context of the interview as well. I conducted partial interviews or informal conversations with dozens more women, many of whom were friends of other migrant mothers. I interacted with mothers and babies in the spaces where they lived, in shopping malls, at restaurants, and in the park. I shared delicious Indonesian and Filipino meals with them. As noted above, I accompanied women and babies to many offices and appointments. I visited several women in public hospitals after their deliveries; accompanied one woman, following her miscarriage, in an ambulance to the hospital; and went with several women to the family planning clinic and with one woman to finish a stage of adoption paperwork.

I regularly visited a shelter for pregnant migrant women, mothers, and their children. The residents welcomed me partly because, as one of the few permitted visitors, I helped alleviate their boredom. For a while, the shelter was almost a second home to me—a place to talk, relax, eat, and hold babies, and through which to keep in touch with women when I left Hong Kong. Some women visited me in my tiny studio flat. I had the opportunity to visit two migrant women in prison. One highlight of the research was attending a child's baptism celebration. I attended countless birthday parties including those marking one month and one, two, three, or four years that were held in public spaces, restaurants, homes or crowded bedrooms, rooftops, and office spaces or shelters of various organizations. As time passed, I encountered women and children I knew on the street, at the park or market, or near the ISS food distribution centers. Several women and babies lived in my Jordan/Yaumatei neighborhood, often with roommates in a tiny room (fifty square feet or less) with a bunk bed in a small, cramped, subdivided walk-up flat. I attended classes for migrant women where they learned haircutting and jewelry-making, and I went to several fund-raising events for migrant organizations.

Although my main focus is on women and children and the bulk of my time was spent with them, I also had opportunities to get to know some men. Gordon Mathews, who conducted research in Chungking Mansions (2011), a haven for men from South Asia and Africa, invited me to attend his Saturday afternoon advanced English classes with refugee and asylum-seeker men. Attending the class numerous times and once serving as the "substitute" teacher gave me the opportunity to meet, over more than a year, twenty or more male asylum seekers, mostly from Africa but also from Pakistan and India, and to engage in many discussions with them about my research. Domestic workers and their babies were topics of great interest to most of these men. In the course of my research, I also got to know several fathers through friends or through their FDW partners.

Besides mothers and fathers, I conducted interviews with dozens of staff members of NGO and charity organizations; lawyers who work with migrant workers and asylum seekers; and numerous activists, advocates, and service providers who worked with current or former FDWs, asylum seekers, or refugees. Although several Hong Kong government officials, including those involved with social work, immigration, and labor, provided valuable written information by email, they were unwilling to meet for face-to-face interviews. Written materials from several local news sources, through the Philippine Consulate, and through various NGOs were also invaluable.

The following story is about Hope and Melinda, the two Filipinas mentioned above who were exasperated about "all the questions" they are constantly asked. Both are former FDWs and mothers of small children; Hope was almost thirty and Melinda close to forty when I met them in 2011. This story raises many themes mentioned above, and others that will be drawn out in later chapters. In contrast to the mistrust and competition described above, their friendship provided reassurance and security in the face of precarity and violence. They approached policies and procedures strategically, and they mistrusted bureaucracy and governmentality. Their stories demonstrate endurance and exhaustion, expectation and survival. They also illustrate subtle ways in which my role evolved from and blurred the lines of confidant, friend, and feminist-ethnographer-activist—a role far from that of detached observer.

HOPE AND MELINDA'S PLACE

To get to their place, I took the MTR to Yuen Long, then caught a Light Rail Train. Hope met me at the station with Liberty—Libby for short—in the stroller, and we walked through a small village, past what was once farmland but was now weedy and overgrown, dotted with old houses expanded with corrugated metal, wood, and concrete. The area was rural only in the sense that it was away from the tall buildings of Yuen Long. The buildings were one or two stories tall; some were warehouses, some housed small factories. Most of the buildings were hidden away behind rusty metal gates and fences, along dirt paths, and guarded by fierce-sounding dogs. Compared with Kowloon, the air was fresh.

Their place looked ramshackle—literally a zone of abandonment from the outside—but was surprisingly homey inside. There was an open courtyard with two chained dogs and piles of building materials and debris. A stairway led upstairs, where Mr. Wang, the landlord, was building another room to rent out. An open-air hallway led to the fenced backyard where Libby and Melinda's son Nicholas played alongside bricks, piles of wood, and rusty old pipes. The kitchen was outside, with a small roof and two partial walls. The bathroom was also outside and was shared by all the tenants. Melinda's room was about halfway down the open hallway. It was more than double the size of any of the mothers' rooms I had seen in Kowloon. The inside was clean and bright, and it housed a big bed, refrigerator, table, couch and television. The first time I visited, I noticed men's clothes hanging above the bed. They belonged to Niko, Melinda's partner who lived with her and Nicholas. The boy, a toddler, stood grinning from the doorway when we arrived, on the lookout for Libby, who was a few months his junior.

Melinda, Niko, and Nicholas had recently moved from an outside room into a more sheltered inside one because winter was approaching. Hope and Libby took over Melinda's old room facing the backyard. It was smaller than Melinda's new room, and there were a few mildew stains on the walls, but the floors were new linoleum. A big bed took up half the room. There was a television, a small table, and stools. Hope shared the refrigerator in the communal outside kitchen. Hope and Libby spent their days there but stayed with Libby's father, Ahmed, every night. Hope cooked Ahmed's meals and prepared his lunch to take to work, then returned each morning to visit Melinda and Nicholas. Given Hope's night-time absence, Melinda helped her find two Filipina boarders (overstayers). The two women worked nearby and were happy to share the place in exchange for paying minimal rent.

The landlord rented out eight or ten rooms. At various times there were Chinese, Indian, Nepalese, and four or five Filipino tenants including Hope and Melinda, and Niko, who had Hong Kong right of abode. Nicholas and Libby were the only children, and they benefited from the attention of many "aunties." With the exception of Niko, the adult tenants were all for-mer domestic workers.

Rent in this area provided twice the space it would in Kowloon or Hong Kong Island. Both Melinda and Hope had filed torture claims, so the ISS provided their landlord HK$1,400 each month for each woman and child. One problem was that the landlord had required a month's rent in advance, which the ISS would not provide. Melinda and Hope expected Mr. Wang to reimburse them when he received the payment from the ISS, but he claimed ISS payments did not start until the second month. Several women I knew complained about ISS payments being late or landlords claiming not to have received them. All they could do was speak to the ISS and hope it would be sorted out. From the ISS perspective, "slumlords" like Mr. Wang were untrustworthy and difficult to deal with, but, consequently, ISS clients like Melinda and Hope were caught in the middle. They went out of their way to be polite to Mr. Wang, bringing him food and "chatting him up." "We share our food with him, but he never shares with us," Melinda said. Their consideration stemmed partly from their vulnerability. He could easily inform the ISS that Hope had boarders and that Melinda shared her room with a Hong Kong resident, and he could alert authorities about the boarders' illegal work, though doing so would likely put him at risk as well, since his tenants were all in the same boat and much of the building was an illegal structure. Melinda and Hope deemed Mr. Wang "very good" because he mostly minded his own business.

Melinda and Hope benefited from strategic omissions when they spoke to their immigration and ISS caseworkers. Both originally claimed not to know their child's father's whereabouts. Although both fathers had reservations about acknowledging paternity, the mothers benefited from this arrangement. It would allow them sole custody of the child if they had to leave Hong Kong, and it meant they could claim food and rent from the ISS. Those benefits would be eliminated or reduced if they were known to be living with legally employed partners.

On one of my visits in 2011, I interviewed Hope. Her family lived in northern Mindanao and was Protestant among the Roman Catholic majority. She was "wild" when she was young, causing her family "many headaches." She graduated from college with a bachelor's degree in hotel management. She worked briefly at a hotel, "but the salary is so low. . . . I was just thinking that I can earn more as a DH [domestic helper] here than I can in Philippines." Like her older sister, who went to work as a FDW in Kuwait after she finished her university degree, Hope left her parents and brothers for Hong Kong. "We did not think that [could happen], working as a DH after getting a BS! But we both did."

Hope arrived in Hong Kong in 2008 and worked for three different employers. Each time, there were problems, and she did not complete the contracts. She said it was probably her fault the first two times, because she was responsible for several children and she did not get along with her Chinese employers. After the first two jobs, she returned home to process another contract. Her third and last employer was a Pakistani man whose wife worked weekdays in China. Hope cooked and cleaned their flat and was happy to work in the man's office, even though it was illegal, because "it was less boring than housework." But when his wife was away, he began making moves. Hope told him she had a boyfriend and repeatedly rebuffed him. On the pretense that she had done something wrong at the office, he fired her.

While Hope had worked for her first employer, she met Ahmed, a young Pakistani man several years her junior. They first met over the phone when a friend gave him her number. At the time, he had worked in Hong Kong for a year doing packing and delivery for a factory. His father had right of abode and sponsored Ahmed as a dependent. Assuming all went well, he would have the right to apply for permanent residency after seven years. At first Hope and Ahmed talked on the phone and exchanged text messages. They met every Sunday until she was terminated and went back to the Philippines for her new visa. Hope was surprised that Ahmed waited for her while she was away. Many women considered him a "good catch" given his good looks, his job, and his prospect for permanent residency.

At first their relationship was good: "We used to love each other, really *love.* . . . But we got in trouble because he is still so young. He's only 22. But he's getting more responsible [now that] he's got the baby. The only problem is he cannot stand up to his father and his family in Pakistan. His father is here in Yuen Long! One town! But he does not know that he already has a granddaughter and that she's one year old." Looking back, Hope realized that there were early signs of trouble. Once, when Ahmed heard a man's voicemail message on her phone, he got angry and hit her. The man was "a friend who knows someone who can maybe help me meet an employer. But he doesn't want to listen to my explanation and he slapped me. I remember that first time slap. Why I didn't leave him at that time?"

"Maybe you thought it would be just one time?" I said.

"Yes, just one time. That's what everyone thinks," she answered.

When Hope was terminated by her third employer, unaware that she was pregnant, she went to live with Ahmed and overstayed her visa for three months. People teased her and said "Just three months! If you overstay, you should have done it much longer!" When she surrendered at the Immigration Department, they gave her recognizance papers and also advice on how to file a torture claim. At the time she did not know what a torture claim was, but they told her to fill out the forms, which would allow her to "use the hospital," so she did:

I surrendered because I was pregnant. And I was thinking that . . . using the Hong Kong ID all the time to go in the hospital is—you know—illegal. So at the time I was thinking, maybe it is better for me to surrender. Maybe I can get more help, because at that time my situation is very delicate. There were twins. One baby is not well. The other baby is, umm, is very weak, so when I surrendered I was thinking that they would help me. . . . But it [one twin] suddenly stopped, two months before being born. . . . I did not know that I lost the baby but it was three weeks already since the baby had passed away in my tummy. So that's terrible. I still felt them moving—the two of them. But after delivery there is one on the table and they said she's the only one. She's preterm, they said, 38 weeks.

At first Ahmed was afraid to put his name on Libby's birth certificate.

> He's scared of his father, because his father doesn't know about me, and he's worried about the family in Pakistan. His older brother and sister in Pakistan and his dad still don't know about us. He keeps hiding us. He's not ready to face his family.

Hope cried, recalling how she went through labor alone because Ahmed was afraid someone would find out.

> When I am in labor he is not there [for me]. Even when I am there [at his place], I have to call the ambulance myself. He couldn't face it. . . . He was there when the water [broke]. . . . I cried when I said "the baby is coming" . . . I put the towel there because water is coming out. He's there but he doesn't know what to do. I said to him, "It's okay, I will go out. I will call an ambulance."

Between contractions, Hope managed to go downstairs to the roadside and call an ambulance.

> And he is at home. But he's so—he cannot do anything—because at that time I don't always understand things. And I think "his father will know," like that. I am always scared *for him*. And I'm in this situation but I always take care of *him*. And I'm in that situation [giving birth].

A few minutes earlier, Melinda had come into Hope's room to turn on the rice cooker, and she gently interjected, "She always cares for him."

Hope continued, "And that time too, I do like that. I'm sitting on the stairs and I said 'I'm all alone.' Alone there and giving birth to the two— and the dead baby—and it is so, you know, hard. It's really hard. You know I feel such pity."

"But she's very strong. And every time I shout at her: 'Why do you do like that? Why do you do like that?!'" says Melinda.

"Did he come to the hospital?" I ask.

> He did not. Because I just protect him. Because maybe [they will ask him] a lot of questions, maybe I tried to cover [for] him. Because when I surrendered I did not tell Immigration that the father is here. I just said, "The father? I don't know. He went back to Pakistan. I will just wait for him." Like that. Why?

Hope is crying, and Melinda and I sit on either side of her at the edge of the bed and put our arms around her shoulders. We sit in silence for several minutes while Hope cries. Then Hope continues: "Later, when he saw the baby, he starting to, you know, open his eyes. And then he said he wants to put his name [on the birth certificate] and he doesn't care if his father knows. . . . He loves the baby. He really loves the baby."

"Do you think he loves you too?" I ask.

"I don't know. That's a question. It's—I can't—I don't know. But he wants me to be here."

After Libby was born, Ahmed asked Hope to marry him, but she was reticent. She struggled with the decision, including her belief that marriage should be permanent and based on love and respect:

> I don't want to get married now, but I want to get married some day. I tried to look at my heart and if I marry I couldn't give—my whole heart. . . . Actually I told him "I did not ask to, and I never meant to, stay here in Hong Kong. I only stay here because I love you and I cannot get away from you. I will not marry just to be in Hong Kong." There's one Filipina, and she said "you have to be thankful your boyfriend wants to marry you. Me, I'm the one who always has to ask my boyfriend 'will we get married? We get married?' like that. You are such a proud girl." I am not a proud girl. I just want to make my life right. . . . If I really want to be a Hong Kong resident, what am I going to do after I marry him? Be a plain housewife? Be alone? And just sacrifice everything like that? . . . I said "I'm not after just being a resident here. If I want[ed] to I can just get a Chinese [husband] here." I am good, even though we have fights, I don't mind. I just struggle with my feelings. How to leave him? How to handle being away? That's my problem, really. But I made a decision already that I have to leave; I have to go back to my country.

Among the concerns Hope mentioned was that Ahmed is Muslim and plans to marry a woman in Pakistan to please his family. She knows Ahmed loves Libby and has been financially responsible, but she does not know if he loves her, and she does not think she loves him anymore, given his abuse. "When you tell him you think of going home, what does he say?" I ask.

> That was before, when I told him that, he says, "you go by yourself and the baby will live here. You will not go with her. She will live here and she will go

to school and she will die here." So I just keep quiet. So now I'm planning to go back to the Philippines. I don't let him know about my plans. I am planning to run away. But when we are good, I cannot think of what is good—what is good for me. When he is nice, it is simple. No fighting and then change plans, change plans again.

When she was pregnant, Hope spent four months at a shelter hiding from Ahmed. Once, when he burst her eardrum, she reluctantly went to the hospital and filed a police report, but she decided not to press charges so as not to hurt his chances of getting residency. She read online about domestic abuse to understand its impact and why it was so hard to leave him:

I want to know what happened to me because I am the victim, you know. And I was not like that before. It is like a twist on my part. Actually, my family has a few resources, but I am just a wild-hearted one and I just want to follow my wants. My mother doesn't want me to come here. What mother wants her daughters to be away as domestic helpers? She says that I can clean at home! But now I want to go home and I understand now, being a mother. I was lost, so lost. It is not wrong to love, but it is killing me. Well I think, think, I think it is calm. Not much story to tell. I am searching because I am here alone. I am thinking what should I do? What should I feel? Maybe too much battering and I lost my memory. I am very forgetful. Maybe it is from slapping. My eardrum is broken; my balance is off.

Hope understood Ahmed's violence to be patterned on his father's behavior toward his mother. Ahmed's mother committed suicide when he was an adolescent, and he blamed her death on his father's abuse. Hope thinks Ahmed wants her to take care of him "like a mother" but he also wants to dominate her. She feels sorry for him because of his mother's death but also resents his selfishness:

When we fight over and over I always want to run away. You know, I am older than him but he shows no respect and then I can see: "Where is the love here? . . . ." It is so unfair, because you sacrifice a lot with him. My parents did not bring me up to be like this. They know about my situation. My mother visited me already; she met him.

A Filipina to whom Hope had confided told her mother about Ahmed's abuse:

So my mother is crying in front of him. She says "Why did you do that?" and he just stays quiet and then says "Sorry" and that he won't do it again. But it *happens*. Again. I know he grew up without a mother, so I just let him experience having my mother. And it's so tiring on my part because I am the older one and he just wants to be cared for a lot. And [she shouts aloud] *"I'm not your mother! I'm not your mother!"* like that. *"I'm not your older sister!"* All around, I'm like that. "Okay, I can be your friend but I cannot be your mother, you know!" . . . It is so tiring because I need someone who is also taking care of me. . . . It's not only the financial part that can make the partner happy. But being secure and being taken care of that's the only thing— the, you know, the girl wants. It is so hard. Those moments I'm alone. I go alone. It is my first baby.

Melinda says gently, "she struggled a lot. She really struggled a lot." Hope's sister was also worried and visited on her way home from Dubai. Hope says:

My sister visited me for just 16 hours. She met the father. And she asked me, "Is this really the one you want to be with for the rest of your life? *Really?*" Because she is still single and she's older than me. I just kept quiet. And she just said, "Think, think!" She said that Muslims are terrorists. She is scared because she thinks maybe someday the father will run away with the baby. I should have gone back when I was pregnant with the twins . . . but I stayed here because of him. I overstayed because of him.

Hope often feels she is walking on eggshells. She watches for the "hard" expression on Ahmed's face when he gets angry. Small things can trigger his temper, like the man's voice on her phone:

The last time he is angry because I can't cook the *paratha* [fried bread] well. "Not cooked too much!" He's angry. Libby is crying and he doesn't want her to, and he is angry. And when Libby cries early in the morning and he is sleeping, he doesn't want the baby to disturb him. I cannot keep her quiet. Little things like that. It is very stressful, very stressful.

After Libby was born, she and Hope were in the hospital for almost three weeks. When they got home, Ahmed had a fit:

I just get a new baby for the first time. How many slaps and kicks he gave me? He hit me after I gave birth. He slaps me, and he bumps his head on my head. I have so many bruises. And that time he hit me I received too much.

I have no towel and I am bleeding [from the birth] and I tell him I need to go out and wash and Libby is crying and he said, "Why didn't you think of her milk and all that [before]?" And our place is upstairs and I need to go down [to the bathroom]. And I am washing [myself] and he's really angry that it is taking too long and she is crying. And at that time he is having trouble with the company [where he works]. So he pushes me. When I receive slaps, so many slaps, with his head he bumps my head and I am swollen here and [have] bruises and so many slaps, and punches on my butt. He's a tall guy and his hands are so big. I try to run away. I am so scared. [I'm] holding the baby, and she is [less than] three weeks.

A Chinese couple saw Hope, bruised and crying on the road, and they offered to call the police.

But I'm too proud to call the police. I cannot do that because I still depend on him, and he will hit me if I call the police. Maybe he will be caught and maybe his Daddy will know. I am protecting him! *Still* I am doing that. The time I finally call the police he has a small knife. It wounded his hand—it is bleeding—and he is blaming me and said it is my fault he cut his hand because he doesn't want to hurt me. But still until now I am staying with him.

Hope frequently suffers from headaches and earaches:

I have medicine for my ear and the music is loud and I ask him "Can you turn down the music?" because he likes it very loud, like a disco. And he doesn't like me to tell him what to do. He told me he won't turn it off. Little things can be fixed, but things like that can't be fixed. I'm so scared when he gets angry. I'm used to slaps. And he throws things. "Don't do like that!" he says and he holds the [cigarette] lighter on my breast. Later on I am just ignoring the pain and it is swelling. I am the big problem to him. He does not see that I am important. That's why I really plan to go back home. . . . When Libby is a baby and we are fighting she is scared, she is [Hope opens her eyes wide and shrinks back pantomiming fear]. Libby hugs me tight and is watching as the father's eyes are getting wide and the face getting red and the voice is so loud, shouting in my face, like that. [As Hope imitates Ahmed's anger, Libby begins to cry.]

I spoke to Hope many times, telling her about organizations that could help and encouraging her to go to a domestic shelter. She gave me permission to tell a social worker about her, and the social worker promised to find her a safe place to stay. I told Hope to call me any time, day or night. She says:

> I want to wait first, because I want to go away immediately, when I have Libby's passport. I don't want to be here for a while and then separate. I have to plan what I want to happen: she can have a passport, and the father will get a visa for her. Maybe it will take three months to work it out. And what will happen in three months? How many fights? Maybe there is an effect from being beaten, you know, being battered? You are very—so down. Depressed and intimidated.

I say I understand, but I urge her to go somewhere else.

> He'll find out. That's why he always says, "There's something you are not telling me." He plans to have a birthday celebration for her for one year and I want her to experience her birthday with him. . . . Maybe I can just stay put for a while. It's not waiting, it's like you are making a puzzle one by one to make it whole.

We talk about her plans to return to the Philippines "for good" and then to leave Libby with her mother and perhaps join her sister to work in Dubai.

> Better to go back. Yes, that's why I'm thinking a lot. Every day, every minute it comes to my mind to go back home. But it is so hard because I cannot tell him because he will turn, you know, like a demon.

She laughs nervously. I say, "Maybe one day soon, you can just leave?"

> Run away. That's my plan. Is it a good idea? I think maybe it is unfair to the father. If I tell him, he will not allow it. It's a problem because last month the father says he wants to get married. He just wants to marry for the custody, for the sake of—and you know it would give him legal rights. And then that's the time I don't have the right to have her. He wants to keep her.

"How would he take care of her?" I ask.

> When I asked him, he said "It's not your business anymore!" I just keep quiet. And I don't mention it again to him just to avoid arguments. I just keep quiet. It's none of my business!? He would send me back to the Philippines—he would buy me a ticket but the baby would stay here!? That cannot!! Now we are good, but I'm worried that he will fight because he

cannot avoid fighting. He will fight us apart. . . . Even just a few hours he cannot handle her. I will lose my mind if I leave her. The family in Philippines is willing to—they are eager to see her. . . . But he told me, "Don't do anything that will make me—" "Like bring her to *my country*?" "Do not do that!" and "I cannot promise what I will do to you if you take her." He said, "I may kill you."

I remind her about shelters where she and Libby could stay. "When you are out of the situation," I say, "you will feel differently." "Yes, it [will be] a relief! Especially with family! Yes, that's my feeling. Watching him being with Libby is, you know, it's very painful."

In late 2011, Hope continued to plan each step to take Libby to the Philippines. Her family would welcome them, help look after Libby, and she would eventually go to work in Dubai with her sister. Following another bitter fight, Ahmed vowed again to change, and, as an indication of his commitment, he insisted on putting his name on Libby's birth certificate. Thereafter, however, the Philippine Consulate would no longer issue Libby a passport without her father's permission. When Hope approached Ahmed about the passport, he demanded that she get a Pakistani passport instead. Tensions were high, but Hope was determined. She withdrew her torture claim and approached an NGO about getting help with Libby's Philippine travel document, despite Ahmed's objections.

Hope repeatedly told me and Melinda how wrong it seemed to separate father and daughter. Melinda said, "He can come to the Philippines to see the baby if he wants to!" Melinda turned to me, "I told [Hope], 'You have a lot of time. You are still young' and the family is still there supporting her."

One day in 2012, while I was accompanying another mother home from the hospital, I got a frantic call from Melinda, saying that Ahmed had found a copy of Hope's letter to the Immigration Department withdrawing her torture claim and explaining that she planned to return to the Philippines with Libby. Ahmed had beaten Hope and taken Libby. Hope was hiding in a nearby park. I recommended that Melinda call the police and gave her the shelter's number. After a few hours, with Niko's help, Hope retrieved Libby, and I arranged to meet them at the MTR station.

When I found them, Hope was sitting on the floor with Libby, behind a wide column, crying and wearing dark glasses that covered her bruised, swollen face. She described Libby's terror when they fought. She refused to call the police or go to the hospital. I phoned the shelter. Eventually—after many hours, several calls, and many questions that Hope could barely answer in her shattered state—she was admitted to a shelter in an undisclosed location. There she received some counseling but kept in touch with Ahmed by phone. He apologized, begged forgiveness, made promises. Hope and I met over the next few days. I brought her clothes from PathFinders and diapers for Libby. Hope said she felt stronger. Ahmed agreed to meet her at the Philippine Consulate and sign the forms for Libby's passport. After two weeks, Hope went back to live with him.

I was not a detached interviewer. As I got to know Hope and Melinda and their children, I offered practical advice and support. As a feminist-ethnographer-activist, I shared my opinion and my phone number, linked women to service organizations and individuals who could help them, and gave them diapers and other things they needed. Hope's story was one of many I heard that were punctuated by violence and precarity—perhaps fueled by a loss of hope in what education would accomplish, in romantic dreams, and in the "capitalist 'good life' fantasy" (Puar 2012, 171). Ahmed struggled with his personal ghosts, fear of his father, and tensions at work. He vented his fears, frustrations, anger, and fantasies of dominance on Hope. Domestic abuse is, of course, not exclusive to undocumented minorities, but for noncitizen or undocumented migrants there is far more to lose from filing police reports or going to the hospital, and shelters where most residents speak a different language provide little comfort. Domestic violence is difficult for every victim, but for outsiders the forms of governmentality associated with assistance are regarded with suspicion and are often experienced as degrading and risky, potentially putting them and their children (and their partners) at even greater risk.

3 Women

> The debates surrounding the TKW [*tenaga kerja wanita*,
> overseas woman labor migrant] reflect gendered tensions
> about modernity. The TKW is a "woman out of place," a
> figure whose transnational mobility and associated gaya
> [style] both threatens the national order and promises a
> way forward. Popular representations of the TKW as WTS
> [*wanita tuna susila*, women without morals, prostitutes]
> cast them as dangerous and shameful women who have
> forsaken their families and their nation in order to satisfy
> their own selfish, consumeristic desires.
>
> — Rachel Silvey (2009, 54–55)

GENDER AND NATION

Women and their morality are often highly charged symbols of a nation's honor. In Indonesia and the Philippines, ideas about women's morality—reinforced by dominant Indonesian Islamic and Filipino Roman Catholic beliefs—are closely tied to women's roles at home as wives and mothers or daughters. Labor migration takes women away from their homes and subjects them to many outside dangers; it creates both an ideological and a practical challenge to the Indonesian and Philippine states. On the one hand, both governments are deeply dependent on migrant women, who are critical income-earners for their families and essential contributors to the national project of economic development. On the other hand, both governments are subject to criticism from the middle-class public, activists, and NGOs because of the harm and violence that migrant workers may experience, with extreme outcries expressed when migrant workers are killed or executed overseas (Rafael 2000; Guevarra 2006). Those who voice such concerns, which are sometimes paired with anxiety about the shame that migrant women bring to the nation by virtue of their subservient roles and potential immorality, call on the government to devise ways to protect vulnerable migrants or put a stop to migration altogether (Blackburn 2004; Constable 2010; Guevarra 2006; Robinson 2000; Rodriguez 2010; Silvey 2007).

Since the 1990s, both Indonesia and the Philippines have passed legislation and imposed controls on migration processes in an effort to allay criticism that they do too little to protect vulnerable workers. Yet attempts to protect and empower migrant workers often create further problems or simply shift the blame to the women. Anna Guevarra argues in the case of the Philippines that "in 'empowering' women, the state, through the support of NGOs and labour brokers of employment agencies, not only endeavours to make them into economically productive workers but also ensures that they are 'good' wives, mothers, and women" (2006, 525). As such, "normative gender roles thus define the moral grounds upon which Filipino women must fashion themselves as workers" (525). New "gender sensitive" measures aimed to protect and empower migrant workers put the state "in a position to appear to appease its public and at the same time continue to profit from the deployment of women into these 'vulnerable' work occupations" (530). Guevarra shows that "the ways the state, and the NGOs it relies on, address such vulnerabilities focus on modifying workers' behaviour instead of addressing the structural conditions that enable the physical and sexual exploitation of women workers" (531). In other words, workers are encouraged to "promote a particular public image by managing their family roles and sexuality" and to follow "cultural norms of femininity" that fit with the state's larger neoliberal economic project, and the workers are ultimately blamed for migration-related vulnerabilities (532).

In a powerful critique of the Indonesian state-sanctioned migration scheme with Malaysia, Olivia Killias argues that it "leads Indonesian domestic workers into bonded labour" (2010, 909). State-sanctioned migration processes and legislation—including the requirement that all workers use employment agencies to work abroad—are allegedly intended to protect workers but instead often resemble conditions of "colonial indentured labour" where migrant women are afraid or unwilling to leave harmful and exploitative work situations because they are heavily indebted to and reliant on employment agencies. Laws exist to protect migrant workers from violence and exploitation abroad, but workers are often discouraged from complaining, asserting their rights, or "making trouble" by a wide range of people, including speakers at state-sponsored predeparture programs, employment agents and subagents, employers, and even relatives and friends who pressure or encourage them to tolerate difficulties. Killias argues that "illegal migration" can thus serve as a means of resisting coercive state-sanctioned systems of migration.

Well-disciplined migrant women, whose bodies are controlled and who are not the subject of criticism, are in the best interest of the sending state as well as the receiving one. Hong Kong and its citizens benefit from having obedient, disciplined, and affordable FDWs to do the work they prefer not to do themselves. The standard "foreign domestic helper" (FDH) employment contract and the surrounding policies set out the rights and obligations of workers and employers. They prohibit workers from bringing family members with them, dictate the conditions of their all-encompassing work lives, and thus distance them from their possible roles as mothers or wives. As noted, from the Hong Kong employers' perspective, ideal workers are devoted to their employers' households. They are always available, obedient, and nonassertive; their sexuality is, ideally, nonexistent or nonthreatening. Politically or sexually active domestic workers, including lesbians or tomboys, are cause for concern among some employers (Constable 1996, 1997, 2000, 2007).

In chapter 5, I will focus on sexuality, pregnancy, and babies; here, I turn to the gender-neutral and sexually nonthreatening construction of FDHs in Hong Kong, to some key policies and practices that structure their vulnerability as workers, and to the gender norms, expectations, and concerns relating to women and migrant workers in their home countries. I begin with work-related policies and their unintended consequences. Next, I turn to the sociocultural profile of Filipino and Indonesian domestic workers in relation to the mothers I knew, highlighting similarities and differences between Filipinas and Indonesians. Stories of Ara, of Ina and baby Angela, and of Marah, her mother, and her partner illustrate how policies and employment practices at home and abroad unintentionally promote overstaying and illegal work, and how workers are encouraged to endure bad work situations.

As I argue here and in the chapters that follow, gender is a key factor in why domestic workers overstay and work illegally. The laws and policies in Hong Kong and their home countries make it essentially impossible to be both a good worker and a good wife/mother/daughter. Migrant mothers challenge Hong Kong's attempt to define them as just workers, and they contest their own state's attempts to label them as bad women. They overstay and work illegally precisely because they aspire to be good mothers and workers, and sometimes wives, which is nearly impossible to do as legal workers in Hong Kong or as single mothers back home.

FOREIGN DOMESTIC WORKERS IN HONG KONG

The number of FDWs reached over 300,000 in January 2012, according to the Hong Kong Immigration Department. This included 149,324 from Indonesia, 145,337 from the Philippines, 3,309 from Thailand, and 3,956 from other countries, including India, Nepal, Bangladesh, and Sri Lanka. The vast majority of FDWs are women in their twenties and thirties, and roughly half are married. Filipino men account for the largest group of male domestic workers, but their numbers are very small. FDWs all come to Hong Kong on renewable two-year "foreign domestic helper" contracts and are legally required to live full time with their employers and do household work. Other than officially giving them a day off a week, the contract does not limit work hours, so many report working sixteen or more hours a day. Work includes mainly feminized duties: child care, elder care, cooking, and cleaning. The contract determines the legal conditions of their stay as well as their rights.

Hong Kong is generally considered a good place to work, and the conditions are much better than most Asian destinations, but several issues create problems for FDWs and increase their vulnerability. These include agency fees and illegal charges, the "two-week rule," which says they must depart within fourteen days of the termination of their contracts, and the requirement that they live with their employers.

Agencies

In order to work abroad, FDWs, especially Indonesian women, often agree to take out "personal loans" and pay exorbitant and often unlawful fees to recruiters and associated money lenders (Killias 2010; Palmer 2010). Despite women's dreams of earning and saving money while working abroad, overseas jobs can lead to mounting debts accompanied by vulnerability. This exemplifies what Laurent Berlant calls "cruel optimism," when "the object that draws your attachment [like a fantasy of the good life] actively impedes the aim that brought you to it initially" (2011, 1). Some workers are fortunate: they pay off their debts while working for reasonable, kind employers, and they contribute to the family's better life. Others are less so: they put up with abusive employers for fear of losing their anticipated income, are unable to send remittances home, and are unable to pay back debts, sometimes risking the loss of mortgaged family property (Ong 2009; Mission 2012; Constable 2007). NGOs in Hong Kong, such as the Mission for Migrant Workers and Helpers for Domestic Helpers, report a cycle of terminations. In those egregious cases, employers regularly terminate workers when (or before) the seven months required to repay their loans has elapsed. The agency provides the employer with a free replacement and charges the worker the full amount again, or close to it, for a new employer. This keeps the workers vulnerable and indebted while the employment and loan agencies get more money.

In the early 1990s, FDWs could avoid agencies and agency fees altogether and could renew their contracts on their own or locate an employer through personal networks without a fee (which was known as "direct hiring"). Today, however, the Indonesian and Philippine governments require FDWs to use recruitment agencies (Constable 1997; Killias 2010). The agency requirement has been severely criticized by domestic worker activists and NGOs because of abuses and illegality. Indonesian workers pay around HK$3,000 per month for seven months (HK$21,000), leaving them only a few hundred dollars of income. If they are prematurely terminated, they are often charged another HK$15,000.[1] Although Hong Kong agencies are only allowed to charge the worker 10 percent of one month's salary (less than HK$390), Hong Kong officials claim there is little they can do, since the excessive costs are charged by overseas agencies and the loan agreements are signed outside Hong Kong. The Philippines does not allow agencies to charge "recruitment fees" per se, and Indonesia had a legal maximum fee of HK$15,000 in 2011, but many agencies find ways to charge workers for such costs as mandatory training, forms, and paperwork. In many cases, prospective workers willingly sign loan agreements for advances from recruitment agents (or subagents) and for the costs associated with migration and training. Indonesian agencies usually require domestic workers to sign loan agreements and have the funds automatically deducted from their salaries. Workers agree because otherwise the agency will not find them employers. Even if a worker locates an employer on her own (for example, through a friend), she is required to pay an agency the required agency fees.

In Indonesia, recruitment agents are not permitted to approach prospective FDWs directly, so they rely on advertisements, recruitment workshops, and informal illegal recruiters. In Java, where most agencies are located, agencies rely on *petugas lapangan* (field agents, or PLs) or *calo* (illegal intermediaries) to approach women (Lindquist 2009, 2010; Palmer 2010). Indonesian domestic workers interviewed on the topic at a Hong Kong shelter mostly reported that they were recruited through *calo* who were often relatives or neighbors (Palmer 2010). As a member of the woman's community, *calo* are likely to be trusted more than agency staff and can effectively put pressure on her family (husband or father) and the local or village leader, whose permissions are required for her to work abroad. Stressing the importance of the "economy of trust" involving agents and subagents and of migrants' reliance on their roles in the "manufacture of legality," Johan Lindquist describes the PL as follows:

> He wears button-down shirts and handles all the paperwork that is demanded in the manufacture of legality—including a birth certificate, an identity card, a medical certificate, various government letters, and, finally, a passport for the recruit. He understands how much money must be handed out along the way and deals with the process that the migrant cannot navigate on his or her own. But he also knows how to speak to migrants in their language and engage them in an economy of trust. (2009, 57)

Women often receive "pocket money" or substantial cash advances from the subagent as incentive for recruitment. According to Wayne Palmer, these financial incentives have attracted notice from NGOs, who claim that agents are effectively bribing women to migrate. Government officials have also expressed concern about the practice, citing cases of migrant workers in Hong Kong and . . . Singapore who say they were persuaded to migrate against their will, usually by husbands or fathers who were keen to use the pocket money to pay off debts. In some of these cases, when women told agents they didn't want to go, their objections were ignored. (2010)

When a domestic worker begins to work in Hong Kong, she must pay back her "debts," including the "pocket money." They usually

make seven monthly instalments of HK$3000 (equivalent to 84 per cent of their wage) to Hong Kong creditors in order to pay it off. Of the debt, HK$3000 is interest owed to public finance companies that provide the loans. HK$7000 is paid to Hong Kong agents for organising things like work visas, and a further HK$11,000 is earmarked for Indonesian agents to cover the cost of training and recruitment, which includes the expense of incentives such as pocket money. (Palmer 2010)

Activists, advocates, and scholars have repeatedly argued that excess fees are illegal and unethical, akin to bonded labor or working for several months for little or no salary, and that such arrangements render domestic workers vulnerable to a range of exploitation and abuse (Lee and Petersen 2006). For fear of defaulting on their debts and falling even deeper in debt, let alone not being able to send money home, migrant workers in Hong Kong—like those in Malaysia (Killias 2010)—put up with difficult or abusive situations. Reports of physical, sexual, and emotional abuse and conditions resembling slavery are not unheard of (Ong 2009). Slaps, kicks, burns, rapes, and "falling" or jumping off of tall buildings are extreme and terrible examples. Less extreme examples include long working hours, insufficient food, no days off, and inadequate shelter. Workers put up with such treatment because they do not know their rights or out of fear of being terminated, losing their income, and taking on ever-mounting debt in the precarious labor market. A few fight for their rights, others choose to overstay.

The Two-Week Rule

When a worker's contract ends, her employer may renew it, or the worker might find a new employer and pay more agency fees. Some women work for one contract and one employer, then return home; some work for several employers. One Filipina I know worked for one family for over twenty-five years. If the employer says it would cause hardship for the FDW to leave, she is normally permitted to delay her return home, or she can go to nearby Macau by ferry for the day to renew her visa. If her contract is terminated prematurely, with a few exceptions (say, if an employer dies or moves abroad), she becomes subject to the notorious New Conditions of Stay, better known as the "two-week rule" that went into effect in 1987 and requires that a domestic worker return home within fourteen days of the termination of her contract if she has not found a new employer.

Like illegal charges by agencies, the two-week rule has been subject to much criticism by activists, advocates, and scholars, all of whom point to the unreasonably short period of time this provides to find a new employer. Other foreign workers who are terminated from their work (especially "skilled" workers) are often permitted to stay for the remainder of time on their visas at the discretion of the director of the Immigration Department, but FDWs, even those who have filed legal cases against their employers, lose their domestic worker visas within fourteen days, thus ensuring that they work or leave.

For those FDWs who have labor claims against their employers, the situation is especially harsh. They must repeatedly apply and pay for short-term visitor visas that prohibit them from working. If they remain in Hong Kong to pursue their cases, they cannot earn money, often accrue interest on their debts, and have little choice but to become dependent on charities and NGOs for several months (sometimes over a year) or to take the risk of working illegally to support themselves and their families. Needless to say, this policy discourages FDWs from filing complaints against their employers. They would rather work or return home than spend months in limbo. Two weeks are often not enough to find a new employer, and several mothers cited the policy as one reason they over-stayed. The two-week rule and debts from overcharging contribute to the reluctance to leave abusive employers.[2] Many workers would rather stay in situations where they are underpaid or abused than risk having no employer or income and being forced to return home.

The two-week rule was allegedly designed to prevent domestic workers from "job hopping" (leaving one employer for another), but it serves—as does the live-in requirement described below—much more broadly to regulate and restrict migrant women, to prevent them from having too much untethered time in which to be someone other than an "FDH." If they are forced to work or leave, these young women cannot roam around, get into trouble, or pose a threat.

Living In

FDH employment contracts bind the workers to one household and require them to live with their employers. For all but the luckiest, this means they live and work in small flats and are on-call twenty-four hours a day, six days a week, often working twelve or more hours a day. Some are caregivers, looking after children, the sick, disabled, or elderly, pushing wheelchairs or strollers, bathing children and the infirm, changing diapers and dispensing medications. They cook, clean, shop, walk dogs, wash cars, run errands, and wash and iron clothes. Even when workers and employers get along well, working and living in someone else's home— often small flats with tight quarters and little privacy—is not easy. Within intimate household spaces, cultural and religious differences are significant. The pay may be good by Indonesian and Philippine measures, where workers face massive underemployment, but it is well below the hourly minimum wage of HK$28 (US$3.60) paid to Hong Kong locals in 2011–12. One reason why FDWs are hired in Hong Kong is that local workers are unwilling to live in or work for such long hours and low wages.

Domestic workers are critical to the prosperity and well-being of Hong Kong people, but as "servants"—much like those of early states described by Hannah Arendt (1958), they are excluded from the rights and benefits of citizens. In Hong Kong, they are also differentiated from other workers and other expatriates. During my field research, the contractual minimum allowable wage for FDWs was raised to HK$3,740 (US$480) per month for workers signing contracts after June 2, 2011—far below the hourly minimum wage guaranteed to other Hong Kong workers.[3] FDWs are the only workers who are required by their contracts to live with their employers, reinforcing the extent to which the employer's household is the focus of the workers' time and energy for at least six days a week, often with extremely long and unregulated work hours.

In June 2012, the famous Hong Kong singer Purple Lee was interviewed for an article about a house she had designed. The article included photographs of the large house, including the domestic worker's "room" with a bed mounted in the bathroom next to the toilet. Critics and domestic worker activist groups were quick to criticize the singer on Facebook, seizing the opportunity to publicize maltreatment of domestic workers and to advocate rescinding the live-in requirement. Building on public interest, media reported on workers who illegally lived out (with the employer's permission). This was followed by an immigration raid and the arrests of twenty-five domestic workers for breaching the conditions of their employment contracts.[4] Little was said of charges against their employers. This was followed by a small demonstration by domestic workers and a few employers who favored allowing FDWs to live out.[5] Attention was drawn to the issue, but anxiety was also raised among FDWs who lived out and their employers. A further push for policy change was in progress in 2013, though critics expressed concern that workers who live out would get themselves into trouble.[6]

Hundreds of thousands of Hong Kong households depend on full-time, live-in FDWs. Such workers are considered a necessity by middle- and upper-class employers whose "dependence" on FDWs is widely acknowledged, especially households with children under age six or with elderly members who require care. Yet this dependence does not translate into equal rights. As Aihwa Ong writes of the wider Asian context, they are considered "an expendable and underpaid servant class" (2009, 158).

In an editorial entitled "An Injustice to Our Most Oppressed Expats," Hong Kong political commentator Alex Lo wrote:

> The maids, as a group, have over many decades contributed far more to the well-being and prosperity of Hong Kong than any other group of expats. We have all benefited, especially local women. How many female executives—or ordinary women workers—would have been confined to the home if domestic help had not been available? Those women have been liberated from domesticity and can now build meaningful—even powerful—careers on par with men, largely thanks to the maids' sacrifices. (2012)

Lo's view is not shared by many locals who welcome FDWs only when they "know their place," which is to work and then promptly return home.

Some locals express significant hostility toward FDWs, as was especially evident during the push for FDW right of abode (2011 to 2013), which prompted fear of competition for low-cost housing, welfare benefits, and other resources.

The rules and regulations placed on FDWs are intended to create disciplined workers' bodies that stay out of trouble. The two-week rule, combined with economic pressures and vulnerability created by recruitment debts, and the requirement that workers live in are all mechanisms of neoliberal governmentality that foster precarity and vulnerability. Such regulations often yield the opposite of the intended results. Rules are broken and policies ignored because, facing outrageous recruitment expenses, women cannot return home, and unreasonable restrictions make it nearly impossible for them to find new employers quickly enough. The stories below illustrate how such policies, paired with exorbitant agency fees, motivate some workers to overstay and work illegally.

ANGELA AND HER TWO MOTHERS

Baby Angela was eleven months old when I met her and her "two mothers"—as they introduced themselves—a month before they returned to Indonesia in 2011. Ara is Angela's birth mother, and Ina says she is her "second mother." Ina looks like a tomboy, and people who know her teasingly refer to her as "the father," but she shrugs it off and says "no, I'm really another mother." I bluntly asked them if they were partners, and Ina patiently explained that people often think so but that they are "best friends, not partners." Ara, Ina, and their close friend Sumiati, who had already returned to Indonesia, overstayed after their contracts ended.

As Ara explained, once her contract finished she could not find a job. A friend told her she could earn much more if she stayed and worked in a restaurant. Weighing prospective earnings of over HK$8,000 a month against the HK$3,700 she made as an FDW, and considering rent and what she would pay an agency, the decision was easy. Ara roomed with several Indonesian overstayers in a cheap boarding house. She was less lonely and had more freedom than with her employers, who allowed her out for only ten hours each Sunday.

Ara, Ina, and Sumiati had become close friends eighteen months earlier when they discovered that Ara was pregnant. Ina was the first to suspect Ara was pregnant; she noticed that her body was changing. Ara refused to believe it, so Ina bought a pregnancy test and confronted Ara with the results. Ara said she had no idea that she was pregnant and had no memory of having sex. Explaining how the situation came about, Ina explained:

> We actually had a sister, not really a sister, but a friend. . . . She is doing bad things. She sold her [Ara] to someone. She gave her some drugs and sold her to someone. Ara could not even remember [anything]. When she told me that story that time I thought she is just bluffing me. So I just don't care for this, but I think, "Why are you crying?" She tells this story. Like this. I tell her, "You just call the police and tell them! Why are you bluffing to me? Tell me the truth!" I feel like she is just lying to me, because this girl [the friend] she [always] treated her very nicely.

Ara interjected, "I think before that she is good person." "Before she always went around with her," said Ina.

Ara described how she had gone drinking with her friend, who introduced her to an African man. She could not recall what happened next, but in retrospect she believed she had been given a "date rape" drug and was raped. She woke up in her friend's place the next day with no recollection of the night before, and she forced it out of her mind until it was clear she was pregnant and she did not know what to do.

Ina said, "We don't know what to do so we try to abort—to throw away the baby."[7] Ara picked up where Ina left off:

> But we do it ourselves with medicine. I know the name but don't know if it is Chinese or what. Cytotek. We pick some up from someone and she said it can throw the baby away. After that I just eat the medicine but even though I eat the whole thing the blood does not come out.

I ask Ara how many pills she took, and she answered:

> Too, too many—maybe around fifty. In a day I take them three times and they say take two capsules and I take four capsules. I don't feel pain come or blood. No sickness, nothing.

Ina said:

> We just realize then that maybe God gives us a chance to have this baby. We
> have one friend [Sumiati], a good friend who went back to Indonesia now.
> She is older than us. . . . Of the three she always gives us help and counsel.
> "What can we do?"

Ara continued:

> Sumiati tells us "You can ask someone who already has baby and you ask for
> help if you don't want this one, maybe give to other parents." She said, "You
> just tell your ISS officer [and ask] what to do." And my ISS officer says
> "Okay, you take care of your pregnancy and after that you meet PathFinders
> and maybe they can help you to adopt the baby." At that time I am really
> confused. But since the abortion [did] not work, I said to the doctor "I tried
> to abort the baby." They did the ultrasound to see and all is perfect, even the
> brain.

I suggested that perhaps the medicine was fake. Ara said, "I could be sick
and the baby too." Ina explained how they bought the medicine from a
friend's friend for HK$1,500 (almost US$200). "We were scared. None of
us knows about it, so she tells us what to take and said not to be afraid. But
we were afraid."

Ina's torture claim had been rejected, and she was told she had to
leave Hong Kong. Ara decided to withdraw hers as well, rather than stay
in Hong Kong without Ina. I asked them about the basis for their torture
claims. Ara answered perfunctorily, "They ask why I don't want to go
back, and I say, 'Because I don't have any family there and now I am
pregnant so I want to stay in Hong Kong for a few years before I go back
to Indonesia.'" Ina's answer was equally vague. Knowing their claims
would not succeed and they are headed home, their stories no longer
seemed important to them. Ina said, "Same, I make up something—my
own story about this." I asked Ara why she cancelled her claim and
whether she would prefer to spend more time in Hong Kong. Ara
reminded me of her "bad luck" in Hong Kong. She was arrested for
working as a dishwasher after only one day at the restaurant. She was
charged with illegal work and overstaying. She spent several months in
Lowu prison while she was pregnant. Ina visited her every two weeks as

permitted and brought her baby formula and baby supplies. Ara found prison difficult and boring. "We feel here we have no life!" Ina emphasized, "We really have no future here!" They both agreed that the hardest part was Ara's arrest. After that, when they worked, they worried all the time. Ina said:

> Actually we do some illegal work but always our heart is like this [she gestures a pounding heartbeat]. That is why it is not good. Anywhere they can catch us! It is our bad luck maybe. We don't know when [we will be caught again]. But we have to think about Angela's future.

Ara concurred, "Yes, we have to think about our baby. We have to do what is good for her. It was hard for her when I was in detention. In the future we must look after her."

Ina's father has some land in Eastern Java, and they hoped to open a small restaurant or coffee shop. "We also can take care of her" she says, as she points to Angela who is pushing a toy stroller across the room. I ask if they will go abroad again, but they say there should be no need to because Ina's family has agreed to help them. Ara said:

> We prefer to stay with Angela. We can bring her up and stay with her. Maybe we will try to survive there. Maybe people will be thinking in Indonesia that we must first get married and then have a baby. But if I come with baby, but no father, they might think there is a fault with me, with us, I mean *with me*. They will think, "How did you get this baby? Maybe she is a prostitute." Many people will say things like that. But I don't care.

Ina adds, "Yes, we don't really care. We really don't care. Whatever they say they can say. But we are going to support our baby. I believe she will have a chance in the future—better than us."

When I ask them about the two-week rule, they both speak angrily at once, saying that this rule and unreasonable agency fees are at the root of the problem. Without the two-week rule paired with exorbitant agency fees, neither of them would have overstayed, they say. They would have sought out new employers, but they could not afford the agency fees again. Not fully aware of the risk, or of the bad luck of being arrested, they had thought they could earn more as overstayers.

PATTERNS AND PROFILES

Many sources contribute to a demographic profile of Filipino and Indonesian domestic workers in Hong Kong, including large-scale surveys by the Association of Indonesian Migrant Workers (ATKI), the Mission for Migrant Workers, and the Asian Migrant Centre (AMC) as well as data from the Hong Kong Department of Census and Statistics. In the pages below, I highlight key features of Filipina and Indonesian domestic workers compared with the mothers in this study. When I use specific numbers or percentages, I am referring exclusively to the fifty-five mothers who took part in my standard interviews and from whom I collected basic demographic information. This included nineteen Filipina and thirty-six Indonesian mothers. In my general discussions and in ethnographic sketches and examples, I do not limit myself to those fifty-five women but draw from a wider group of around a hundred mothers I knew.[8] In many ways, the fifty-five mothers are like other Filipina or Indonesian domestic workers, but in other ways, such as marital status, they are not.

My research mainly involved qualitative methods that are most useful to understand the lives and everyday experiences of migrant mothers and their babies, but quantitative material and survey data help to place the mothers in a wider context. That said, it is important to stress that the fifty-five mothers are not necessarily representative of all FDWs who become mothers, nor do they and the other mothers I met, talked to, or heard about constitute a representative or random sample. I met about two-thirds of the mothers I interviewed through PathFinders, whose clients are mostly Indonesian. I met other mothers through various migrant organizations and earlier research contacts and through mothers like Hope and Melinda (see chapter 2) who introduced me to their acquaintances.

Based on the mothers in this study, it might be tempting to think that there are more Indonesians than Filipinas who become pregnant in Hong Kong, or that there are relatively few women who have children with Chinese men, but this is not likely the case, for several reasons. PathFinders' clients (as opposed to other FDW mothers) may have nowhere else to go for help. Women who have local Chinese partners may have other options and resources to turn to for legal, bureaucratic, and child and maternal health-related assistance. Filipinas have been in Hong Kong longer than

Indonesians, have a greater range of migrant worker organizations to turn to, and may have better-established networks of friends and relatives in Hong Kong to advise them. Filipinas might also have better access to online and printed information. Indonesians are especially reluctant to return home pregnant and try to avoid doing so at any cost, whereas one study suggests that more Filipinas who get pregnant in Hong Kong may give birth in the Philippines (Ullah 2010). Anecdotally, Filipinas seemed to anticipate more social acceptance of single motherhood than Indonesians, a topic I return to later in this chapter. The higher number of local marriages involving Filipinas also suggests that there would be more Filipina former FDWs with Hong Kong–born children than my sample suggests. According to Immigration Department figures, which do not identify occupation, marriages of Filipinas registered in Hong Kong from 2008 to 2011 averaged 420 annually, whereas marriages of Indonesian women averaged 240.[9]

When and Where?

The history of Filipino and Indonesian FDWs in Hong Kong also differ. Filipinos began working there in the 1970s, first for English-speaking expatriate employers, then becoming popular with Chinese employers, partly because they could help teach English to the children. Local women increasingly went to work outside the home, and middle-class families could no longer rely on extended family members or Chinese amahs for household work (Constable 2007; Cortes and Pan 2009; Lan 2006).

The Indonesian government began to allow recruitment of women to work as maids in the Middle East in 1983 (Silvey 2004), but in the early 1990s few Indonesians worked in Hong Kong. By 1994 their numbers had begun to grow, and Indonesians overtook Thais as the second largest nationality of FDWs. In December 1994, Hong Kong hosted 10,000 Indonesians, 7,000 Thais, and 120,000 Filipinos (Constable 2007, 4). In 1997, when the Asian financial crisis hit Indonesia, and 1998, when President Suharto and his New Order regime fell, the Indonesian government and recruitment agencies actively promoted women as overseas workers, and their numbers jumped significantly. By December

1999, there were over 40,000 Indonesian FDWs, fewer than 6,000 Thais, and over 140,000 Filipinos in Hong Kong.

By the late 1990s, Filipino grassroots organizations, NGOs, and activists had become well established and highly effective at educating and assisting migrant Filipinos to assert their rights in Hong Kong. Surveys show that the abuses Filipinas faced at work a decade earlier had decreased significantly, though Indonesian domestic workers (who were younger, less experienced, and less educated) were more likely to suffer an array of abuses. Indonesians experienced more breaches of their contracts, such as underpayment, no weekly day off, inadequate food and shelter, and physical and emotional abuse (ATKI 2005; AMC et al. 2007; Mission 2012).

Indonesians rapidly gained popularity in Hong Kong at the turn of the century. Some Hong Kong Chinese employers prefer Indonesians because they are more conversant in Cantonese, having had language training before arrival. According to employers, Indonesians "know their place" and are less likely to complain of underpayment or other abuses. Indonesians are also considered less assertive and less savvy than Filipinas, with less effective social and activist networks and less knowledge of their rights and recourses. Employer preferences correlate with their educational and occupational status: Chinese employers who hire Filipinas are more likely to have college degrees and to have administrative, managerial, or professional jobs than those who hire Indonesians (Wang 2011). In 2001, the number of Filipino FDWs reached a peak of over 155,000; by 2006, it had dropped to under 118,000. By 2009, the number of Indonesian FDWs in Hong Kong reached over 130,000, overtaking Filipinas for the first time. Since then, Indonesians have remained the largest group by a small margin. Although numbers of both Indonesians and Filipinos have continued to increase in recent years, the media report growing shortages of domestic workers overall.[10]

The Filipina mothers, like other Filipina FDWs, migrate from many regions of the Philippines, but the largest numbers of FDWs come from Luzon, with many from Manila and the surrounding regions; most come from the more urban areas of the Philippines (Sayres 2007). The vast majority of Indonesian domestic workers come from rural areas of Java, the administrative and economic center of Indonesia; over 60 percent are from East Java (Jawa Timur), the poorest region of Java; over 25 percent are from Central Java (Jawa Tengah), 5 percent from West Java (Jawa Barat), and smaller numbers from other regions of Indonesia (ATKI 2005; AMC et al. 2007). The origins of the fifty-five mothers I interviewed echo these patterns.

Indonesians are generally newer to Hong Kong than Filipinas. In 2006, Filipino FDWs averaged 6.4 years in Hong Kong and Indonesians 3.3 years (Wang 2011).[11] Other surveys found that more than half of Indonesians were in Hong Kong for two years or less, whereas Filipinas averaged five years (AMC 2001; AMC et al. 2007). Some Filipinas I knew had spent over two decades, most of their adult lives, in Hong Kong, but I knew very few Indonesians who had been there more than a decade. The mothers I interviewed echoed the pattern: Filipinas had been in Hong Kong several years longer than Indonesians, but mothers of both nationalities had been—not surprisingly—in Hong Kong almost twice as long as the average Filipina or Indonesian FDWs. Eighty percent of the Indonesian mothers arrived in Hong Kong between 2003 and 2009 and had been there an average of 6.5 years. The two earliest arrivals came in 2000 and had been there 12 years at the time of the interview. The Filipino mothers had been in Hong Kong twice as long (on average 12.5 years, a median of 11 years). Two Filipina mothers arrived in the late 1980s.

Age and Education

Sending countries often set minimum age requirements intended to protect young and vulnerable migrant workers. The Indonesian government set a minimum age of eighteen for women migrant workers.[12] In 2006, the Philippine government set the minimum age of men and women "household service workers" at twenty-five but, in 2007, facing many complaints, reduced it to twenty-three. Unlike Singapore, whose minimum age for FDWs was increased from eighteen to twenty-three in 2005, Hong Kong has no age requirement but requires FDWs to have two years' work experience before coming. Many Filipinas claim to have work experience in the Philippines, but many Indonesians have worked elsewhere before Hong Kong.[13] Over half of the Indonesian mothers (57 percent) had worked in another country, most often Singapore, followed by a few who had worked in Malaysia or Taiwan. None of the Filipino mothers had worked in another country, but several of them had sisters or friends working in the Middle East.

Given their history in Hong Kong and sending country age requirements, Filipina domestic workers tend to be older than the Indonesians. In 2006, Filipinas averaged thirty-six and Indonesians twenty-eight years of age. Average age on arrival is 29.7 for Filipinas and 25.6 for Indonesians (Wang 2011).[14] The three oldest mothers I knew were Filipinas in their late forties and early fifties, but most were in their thirties, and the average age was thirty-eight. The two youngest Filipinas were in their late twenties. The oldest Indonesian mothers were in their late thirties; 80 percent were in their mid- to late twenties and early thirties, and their average age was thirty. The youngest Indonesian mother said she was nineteen, but her passport said she was twenty-one.

If anything, Indonesians are younger than their official records indicate. I learned to ask Indonesian mothers, "Is that the age in your passport or your real age?" In most cases, her real age was two or three years less than her documented age. It is not uncommon for an Indonesian teenager who has finished middle school to get false papers to work abroad (Silvey 2006; Palmer 2010). A high school diploma was sufficient for a field agent or *calo* to get her a passport, and it was easy (at least in the past) to get a school certificate from someone a few years older.[15] Several women were under eighteen when they first went to work in Singapore or Hong Kong. Indonesian women remembered with humor how their first employers called them by the name on their passports and got angry when they did not immediately respond. Indonesian women who married locally all used the "new" name, lending it permanence.[16]

Filipina domestic workers tend to be highly educated; many have college or university degrees (French 1986a, 1986b). A study by the International Labour Organization (Sayres 2007) found that over 60 percent of Filipina FDWs in Hong Kong completed tertiary (post–high school) education. Indonesian domestic workers are less educated; one survey of over 2,000 Indonesians found 12 percent had completed primary school, 58 percent junior high school, and 30 percent high school (AMC et al.

2007). In contrast, it is rare to meet Filipina domestic workers who did not complete high school, and many of them have college degrees. Given unemployment and underemployment in the Philippines, highly educated Filipinas (like Hope and her sister) often work abroad as FDWs. Of the mothers I interviewed, all Filipinas had finished high school, and many had some college education or a college degree. Two Indonesian mothers had some college education; one had completed only primary school. Most others had finished middle school, and a few had begun or finished high school.

Religion

Besides age and educational differences, there are also religious differences between Filipinos and Indonesians. Over 80 percent of the Philippine population is Roman Catholic, roughly 10 percent are Protestant or other Christian religions (such as El Shaddai and Jesus Is Lord, both of which have growing popularity in Hong Kong), and 5 percent are Muslim. Indonesia is almost the reverse, with a population of over 85 percent Muslim, 8 percent Protestant or Roman Catholic, and less than 2 percent Hindu.

Filipino domestic workers are mostly Catholic, but, given the growth of evangelical churches over the past two decades, the rate of conversion to evangelical Christianity is increasing. Few women from Muslim regions of the Philippines go to work in Hong Kong, but some Filipina domestic workers are Muslim or convert to Islam in Hong Kong. Conversion to Islam is noteworthy, given the common animosity toward Muslims in the Philippines (Constable 2010; Hawwa 2000a). The number of Filipinas who converted to Islam in Hong Kong over the past decade and a half is likely several hundred. Sithi Hawwa's groundbreaking research found that a "very high percentage of converts to Islam in Hong Kong are migrant domestic workers" (2000a, 348). A fact sheet she obtained from the Masjid Ammar Mosque in Wanchai documented that "from 1993–96, about 100 Filipinos embraced Islam" and that over 70 percent of Muslim converts in Hong Kong are Filipinos (353). On her first visit to the mosque, Hawwa met "five newly converted [Filipino] women; two of them were married to Pakistani men and three of them planned to marry their Pakistani boyfriends in the future. They came to the Mosque to learn about the religion of their men" (353). In interviews I conducted a decade after Hawwa, I was told that three or four conversion ceremonies occur each year, with approximately twenty Filipina converts each time. Most of the dozen or more Filipina converts I met (none of whom are among the fifty-five mothers I interviewed) had Pakistani boyfriends or husbands, and most were still working as FDWs.

Indonesians are mostly "born Muslim," but the extent of their religious adherence and practice varies (Constable 2010). Among the Indonesian mothers I interviewed, two were raised Roman Catholic and one Protestant; the men who fathered their children were Chinese or Western (not Muslim). The Protestant mother was married to the Chinese Protestant father of her child. The two Roman Catholic mothers did not know the father's religion but were adamant that they were not Muslim. Two more Indonesian mothers converted from Islam to evangelical Christianity while working abroad. One converted in Hong Kong and the other in Taiwan. Both of these Christian converts had children with African Christian men they had met in Hong Kong. Three Indonesian mothers were married to Indian Sikh men and did not plan to convert, but they agreed to raise their children Sikh. The largest group of Indonesian Muslim mothers had children with Pakistani Muslim men. Of the nine Filipina mothers whose children were fathered by Pakistani men, three had converted to Islam. One Filipina who was born Muslim had a South Asian Muslim partner.

Men's and women's religions are clearly relevant to their relationships. Women reported that religion often comes up during fights and arguments. Filipinas told Hawwa about the greater respect they receive from Muslim men after they convert: "The moment we told our friends (Pakistani men) that we are going to convert, they were pleased. . . . Since then, their attitude is changed. They respect us. We can feel that they treat us 'special', different from other Filipinos" (2000a, 360). Similarly, one Indonesian Muslim told me she received better treatment from her African Muslim husband and other Muslim men when she began to wear a *hijab* (a modest head cover). Christian Filipinas who did not convert reported that, during fights, especially those involving other women, jealousy, or mistrust, their

Muslim partners criticized their religion, morality, and *haram* (prohibited) relationships.

Marriage

As a Roman Catholic country, once a Spanish colony, the Philippines has strict views on marriage and prohibitions against divorce and abortion. Philippine gender norms are often characterized as patriarchal, historically influenced by Catholicism, with an ideological emphasis on women's sexual purity and women's marital fidelity. As women's migration has outpaced earlier patterns of Filipino male migration, women have played a greater economic role in their families. The wider impact of migration on gender roles is debated. Rhacel Parreñas (2005, 163) describes enduring Filipino notions of the father as the "pillar of the home" (the main support) and the mother as the "light of the home" (shedding radiance). She argues that women who migrate are often blamed for not doing their jobs as mothers, whereas fathers who go are said to follow their proper economic roles, just at a greater distance. Male migration is considered less disruptive to families, since the mother normally stays to care for the children, but female migration is morally problematic because children do not receive their mothers' care. Despite the fact that gendered inequalities and ideologies persist, Filipina migrants nonetheless gain some authority and independence through migration. Some migrant workers become politically active, some convert to new religions, and some establish new intimate relationships with men or women (Constable 2007, 2010; Sim 2009; Johnson and Werbner 2010).

In a study of the Philippine state as labor broker, Robyn Maglit Rodriguez describes the fear that women's migration undermines the "social and moral fabric of the Filipino family and ultimately the Philippine nation-state" (2010, 115). The state promotes labor exportation but is ambivalent about nationalistic anxieties. "Unruly sexual conduct of women" is especially "problematic for the state," Rodriguez explains, since "one means of being respectable women is through maintaining their roles as mothers" (114). She quotes a nun, an instructor at a Philippine predeparture orientation seminar for domestic workers, saying:

More and more Filipinas are becoming pregnant before getting married. They are having sex as often as they change clothes. Nowadays the wedding march is "here comes the bride, six months inside." . . . Even when a Filipina attends Mass, she's dressed so sexy that instead of the "body of Christ" the priest says, "Wow what a body!" (113)

The nun went on to urge migrant workers to turn to God, not to sex, for comfort (214).

Filipinas and Indonesian women are expected to marry and be obedient wives who bear children. Women are to blame if a marriage fails. Women are expected to be virgins at marriage, but recent studies suggest that premarital sex may be common among both groups of migrant workers (Ullah 2010). In Indonesia, as mothers and wives, women are expected to devote themselves to maintaining a "stable, nurturing, domestic environment," which is "central to the state's vision of an orderly and morally controlled nation" (Silvey 2004, 252). The Indonesian state reinforces the expectation that women obey their fathers before marriage and their husbands after marriage. Unmarried women under twenty-five need their parents' permission to work abroad, and married women under twenty-five need their husband's permission. Women who have children under a year old are not permitted to work abroad, whereas men face no such requirements (Silvey 2004, 251; Silvey 2007).

Javanese women reported that arranged marriages, often based on parental introductions, are the norm in their communities. At home, if an unmarried couple is known to be having sex, they may be forced or pressured to marry. Polygamy is rare but not unknown. Some women delayed their return home to avoid the pressure to marry. Several had experienced a failed marriage, which added incentive to work abroad.

Large-scale surveys of Hong Kong FDWs show that just over half of Filipinos and just under half of Indonesians are married (see Wang 2011).[17] The mothers I interviewed reflected the same pattern for single (never married) Indonesians: over 50 percent were single when they came to Hong Kong. Compared with all FDWs, not surprisingly, the number of Indonesian mothers who were "married" in Indonesia was much lower (only 15 percent) and those who were divorced/separated (33 percent) was higher than the norm. The pattern for Filipina mothers differed even more from FDW surveys. Close to 60 percent of Filipina mothers were single (never married) in the Philippines, 15 percent were married, and 30 percent were separated/divorced. FDWs who become mothers in Hong Kong include a significantly higher proportion of single and divorced/separated women than the general FDW population. Within the context of migration, given long absences and separations, marriages often end (Pratt 2012).

Divorce is permitted in Indonesia but not in the Philippines. Before conducting this research, I had assumed this might correlate to a more tolerant attitude toward single or divorced mothers in Indonesia, but, at least in rural Java, this does not seem to be the case. Indonesian FDWs stressed the shame of divorce and single motherhood for women. Nani Zulminarni, founder of the Indonesian organization PEKKA (Women Headed Household Empowerment), argues that unmarried women, divorcées, and single mothers face serious discrimination in their communities:

> In order to meet the criteria of a "good woman," one must get married and obey her husband. The negative treatment of unmarried women and single mothers by their communities includes the suspicion that they "will instantly become someone's mistress or a home wrecker," sexual harassment in the workplace and in the neighbourhood, and stigmatisation "as lonely women badly in need of a man." In addition, divorcées and remarried widows are perceived as having failed as wives, as mothers and as women. . . . The negative perception of widows and divorcees is similar to that associated with former prisoners and ex-prostitutes. (Refugee Review Tribunal 2010, 1)

Zulminarni and the Refugee Review Tribunal say that single mothers are considered a "disgrace to their families. Within the wider society, having a baby alone is viewed as sinful and unacceptable," and in some areas they are "excluded from village councils, shunned as immoral" and experience "difficulties in finding employment" (2). Besides social exclusion, "single mothers in Indonesia face discrimination from the authorities" and "financial hardships and severe challenges in providing for their children" (2).

Filipinas mentioned regional differences but seemed overall less concerned about the stigma of single motherhood than Indonesians. When religious or official marriages dissolve in the Philippines, couples separate but cannot divorce. A new partner may be referred to as "husband" or "wife" even though they cannot be officially recognized by the Roman Catholic Church or the state. Only very wealthy or well-connected Filipinos are able to obtain annulments. By contrast, Hong Kong's divorce policy is quick and easy. A couple can get divorced on the basis of having lived apart for one year if both partners agree, or for two years without the partner's consent.[18] Some resourceful migrant workers obtain divorces in Hong Kong (Constable 2003). Although such divorces are not recognized in the Philippines, they are recognized in Hong Kong and many other parts of the world.

Nellie, a Filipina former FDW who is legally married to Cesar, a Filipino Hong Kong permanent resident, described how she paid for her estranged husband of many years and his partner to come to Hong Kong to file jointly for divorce and officially marry there. Such an arrangement was not recognized by the Philippine Consulate or the Catholic Church, but it was recognized by her new Protestant church and by Hong Kong law. This arrangement insured that neither ex-spouse could sue the other in the Philippines for bigamy, since both would be guilty. Illustrating the position of the Philippine state in relation to marriage, when Nellie and Cesar married and had a daughter, Lilly's Philippine birth certificate (which was needed to obtain her Philippine passport) marked her as "illegitimate" on the basis that her parents' marriage (and her mother's divorce) was not recognized. The Roman Catholic view of "legitimacy" also impinges on the ability to have a child baptized and may help explain why religions that allow divorce and remarriage and the baptism of "out of wedlock" children are growing in popularity among migrant workers.

Whether or not a woman is married back home in Indonesia or the Philippines is not straightforward. The "official" designation of whether someone is married in the Philippines or Indonesia is indicated on her passport or identification card, but, if she were married in a religious ceremony, it might not be an "official marriage." Filipinas who are separated from their spouses might answer either way (married or single). A woman's relationship with her child's father is equally complex. Indah and her partner had no ceremony of any kind but considered themselves "married" (committed). Some women had Muslim *nikah* ceremonies (a religious blessing) in Hong Kong, but they are not recognized legally unless they are officially registered, which requires that both prove they are single.

At the time of their interviews with me, fewer than half of the Indonesians (45 percent) and Filipinos (44 percent) considered themselves "married" to the child's father, and roughly half of the Indonesian and Filipina mothers referred to their child's father as a "husband" even if they were no longer together. Far more Indonesians considered themselves single (40 percent) versus Filipina mothers (17 percent). As will be discussed in chapter 5, saying a man is or was a "husband" asserts the woman's morality but does not necessarily mean there was a marriage ceremony, though many Indonesian mothers with Muslim "husbands" had a Muslim *nikah*. More Filipinas (39 percent) than Indonesians (15 percent) called the father a "boyfriend"—a way to refer to ongoing relationships without the expectation of marriage, whether for religious reasons, because one or both was already married, or because they had no plan or desire to marry. Indonesians use the term "boyfriend" to indicate more short-term or casual relationships, or men with no intent to marry.

Although regional differences existed, most Javanese mothers were loath to return home with their children and stressed the shame back home of having children out of wedlock. Some planned to say they are married in Hong Kong (regardless of the actual circumstances), but, unless the man is with her or sends her regular remittances, she is usually considered a single mother along with the stigma that entails. Indonesian single mothers were clearly more reluctant than Filipinas to tell their parents about their pregnancies, and they often waited for months or years to break the news, for fear of the anger and shame it would bring. In Java, as compared with the Philippines, there seemed to be less institutional support for single mothers. One home for pregnant women outside of Jakarta required women to pay rent and was more like a boarding house than an assistance program. Indonesian women expressed greater concern than Filipinas about finding work to support their children back home. Filipinas, in contrast, while aware of stigma and economic difficulties, expressed less reluctance to go home and believed there is "always a way to earn money and not to starve" if you are willing to work hard and live frugally. In the Philippines, there may be greater acceptance of women having partners who are "elsewhere" because of its long history of migration. Perhaps a man's absence raises fewer suspicions and does not automatically stigmatize her.

MARAH: MOTHER, DAUGHTER, PARTNER

When I interviewed Marah, a Muslim Filipina, in 2012, she was in her early thirties and had been in Hong Kong for seven years. She was never married in the Philippines but had a partner and a child in Hong Kong. Unlike most Filipinas I knew who were Christian or had converted to Islam, Marah was born Muslim. Her father was Muslim and her mother had converted from Roman Catholicism when they married. Born in southern Mindanao, Marah had vague childhood memories of Muslim violence, of villagers being killed, and of her family fleeing to the north. After leaving Mindanao, they adopted new names and cut their ties to that region. Marah was too embarrassed to wear her Muslim *hijab* in the north, because no one else did, and she only took up religious practice again in Hong Kong.

When Marah was in grade school, her parents separated. Her father was a seaman and had a second family. Marah thinks her mother was "too proud" to accept his money and instead took a job overseas as a domestic worker; during this time, Marah and her brothers lived with their maternal uncle and grandparents in Iloilo. Her mother first worked in Kuwait, then Dubai, before returning home sick. Two years later, she went to work in Hong Kong and stayed for almost twenty years. As Marah explains:

> [My mother] stayed in Dubai only a few years and then someone from another country did magic [on her]. I don't know if you believe that. She goes to all the doctors and they cannot do anything. . . . Some people think she has AIDS but really somebody did magic. . . . For almost two years my mother cannot stand up. She has pain here [pelvic area].Then slowly, slowly she gets better because my grandparents found an old woman who is very good at taking out magic.
>
> Some don't believe it at the time, but someone in that country did it. She was working in a big palace in Dubai with many helpers and she is the one taking care of the kids. There were two kids and they were Arabic people

and of course my mother is Muslim. I think the Arab guy's wife died when the baby was small. So, I think the Arab man likes my mother and some girl is jealous, and the helpers fight. So they take her underwear and use it to make her sick.

[When she came home] my grandmother finds an old lady who can help. Medicine cannot help. She had to go to the sea and find water only from one place and drink it with some special leaves that are very difficult to find and then go to another place and find this and that. Wah! Almost two years and then she goes to Hong Kong. My grandparents didn't want her to go back to Dubai. When she is okay again I think the person making the black magic died.

Marah's mother insisted that Marah and her brothers go to school and college, but when Marah graduated she could only find a low-paying job in a shop. She worked there almost two years, begging her mother to help her find work in Hong Kong:

I want to be with her. . . . Growing up I miss her. Growing up, there are three of us and at that time we have no phone and you have to go to the public phone in the center. No one had cell phones then. . . . Then we talk only a few times a year. If she comes home for vacation or she arrives at the airport I cry. That's why she doesn't like to see me at the airport. So later I say "you help me apply here." And of course I am thinking of [being with] her and she said "of course, but you go to school first. We have dreams." She says, "I am not eating [i.e., going without food] here because I want you to go to school!" And then, when we are older we finish our studies—all for her. Really, I love my mother so much. I study and go to school . . . I am naughty and I am the only girl. . . . My uncle says, "You are the girl and too much of a headache for me, but the two boys are good!" Yes, I am in school, but because I have no allowance I withdraw from the school so I can spend the tuition money! My mother says "Why did you withdraw?" And then she says, "Okay you go back again . . . ."

My grandparents are already old, so we live with my uncle in the city at a boarding house. Everything we ask for he gives it to us. She buys things in Hong Kong and then sends it, even though she is not eating or spending on food. She is saving for us.

Marah finally does join her mother in Hong Kong:

Now here in Hong Kong I finally understand how hard it was for her, and I cry too much [about it]. In Iloilo we really do not know how much she is working. Everyone works very hard in Hong Kong—mostly—really very hard. She only got a Western employer at the end. Before, it is too hard.

Marah's first Hong Kong employer was Chinese and did not pay her the legal wage. The work was exhausting, but her mother urged her to stick with it:

> Instead of giving me the HK$3,280 in my contract she [the employer] is giving me only HK$2,500 per month. When I learn that it is wrong, I am afraid to say something. The work is hard. Every day I prepare the food for more than ten people. There are so many people in the house! Every day I call my mother, crying. She says "You are okay!" If they are okay—or if they are good—we try to keep that employer, because if you break contract it is too hard to find another one. So even though it is too hard, I try. . . . After my employer's sister has a baby, I take care of them too. Every day I make the soup and everything for twelve or thirteen people: the mother and father of my employer, the parents stay there with one daughter, and then my employer's two brothers and the sister, and the husbands and wives. . . . Wah! Every day I wash the towels. After they use them once they throw them in the bucket! Work is so hard but I finish the contract.

While Marah worked for her first employer, she met Kareem, a Sri Lankan Muslim a few years her senior who came to Hong Kong as a foreign domestic worker before 1997. They met in Tsim Sha Tsui when she was there with friends on their Sunday off. He was working at a shoe shop in Chungking Mansions. By the time Marah went to work for her second employer, she and Kareem met every Sunday. Her employers were a French couple with a baby. The work was considerably easier. While she worked for them, she had a miscarriage. When she got pregnant again, they helped her obtain medical care. At first, Kareem did not want a child. Marah says:

> We didn't plan to have a baby. I'm supporting my mother and he's supporting his father. When I get pregnant again [after the miscarriage] I tell him I will have a baby next year. He said, "Then no need to come to my house." But I decided to have it anyway, even if he doesn't want it. I say, "Okay, I will have the kid alone even if the kid has no father. I will take him to the Philippines." And then I told my good friend from the Philippines who is in Hong Kong and has a Pakistani husband, and she says, "We don't have

any boys and they [Pakistanis] like boys, so maybe if it is a boy, he will like it and we will adopt him? We can tell him who the real mother is."

At that time I am scared of my mother, and I still do not tell her. She knows that I have a boyfriend who is from Sri Lanka, but she doesn't know that I am pregnant. My boss takes me to the hospital for the ultrasound because I am bleeding. They give me a photo from the ultrasound. Then for three days I do not call the father and I say, "Okay. I will try to forget him." And then he calls and says, "Why are you not coming home?" I said, "You told me there is no need for me to come," and then when I go there that night and show him the picture and he shows it to all his Sri Lankan friends, he is so proud. He is very proud. . . . In the ultrasound they can see it is a boy. He likes that it is a boy. When he sees the picture in the ultrasound, it changed his mind and it changed his heart. He said, "It is my first child, a son, and I don't want to let him go."

Marah's pregnancy was difficult, but she continued working. During the seventh month, long before the due date, she had severe pain and bleeding so her employers took her to the hospital:

I think maybe my baby is already lost. I say, "I want this baby!" They say the baby is very strong and is holding on inside. It is only seven months. Then they induce me because I have been three days in the hospital and the water breaks. . . . The father comes to visit. He thinks I am nowhere and he asks, "Where is my wife?" I am not in the hospital bed. He comes inside the delivery room. I am shouting. He is watching and he is crying. He can hold him [the baby] in one hand. He has to stay for three months in the hospital. . . . The father brings him home by bus because I have a [job] interview; all the people are looking because he is so, so small.

While the baby, whom they named Mohamed, was in the hospital, Marah's maternity benefits ended and her contract expired. Her employers "did not want to hire someone with a baby," and she could not find a new employer, despite her efforts. She allowed her visa to expire and filed a torture claim.

Marah and Kareem had a Muslim *nikah*, the three of them lived together as a family, and Kareem referred to her as his wife, but Marah spoke of him as "the father" or as her "partner." The first time I heard her use the term, I was surprised, because other Muslim mothers I knew referred to their live-in partners as husbands, even without a religious blessing, and those who had the *nikah* were adamant that they were "married in the mosque." Marah laughed at my question and said Kareem objects to the term and says, "What?! Am I *not* your husband?" Marah and Melinda were both reluctant to use "husband" but for different reasons. For Melinda, it was because she and Niko were both still legally married to other people. Although Niko and his estranged wife planned to divorce in Hong Kong (where they were married), Melinda would technically remain married in the Philippines, even if she divorced in Hong Kong. For Marah, who was never married in the Philippines, the reasons are different but reflect a similarly complex vision from the multiple vantage points of the Philippines and Hong Kong (Constable 1999). She does not call Kareem her husband because she is not sure if and when she will have to return to the Philippines, and because they would not be considered married there since they did not have a civil marriage. When I interviewed her a few weeks later, I asked if she and her partner were "married in a mosque":

> It is only *nikah*. It is only like a blessing, different from a wedding. Because you are Muslim and you stay together without the blessing it is *haram* [prohibited]. So we have the blessing. *Nikah* makes it *halal* [permitted]. It is not a marriage, only a blessing. For a *real* marriage, all your family are there and you wear nice clothes. The blessing is very simple and is only praying for you. He can't have a wedding because we don't have the money. For them [Sri Lankan Muslims] the man has to give gifts for the girl. Because we are talking with his auntie, and his auntie says, "What did you give to your wife?" Because they must give gold and he only gave me this necklace—this small one. I don't care about the jewelry. I told him the important thing is that you are there and you are with me and with your son. It is okay.

In other words, the *nikah* lacked the presence of family members and other social relations that would lend it greater legitimacy, and it lacked the usual economic trappings. This stripped-down version of marriage allowed them to live together without sin but was not the marriage Marah had imagined or hoped for.

In other ways, as well, Kareem, Marah, and Mohamed's family situation and their future together is highly precarious and uncertain, located in Hong Kong's marginal spaces. The man who signed Kareem's last few contracts had never intended that he do "domestic work." He initially hired him as an FDW because it was much cheaper than hiring a shop clerk or warehouse worker. Kareem got along well with his employer, who continued to sign his contract each time it expired though he rarely saw Kareem and had not paid him or employed him for many years. Kareem did not feel exploited by his "employer"—who would also be vulnerable if Kareem was caught working illegally. Kareem felt grateful that the man allowed him to have a contract. I was unsure whether Kareem had paid him to sign his contract. I knew one person had offered to sign for a substantial sum, and I knew of women who paid "employers" to sign a bogus "contract" while they did other work. In some cases, the domestic worker only did part-time work for the employer and earned more with other jobs.

At the time of our interview, Marah was very worried. Kareem's contract was due to expire in ten days, and he had been unable to reach his "employer." Every time, he told Kareem it was "the last time" he would sign, and Marah feared the worst: "This time I think we have a real problem." The related problem was that Mohamed's legal status in Hong Kong, which allowed him to attend kindergarten, required that one of his parent's have regular (legal) status in Hong Kong. For the time being, his visa matched his father's. After seven years, in less than two more contracts, Mohamed would technically qualify to apply for permanent residence. The stakes were high, and, with only two days to spare, Kareem's "employer" signed his contract. Kareem and Marah breathed a sigh of relief until the next time.

Kareem's renewed contract meant that he could continue to "freelance" and work odd jobs. Although this was "illegal work," the fact that he had a FDH visa meant he had a Hong Kong identity card. This gave him some degree of protection. He would be safe from immigration if he was asked to show identification, and he was at an advantage over other workers without ID cards. He was nonetheless vulnerable if he was caught. Some months, Kareem earned less than HK$3,000, which made it difficult to cover the difference between what Marah received from the ISS as a torture claimant and what they owed for rent. Other times, Kareem earned "a lot of money," and Marah would send some to her mother in the Philippines:

> He says, "Okay, you send this to Mama." He has a heart, not like the other partners who are not thinking of their partners and sending money. I am so

lucky. If he is working and has a big salary, he asks me to send it to my
mother. If he sends money to his father, he sends it to my mother also. . . .
Some people say [his mother] died and some say maybe she went to another
country and found another husband there. . . . He didn't grow up with a
mother and dad. It is different when you have parents, especially a mother.
That's why he told me, "I don't want my son to not have a mother, like me."
Of course if you must go you must. I would bring my son to the Philippines.

Despite Indonesian and Filipino gender ideals regarding marriage and
motherhood, and despite Hong Kong's constraints on workers, countless
FDWs and former FDWs have babies and families there. Ara and Ina
formed an alternative family of two mothers and a baby. The two women
thought about the risk of getting caught working illegally, and ultimately
they agreed to raise Angela together in Ina's community. Well aware of the
criticism and speculation Ara would face as a "single mother" of a mixed-
race child in Indonesia—an identity that is easily blurred with ideas about
wanita jalang (bad women) or *wanita tuna susila* (women without morals)—they left Hong Kong, determined to ignore gossip and to make a go
of it as they had done during the first two years of Angela's life in Hong
Kong. They left with some money in their pockets. Yet, as will be described
in chapter 8, they did not know the strength of social pressures or how
short-lived their alternative family dream would be.

Marah, her mother, and her partner Kareem illustrate other aspects of
migrant motherhood. Despite the idea in the 1970s that labor migration
would provide a temporary solution to the country's economic difficulties,
Marah—like Hope, discussed in chapter 2—is among countless college-
educated Filipinas whose parents worked abroad for their children's education and a "better life," only to see them later go abroad as domestic
workers. Despite the Philippine reverence for family and marriage, strict
policies prohibiting divorce (as in Nellie and Cesar's case) serve not only
to deter remarriage among parents like Melinda and Niko, and to mark
children as "illegitimate," but also to influence Marah's thoughts about
marriage. Despite the Muslim *nikah* ceremony, she fears it is not "really"
a marriage and perhaps cannot be one because of its likely impermanence.
Like Hope, Marah's ideas about what marriage "should be" influenced her
reluctance to define herself as married, but it did not deter her from having a committed relationship and a child.

Despite Philippine and Indonesian predeparture orientation seminars that preach abstinence and family values, despite restrictions on age of migration that aim to protect young women, and despite legal prohibitions against divorce or laws requiring marital cohabitation as well as Hong Kong policies requiring domestic workers to live in and then leave quickly when their jobs end, paying them low wages and separating them from citizens as "FDHs," these policies do not prevent people from having sex, relationships, and babies or forming families. These families may not be permanent or traditional in structure, and they may not travel intact back to Indonesia or the Philippines, but they exist and thrive in Hong Kong.

At my first PathFinders' meeting in 2010, I spoke to an Indonesian woman who said that, at home, male relatives would pressure men to honor their obligations. Within the upheaval of migrants' lives in Hong Kong, however, few social pressures can be brought to bear to maintain gendered roles and responsibilities. Social pressures and patterns that otherwise define and formalize men and women's relationships, marriages, and parental obligations in parts of Africa, Southeast Asia, and South Asia simply do not apply. The paternalistic state cannot fill this role despite its assertions to the contrary. I end this chapter and bridge to the next with a paraphrase of an alleged statement from a senior Indonesian Consulate official (the representative of the "state" abroad) who had been briefed about the problems faced by Indonesian domestic workers who become mothers. As several of the meeting's attendees later said, his response was not, as they had hoped and expected, "How can we help these women?" Instead, it was, "Who are these men? Give us their names and we will find them!"

4 Men

Sometimes having a husband of another race or nationality
is what we call "Wow!" "Wow!" is usually White or
American. But if he comes from an Asian country or a
Third World country like the Philippines they will say,
"Why not chose better one? If you chose that one, then you
are better off choosing a Filipino."

— Nellie, a Filipina former FDW, in 2011

DIVERSITY OF MEN

The men who become fathers in Hong Kong are much harder to general-
ize about than the women who become mothers. Unlike the women—who
all entered Hong Kong as FDWs and who come from Indonesia or the
Philippines—the men represent a vast range of backgrounds and status.
They come from South Asia, East Asia, Africa, Europe, and the Americas.
They run the socioeconomic spectrum from well-off, well-educated professionals, businessmen, and tourists to small-scale traders and low-level
bureaucrats, manual laborers and "illegal" workers, and asylum seekers
who may be well educated but are dependent on social services and charities for survival. Nationality, legal status, purpose of stay in Hong Kong,
occupation, class, race, religion, and marital status are among the factors
that differentiate men and influence their relationships with and attitudes
toward women in general, foreign domestic workers in particular, and the
status and future opportunities of their children.

The diversity of fathers, as illustrated below, is tied to Hong Kong's history and its ambivalent relationship to asylum seekers and ethnic minorities. Described early on as a barren rock with but a few fishing villages

when it was ceded to the British in 1841, its current population of seven million is over 95 percent ethnic Chinese, most of whom are descendants of political or economic refugees from the mainland. Some South Asians are descendants of men recruited by the British for defense, or who are tied to its history of trade and finance. In the 1970s and 1980s, over 200,000 Vietnamese boat people landed in Hong Kong with its "port of first refuge" policy, which meant no one would be turned away.[1] Asylum seekers have continued to arrive in recent years from South Asia and Africa. Despite its generous entry policy, however, Hong Kong does not allow refugee settlement, so approved refugees must often wait in Hong Kong for many years (without the right to work) before they are resettled elsewhere. Moreover, as a Special Administrative Region of China since 1997, Hong Kong has struggled with the concept of "one country, two systems"—torn between identification with and dependence on the mainland and a desire to keep mainlanders out and maintain the uniqueness and privilege for "locals."

Residential status in Hong Kong and the right to work are critical factors in relation to privilege and precarity (see Figure 1). At the most privileged end of the continuum are Hong Kong permanent residents of various nationalities—most of whom are Chinese—who have right of abode in Hong Kong, who can work there legally, whose children automatically become Hong Kong permanent residents, and who can potentially sponsor a foreign spouse as a "dependent." Next most stable are those who are legally permitted to work in Hong Kong but are not yet permanent residents. This includes men and women who are admitted for certain types of work (usually skilled) or those who were admitted as "dependents" (usually of resident fathers) but who have resided there for less time than the seven years required for permanent residency (like Hope's Pakistani partner Ahmed in chapter 2). Less privileged are those who work legally in Hong Kong as contract workers but have only temporary visas, like Marah's partner Kareem, an FDW (chapter 3). Under special circumstances, and as long as the parent continues to have an FDH visa, Hong Kong–born children (like Kareem's son Mohamed) have some opportunity to become a resident, but the domestic worker parent does not. Next are those who are in Hong Kong legally and temporarily but who have no legal right to work, such as tourists and

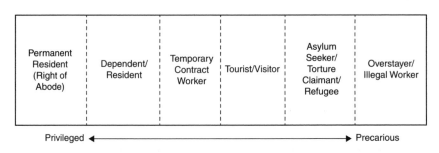

Permanent Resident (Right of Abode)	Dependent/ Resident	Temporary Contract Worker	Tourist/Visitor	Asylum Seeker/ Torture Claimant/ Refugee	Overstayer/ Illegal Worker

Privileged ◄————————————————————————► Precarious

Figure 1. Residential Status in Hong Kong, from Privileged to Precarious.

students. At the least privileged, most precarious end of the continuum are a range of people who hold what are commonly referred to as "immigration papers" (or recognizance papers). This includes asylum seekers, torture claimants, and recognized refugees who have not yet been relocated—mostly from South Asia or Africa. These men (and women) are permitted to remain in Hong Kong while their cases are under review, but, since Hong Kong does not accept refugees for resettlement, it is unlikely they can stay. In the meantime (sometimes for many years), they cannot work even when officially recognized as "refugees."[2] Many people who are not permitted to work do so anyway, but some asylum seekers/refugees do not, for fear that, if they are caught, it will jeopardize their chances of asylum and resettlement. Among the least privileged are "overstayers," who usually enter Hong Kong legally (for work or tourism) but exceed the permitted stay and work illegally. As described below, whether a man is a permanent resident, a domestic worker, an asylum seeker or refugee, or an overstayer, and whether or not he works (legally or not), has a huge impact on his life, the status of his Hong Kong–born children, and the child's mother.

HAKIM

Hakim is an asylum seeker and trader in his mid-thirties who came to Hong Kong from Pakistan around 2005. When I met him, he had recently married a Hong Kong Chinese woman. Before that, for three years, he had an Indonesian girlfriend whom he had not married but considered his "wife." Although they did not have children together, his story offers insight into such relationships. Introduced by a friend, I met Hakim at teatime in a small restaurant on the ground floor of Chungking Mansions. Hakim allowed me to record our conversation.

In keeping with the Pakistani ideal of marrying one's father's brother's child, when Hakim was young his family planned him a match with the daughter of an uncle who lived in Hong Kong and had Hong Kong residency (Weiss 1991, 423). This match would have provided him with a valued legal opportunity to work in Hong Kong and remit money to his family, paving the way for business ties and future migrations. Before that occurred, however, Hakim's other uncle's family in Pakistan, whom he saw regularly, encouraged him to marry their daughter. They told him of her beauty and of her interest in him; eventually he gave in to the idea, fell in love with her, and they were married. From the start, it was what Hakim called a "disastrous marriage": "The first night of our marriage she said that her parents had asked her to marry me and she had to do it. But she said, 'Don't ever touch me! I belong to somebody else.' My heart was broken. I loved her, but she tricked me." She had only agreed to marry Hakim so that her own brother could strategically marry the Hong Kong cousin. Moreover, she was in love with a higher-caste man whom she was prohibited from marrying. Refusing to be "shamed," Hakim ignored his wife's resistance, consummated the marriage, and conceived a child. But the marriage was doomed from the start.

A few years later, after his father died and his business was failing, Hakim decided to get to Hong Kong on his own. He was determined to follow his intended fate. Once in Hong Kong, he worked and filed an asylum claim. Without any help from family members, he started a small business and slowly built up his work experience, contacts, and clientele. He became a successful trader among the many other South Asians and Africans who deal in watches, mobile phones, or electronic goods imported to Hong Kong from China. Hakim is highly resourceful, well respected, and very busy—as evidenced by the several business calls he received in the course of our conversation. As he said, "Technically I should not work. I am still considered an asylum seeker. In one and a half more years, I will have a Hong Kong visa. Then I will be allowed to work. I live to work."

Given the topic of my research, much of our conversation focused on his former girlfriend, an Indonesian domestic worker who was in her mid-twenties when they first met:

> I had a very nice girlfriend whose name was Dini. In those days I just went to Kowloon Park with some friends and we accidentally met. She is from Surabaya [East Java]. She was with her girlfriends and one of them has a boyfriend who is with us and they introduced us. She was working as a domestic helper and it was her day off. We started talking and met a few times, sat together, and it was like we could read each other's minds. After I met her a few times, I think she is intelligent and she can help me in my life. So that is when I started taking interest in her. We started meeting each other and the relationship grew automatically. I said to her that "I started liking you and you are so good for my heart." After two months we decided that we should be girlfriend and boyfriend. . . . She was working, but we saw each other every week and on holidays for three years. We never fought; we never quarreled. We read each other's minds. We never had different views on anything in three years. That was so absolutely perfect. So I miss her, you know.
>
> She used to come to my home. Her boss let her leave at 6:00 and it takes 45 minutes to reach Chungking Mansions and she was at my place making breakfast for me every Sunday at 6:45. She was pressing my clothes, she was cleaning the home, cooking. Until 10:00 at night she was with me.
>
> It was my wish that I should marry her. I was very loyal to her. One day she came on her holiday and I said, "We are together for a very long time, so we should be together for the whole life now. Because I know you are intelligent enough to support me and I will support you for the whole life—the rest of my life." I said, "I want to marry you because it is now three years that we have understood each other. We can spend a very happy life, a life, very happy life." That is true. I was not trying [to marry] some Chinese girl to get an ID card. I offered her [marriage] very sincerely. "Okay, Dini, we should marry now." But she has some other plans. She told me that she cannot live outside Indonesia and if she marries me she will have to go to Pakistan at some stage of her life, and she is very firm about living together with her family in Indonesia. That is the way she explained it to me. She is very sincere [honest] to me; there is no doubt about that. Actually the other reason for Dini's refusal was my status here in Hong Kong, because I am still an asylum seeker and she thought that I don't have a future. So it is very hard for her to marry someone who is an asylum seeker here. It was her choice. Of course if she marries me I could go back and visit Indonesia and Pakistan, but she had other plans. That is what I offered her.

When it was three years and we knew each other very well, we had to decide something. I had not yet met the Chinese girl. The first time I met the Chinese girl, my heart was totally Dini's. . . . Sometimes she sends some [text] messages. The messages are very short and she says "call me" and I call her. She knows I am married now. At the last stage, when she was about to leave Hong Kong, she met me one day and said she has started regretting that she refused me. So I told her that now is very late because I have been married to a Chinese girl, and why should I destroy my married life once more, because my marriage in Pakistan ended in divorce before, so why should I destroy my marriage? It is my life, you know. We cannot play with our lives, so it is very hard to go back.

My first marriage was a love affair. When I was twenty years old, I used to think I would marry the most beautiful girl in the world. I was able to marry a very beautiful girl but her heart was not. The second wife was my necessity. Dini was not an Angelina Jolie. She was just an ordinary human being—but her heart was absolutely brilliant. I do not care about the color of the skin or the eyes, or the face, only what is beautiful inside. Dini, I think she was my real wife because she took care of me for three years.

And now my third wife. I have experience now with three wives. I have been betrayed once in my life and then I lost Dini. At some point in your life you think you should start something serious. I was serious right from the start, but my wife in Pakistan was not. And here Dini was a domestic helper and it wasn't to be. I am sincere about my Chinese wife. . . . For me it is okay if she stays with me the rest of her life. Because I am dedicated to my life. I like working. So these are three different stories; these three different characters. My wife now is happy because she doesn't have to work at home. . . . I am being a loyal person. I take care of her.

With his marriage of convenience and his prospects for future residence, Hakim was considered very lucky by his peers.

WHO ARE THE FATHERS?

The wider portrait of the men presented here draws from the fifty-five mothers I interviewed, men I met through their partners, conversations and interviews with dozens of men like Hakim who are not fathers, and material gleaned from a range of scholarly sources. The fifty-five mothers had sixty-six children in Hong Kong with fifty-seven men who spanned sixteen nationalities. In terms of broad geographic categories, the largest number of fathers were South Asian. Among the fifty-seven were twenty-nine South Asians (seventeen Pakistanis, five Indians, three Nepalese, two Bangladeshis, and two Sri Lankans), nine Africans (from Niger, Nigeria, Congo, Ghana, Mali, and elsewhere), eight Southeast Asians (five from the Philippines and three from Indonesia), eight Chinese (including six Hong Kong Chinese and two mainlanders), and three others (one each from the United States, Mexico, and the Netherlands). Other fathers whom I met or learned about (but who were not partners of the fifty-five mothers) came from many of the same countries mentioned above as well as England, Germany, and Australia.

In terms of residential status in Hong Kong, by far the largest categories of fathers were Hong Kong permanent residents and asylum seekers/torture claimants/refugees. Most of the men fit into one of these two categories. Nineteen of the fifty-seven fathers, including most Chinese fathers, several South Asians, two Filipinos, and one American, had permanent residence in Hong Kong. Some were born and raised there; others obtained residence after living there legally for seven years. Nineteen other fathers were asylum seekers/torture claimants/refugees. Many South Asians and most of the African fathers were in that category; one African father said he had official refugee status and was awaiting resettlement.

Five fathers were in Hong Kong as visitors or tourists. One was a tourist from Indonesia. The rest were traders or businessmen: one from Mexico, one from the Netherlands, and two from Africa. The Africans traveled regularly between Hong Kong, China, and their home countries, trading electronics, watches, and others consumer goods.

Five fathers who had worked illegally had been voluntarily removed from Hong Kong after serving prison time. The mothers had lost touch with them. One father was currently overstaying and had not yet filed an asylum claim. Many others were overstayers who later filed asylum/torture claims after being arrested for working. Overstayers tend to blur into the asylum-seeker category and also the visa category, since most of them originally entered Hong Kong legally with visas or were granted permission to stay for fourteen to ninety days upon arrival at the airport; they might have renewed their stay, but eventually they overstay, file asylum or torture claims, and, once their claims are rejected, return home or perhaps overstay again.

Three Filipino fathers and one South Asian father had domestic worker visas. Male FDWs commonly do "masculine work" such as gardening and driving and are often paid double or more what women get. Some wealthy employers with large homes hire Filipino married couples. One couple I interviewed worked in a household with three other FDW couples. Some such employers are amenable to allowing a couple's Hong Kong–born children to stay with them, either in their spacious residence or "living out," even though this may constitute a breach of the employment contract. Without the employer's agreement (real or professed) that the child can reside with the domestic worker parent, the child's visa will not likely be granted.

Two fathers lived and worked legally in Hong Kong and had Hong Kong identity cards but had not yet obtained permanent residency. Two were dependents of permanent resident fathers—one who had not yet been there seven years, the other who had not bothered to apply. Two other fathers had, by 2013, married Hong Kong Chinese permanent residents and were waiting for dependent status and permission to work. Another father had "unconditional stay" to remain and work in Hong Kong for seven years, after which time he could apply for permanent residency.

In a fascinating study of Hong Kong's famous Chungking Mansions, described as a "Ghetto at the Center of the World" and as a site of globalization from below, Gordon Mathews (2011) divides the diverse collection of people who live and work in its many small shops, restaurants, guest houses, and small businesses into several categories. These include traders, owners and managers, temporary workers, asylum seekers, foreign domestic workers, sex workers, heroin addicts, and tourists. Chungking Mansions represents not only a "microcosm of globalization" but also a condensed distillation of Hong Kong's ethnic diversity and interrelations. As such, these categories are useful for thinking about the fathers in this study, who they are, and where they come from. Indeed, a few of the people of Chungking Mansions *are* the fathers in this study.

Traders in Chungking Mansions are mostly African men (though Africans increasingly live and work in other parts of Hong Kong, as well). The women I knew sometimes referred to them as "businessmen" despite the small scale of their trade. They either obtain a visa before coming to

Hong Kong, if they can afford it and it is required, or, if their home country is allowed visa-free entry, they are admitted at the airport, usually for two weeks, thirty days, or ninety days and can leave Hong Kong and reenter (Mathews 2011, 58). Some traders go to Hong Kong every few months; others constantly move back and forth, buying Chinese-made goods and taking them back to their countries. One trader I knew of was on a business visa and was said to trade in diamonds. He rented a flat in Hung Hom, where his pregnant, former-FDW girlfriend lived. American and European business travelers usually stay at more upscale hotels than the budget guesthouses of Chungking Mansions but echo the pattern of coming to Hong Kong for a few days several times a year, or less often for longer periods, and they too meet and have short-lived relationships with FDWs.

Most of the *owners and managers* of small businesses in Chungking Mansions, like those in other parts of Hong Kong, are Chinese or South Asian permanent residents, some of whose families have resided in Hong Kong for generations. One South Asian father lived and worked near Yuen Long and owned a clothing-packing business that ships goods to parts of South and Southeast Asia. Like many of the owners and managers at Chungking Mansions, he was a Hong Kong permanent resident with a wife and children in Pakistan, but he had a Filipina former-FDW girlfriend who overstayed her visa, worked for him alongside several other overstayers, and bore him a son. One Chinese father also illustrates this pattern: he owned a business in the New Territories, was married to a Chinese woman with whom he had adult children, and had a child with a Filipina domestic worker ex-girlfriend.

Temporary workers in Chungking Mansions and elsewhere in Hong Kong are often South Asians who initially came as visitors, then overstay and work illegally. Typically they earn far less than locals for the same work. Some employers justify this as providing wages that are far more than men would earn in their home countries. Other employers reason that they are taking risks by hiring illegal workers. In Chungking Mansions, they work as shop clerks, waiters or dishwashers at restaurants, cleaners or managers at guesthouses, goods carriers, or touts for various businesses (Mathews 2011, 74). Outside of Chungking Mansions, temporary workers from South Asia, Africa, and China do many of those same jobs, and they also work at construction sites, in automotive junk-yards, in transportation and shipping, and at loading docks, warehouses, and factories. Temporary workers also overlap with asylum seekers and torture claimants; although the latter are not permitted to work, some do so anyway. Men with the right to work in Hong Kong do many of the same jobs: drive trucks, transport cargo at the airport, install power lines or pipes along transportation lines, work as guards or night watch-men, or do automotive work.

RASHID

Rashid is an asylum seeker and torture claimant. He came to Hong Kong overland from Pakistan through China, then by boat to Hong Kong. His initial aim was to work for some relatives and to earn and remit as much as possible before his claim was rejected and he would be forced to leave. By the time I met him in 2012, his aim had changed somewhat because he had met Lilik (chapter 2), with whom he had a Muslim marriage blessing at the mosque, and together they had a son, Husain, who was three months old. Lilik had not found a new employer before her visa expired, so she had recently overstayed. She then filed a torture claim so they could remain together "as a family." When I visited them in their new home and offered to take a "family photograph," Rashid insisted on showering and changing his clothes first. As they posed, he proclaimed that he was a "very lucky man" because Allah had blessed him "with two wives and two sons." When he was a teenager he had told his parents that he would have two sons "and now it has come true," though his parents do not know. When Lilik teased Rashid that he "need not be so proud," he shrugged it off, say-ing, "I am not proud, just grateful to God for the blessings he has given me!" He affectionately embraced his son before going downstairs to work in the market.

After Husain was born, Rashid stopped working in the relatively safe home of a Pakistani relative who is a resident, and he took up much riskier but far more lucrative work setting up and taking down market stalls. The number of stalls grew as did his reputation for hard work, and he earned over HK$12,000 a month, enough to send money to his parents and wife and children in Pakistan and to rent a room in a flat near the market. Rashid and Lilik were very happy with the space, despite the many flights of stairs in the dilapidated old building. Another Pakistani-Indonesian couple and baby rented the second bedroom and shared the flat with them. Before, Rashid had lived in a dormitory-like room with several other Pakistani men.

Rashid's wife in Pakistan had heard rumors from her relatives in Hong Kong that Rashid had a girlfriend and a baby. Lilik heard them argue on the phone. Rashid told his Pakistani wife it was just "jealous gossip." He was afraid to tell her about Lilik and Husain for fear that she would tell his parents and that her relatives would report him to immigration. He preferred to tell his parents himself "in person, when the time is right." Meanwhile, he avoided being seen with Lilik and Husain. As he explained, and Lilik recounted with frustration, "he thinks if people know he has a girlfriend it is okay. It is expected. But he doesn't want them to know he has wife and baby." As a result, they live their family life in private or in the shadows. Lilik goes out with the baby at odd times, has friends visit her at home, or goes out while Rashid stays with the baby. Rashid does not let Lilik and Husain go out together while he works nearby lest his wife's Pakistani relatives see them. Once, Rashid's uncle paid a surprise visit, and Lilik and Husain had to hide on the sweltering hot roof for an hour until he left. Lilik was angry, but she shared Rashid's concern that if someone told his wife he could be reported to immigration, put in prison, then deported, and their life together as a family in Hong Kong—and his ability to support her—would end.

Rashid had a visibly close bond with Lilik and Husain. He said that he had learned to be a "real husband" and "real father" in Hong Kong, that theirs was a "love relationship" in contrast to his arranged marriage to his uneducated cousin in Punjab. Rashid and Lilik planned to stay in Hong Kong and to earn as much money as they could for as long as possible. Rashid had given a trusted cousin (a Hong Kong resident) money to support Lilik and Husain should he be arrested, and he had given Lilik some gold jewelry. He said he could not imagine Lilik (with her style and independence) "surviving" in Pakistan. Lilik had little desire to go there, and he could not live in Indonesia, even if Lilik and Husain went, because he could not earn enough money there. He was adamant that he would support Lilik and Husain regardless, even if he had to make his way to England to work, where he also had relatives.

British colonial history provides an essential backdrop for understanding why Rashid, Hakim, Kareem, and many other South Asian fathers went to Hong Kong in the first place and how it colors their experiences there. Long before India's partition in 1947, Indians (some from the Sind and Punjab regions that later became Pakistan) were recruited to serve in the colony's police force and the British military. After partition, Gurkhas from Nepal replaced Indians in the British Army in Hong Kong. Throughout and after the British period, Indians and Pakistanis went to work in Hong Kong as private security guards; they also worked in construction and other low-skilled jobs with their English-language ability offering some advantage, especially before Hong Kong's reunification with China in 1997 (Weiss 1991; White 1994).

Today, Hong Kong's South Asian community spans socioeconomic extremes—from very wealthy, long-established families of traders, successful international businessmen, and famous philanthropists whose families reside in Hong Kong on one end of the spectrum, to poor manual laborers and asylum seekers who are recent arrivals and often come alone, without their wives and children, on the other. Marginal South Asian men are generally shunned by more elite South Asian and Chinese women, and they are more likely to have relationships with FDWs. Relationships between Pakistanis and Filipinas began in the 1980s when there were very few Indonesians in Hong Kong. One man is quoted as saying, "We Pakistanis get on well with the Filipinas because we are all foreigners here in Hong Kong and the Chinese don't like us" (French 1986a, 217; see also Weiss 1991; White 1994).

The Hong Kong South Asian community has long had far more men than women. In 1994, approximately 85 percent of the 15,000 Pakistanis in Hong Kong were men, and around 7,000 of them worked as guards in banks, dockyards, factories, shops, prisons, and elsewhere (White 1994, 143, 118). The goal of Pakistani and Sikh watchmen, like South Asian male migrants today, was "to earn as much money as possible and to return home to their families" (White 1994, 118). Most Pakistanis left their families in Pakistan because they could work longer hours, reduce expenses, and "their wives are not exposed to the corrupting influences of Hong Kong" (White 1994, 118). Pakistani watchmen sometimes married local Chinese women who converted: "Sometimes, a man may have a wife in Pakistan to whom he will return to upon his retirement, but live with a Chinese (converted) wife and his children in Hong Kong" (Weiss 1991, 437). In the 1980s, these men lived "workaholic lives in close living quarters in Hong Kong so as to enrich their families back home. Given such filial orientations, they would not be expected then to defy tradition and marry outside of their family's wishes, nor would many of them want their wives to mix in Hong Kong's culture" (Weiss 1991, 437). One young watchman said that Pakistanis do not want to marry Chinese or Filipinas because "they will wear a skirt or dress after marriage," reflecting his view of their lack of sexual modesty, in contrast to proper Pakistani wives (Weiss 1991, 437).

In 2012, Pakistani men in their twenties or thirties, like Hakim and Rashid, were still going to work in Hong Kong. They were married in Pakistan but appeared "single" in Hong Kong. Some of the Pakistani fathers like Ahmed (Hope's partner) were sons of earlier Pakistani immigrants. Among the twenty-nine South Asian fathers, the largest nationality was Pakistani. Of the seventeen Pakistani fathers, nine had children with Filipinas (some who converted to Islam) and eight with Indonesian Muslim women. Sithi Hawwa's study of Filipinas who convert to Islam illustrates the extent to which relationships between Pakistanis and Filipina domestic workers are institutionalized, though not necessarily permanent:

> Pakistanis and Filipinas in Hong Kong share many similarities, such as their relatively low position in Hong Kong society, a large component of single people among each group, the status of a relatively sizeable large minority group, and English language ability, [but] they have two sharp distinctions between them—their educational attainment and religious affiliation. Filipinas are generally credited with high educational attainment, whereas Pakistanis' literacy rate is low compared to the developing world's standard. As far as the religious difference is concerned, Islam is the dominant religion in Pakistan, and Christianity, especially Catholicism, is the dominant religion in the Philippines. (2000a, 353; see also Hawwa 2000b)

The mothers I knew described how Pakistani men, like Rashid, often failed to mention until after their relationship became serious or sexual, or after they were "married in the mosque," that they have a wife in Pakistan or plans to marry in Pakistan. Men sometimes told their partners it was a "family obligation" to marry a partner of their parents' choice. Many Hong Kong relationships fail. The men may have other girlfriends or "sleep around." Jealousy and misunderstandings are common. The idea of going to Pakistan can also be a source of conflict. Some women are unwilling to do so; others would like to but are told by partners "you won't last a day" or "you wouldn't survive" because of *purdah* (seclusion) and modesty restrictions. I knew two Indonesian mothers—both of whom always wore Punjabi-style Muslim clothing—who went to Pakistan with their husbands and young children in late 2012 to "see what it is like" despite the warnings and horror stories they heard from friends.

By 2010, relationships between Indonesian women and South Asian men were common. Many Muslim men consider Muslim Indonesians better-suited and say their lower education makes them more approachable than Filipinas. Although Filipinas generally speak better English, increasing numbers of Indonesians also speak English from working in Singapore or socializing with English speakers.

A South Asian businessman and self-ascribed community leader told me that FDWs are a logical solution to men's loneliness and sexual needs: "Punjabi men are mostly from rural areas and are not well educated. They come here as 'bachelors' with no wife here. They are used to seeing Muslim women all covered up and men and women being separated. Then they see all the Filipinas and Indonesian helpers looking very beautiful and wearing so little clothes." In his experience, some such relationships are long-lasting. He described two couples he knew who had gone back to live in villages in Pakistan and who he insisted are "very happy there" and are not treated "like maids" as women commonly fear. But other relationships are violent and troubled, and he attributed this to the fact that the men and the women have no family members or community members in a position of authority in Hong Kong to enforce proper behavior. He also said, "Of course men will get angry if their wives constantly criticize and cause him shame," but he said this was more of a problem with South Asian wives than Southeast Asian ones.

Hakim, too, insisted that there are successful "marriages" between Pakistanis and FDWs, but from his perspective "successful marriages" can also be short-lived:

> So many Pakistanis have been married to domestic helpers, and happy marriages. Lots of them! If both parties are sincere to each other this is a love affair. So the ultimate result is if you live with someone for one, two, three, four years, it is marriage! I have known so many. If I know fifty Pakistani guys, thirty have been happily married to the Indonesian girls or Filipinas. This is a very high proportion. I'm talking about people who have been here for five or ten years, because they are mature. But all of them are asylum seekers and, ultimately, somebody will have to go to Indonesia and someone will have to go to Pakistan. This will ultimately have to happen.

Among South Asians, Nepalese are also a significant minority in Hong Kong, their presence likewise tied to British colonial history. Gurkhas were recruited from Nepal to serve in the British Army in Hong Kong after partition. There were 6,000 Gurkhas in 1994 (White 1994, 118). Children of Gurkha soldiers born in Hong Kong before 1983 were granted permanent residence. Before the 1990s, few Nepalese exercised that right, but during the 1990s, the largest period of emigration in Nepal's history, many did, and the number rose to almost 18,000 (Frost 2004, 366). Former Gurkhas were permitted to stay in Hong Kong after 1997 when their brigades were disbanded, and they could sponsor dependents who were not born there. The Hong Kong Immigration Department listed 19,700 Nepalese and 18,500 Pakistani "foreign residents" in December 2011, making them the seventh and eighth largest minority groups, respectively. Echoing the gender-skewed pattern of Pakistanis, two thirds of Nepalese in Hong Kong are men (Frost 2004, 367), but, unlike Hong Kong's Pakistani and Indian communities, which have deep historical and generational links and community ties (including businessmen who can help new immigrants find work), Nepalese are relative newcomers who often speak neither Chinese nor English fluently, and their community has fewer occupational opportunities and resources. Sixty percent of Nepalese work in construction; many work as guards, bouncers, and bartenders (Frost 2004).

For many decades, Gurkha soldiers' children returned to Nepal with their mothers, grew up there, and only returned to Hong Kong as young adults. When they married and had children, many of these "third genera-tion" children were raised in Nepal (Tam 2010). Given their lack of literacy in Cantonese and their lack of formal education in the Nepalese language, they are "caught in cultural limbo" (Tam 2010). One Nepalese community activist explained to me that some members of this "third generation"—which includes the Nepalese fathers in this study—are socially troubled, turn to drugs and alcohol, and live on government handouts. Vikram, a Nepalese father whom I saw around the Jordan/Yaumatei neighborhood where I lived, was described by his ex-girlfriend, Eka, as an unemployed "partyer and playboy." Most of Vikram's friends were Nepalese residents or dependents who "grew up, settled down, and got married," but he was an overstayer. He met Eka, an Indonesian former FDW and torture claimant, at a bar near Jordan Road. They moved in together but broke up when she got pregnant.

Two other Nepalese fathers had children with FDWs who overstayed their visas when they became pregnant. Both men were in Hong Kong legally: one as a resident and one a dependent. They were initially kind and responsible partners until their addictions took over. Gopal illustrated a common pattern. He began by drinking cough syrup in Nepal, then pro-gressed to methadone in Hong Kong, which was cheap and easily avail-able. He was normally quiet and shy, but the drugs made him "happier, friendlier, and more confident." When he moved to an area where metha-done was not easily available, he took up heroin. The addiction took over, despite the threats and pleas of his partner and his parents and my attempts to have him meet a Nepalese drug-addiction counselor. He lost his job, and eventually his partner and children left Hong Kong, broken hearted. The stereotype of Nepalese drug addicts is well known in Chungking Mansions, where they are reputed to be lazy and spoiled, spending their welfare checks on heroin and wasting their much-envied status as legal residents (Mathews 2011, 88, 181).

A Chinese drug counselor who worked with South Asians explained to me that drug and alcohol addiction may be worse among Nepalese than other South Asians but that the problem is likely overstated. Among Pakistanis, she said, "drinking and drugs are more likely to be taken in private and to be kept within a household, so it is less well known. Since it is considered shameful for Muslims to drink or do drugs, they are hesitant to do so publically and may try to deal with the problem individually or keep it hidden out of a sense of shame." Sociohistorical factors are also relevant: "Gurkhas used to have clear occupational roles and organized and disciplined communities (military camps) but, now that those are gone, young people have a much less clear sense of occupational direction. The fathers did not do drugs, but drinking may have been an issue." Moreover, given Nepalese views of Hinduism and Buddhism, "they may consider alcohol and ganja are fine and okay in festivals. There is also the community factor, where much of it is peer activity and if one person does it they all do. Also, they drink together and smoke hashish together. The young people are fairly alienated in Hong Kong. The Pakistanis were better integrated into Hong Kong society and Indians too, but the new immigrants are also at risk." Although many Nepalese are legally entitled to be in Hong Kong, they lack the clear occupational path of their fathers' or grandfathers' generations and lack the educational and language skills to compete for better jobs. Nepalese are more likely than other South Asians to work in bars as waiters, waitresses, bouncers, and bar tenders, putting them in closer reach of alcohol and likely drugs, as well.

The numbers of Bangladeshis and Sri Lankans are small, and their arrival in Hong Kong is more recent than Indians, Pakistanis, and Nepalese. Neither group is among the top fifteen nationalities of "foreign residents" in Hong Kong (with 5,000 or more). In the mid-1990s, there were 150 Bangladeshis (White 1994, 143), but the number has likely multiplied in recent years (Ullah 2013). A. K. M. Ahsan Ullah estimates that half the Bangladeshis in Hong Kong entered initially on tourist visas and work illegally. Based on his survey (2013) of fifty-six Bangladeshi migrant workers in 2005, they take on a variety of low-level, part-time jobs at an hourly rate (at wholesale shops, factories, or construction sites, or as touts soliciting customers in the tourist areas). Most of them entered Hong Kong multiple times on two-week tourist visas that they renewed for as long as they could, using multiple names and passports. If they were caught working, they would initially get a six-month sentence and eighteen months for repeat offenders. One-third of them were married but "almost all of them admitted directly or indirectly to having girlfriends, no matter whether they were married or unmarried . . . two-thirds of them have multiple girlfriends . . . mostly from the Philippines and Indonesia" (174). As Ullah points out, since FDWs have Hong Kong identity cards, they help their boyfriends to open bank accounts and to rent rooms, things they cannot do themselves.

Of the South Asian fathers with Hong Kong permanent residence, two were Indian (Sikh) men who married Indonesian former FDWs and sponsored them as dependents. One Pakistani father with legal residence was in prison for carrying a knife; another for selling drugs. Two Pakistani men I knew were still on dependent visas (sponsored by their fathers, including Ahmed). One unfortunate Pakistani man, who was in prison for illegal work, had three older brothers who were dependents, but his father died before he could be sponsored as well. Most South Asian nonresidents stayed in Hong Kong illegally for a period of time after their tourist visas expired.[3] Many then filed asylum or torture claims—not expecting to "win" them but hoping that, during the years it would likely take to process their cases, they could work and send money home. Unlike "political" asylum seekers, these often self-identified "economic" migrants are usually resigned to the idea of eventually returning home.

AFRICAN MEN

Africans are more recent arrivals in Hong Kong. Their numbers are very small, but the past decade has seen a massive increase in the number of sub-Saharan African traders traveling to South China (Mathews 2011, 58; O'Connor 2012). In addition to traders, African asylum seekers began arriving in Hong Kong in the early 2000s. African women are also traders and asylum/torture claimants, but the majority of Africans are men who come without their families. Many African asylum seekers are "middle-class in background and are among the well-off in their home countries as shown by the fact that they were able to come to Hong Kong. . . . The majority were able to pay the price of airfare from their home countries" (Mathews 2011, 172). Racist local attitudes toward Africans and darker skinned people—viewed with a combination of fear and curiosity—are well known in Hong Kong. I have seen Chinese passengers change seats or refuse to take the only vacant seat in a crowded subway or bus because it is next to an African. One Congolese refugee described how her children were taunted about their skin color by schoolmates, even by South Asians.

Mathews notes that the way some African men "are used to accosting women in Africa is considered aggressive in Hong Kong," which perhaps adds to the fear with which they are regarded by locals (2011, 60–61). Given fear and racism, it is not surprising that Africans stick together and congregate in particular locations such as Chungking Mansions and Sham Shui Po. Africans are seen at the Kowloon mosque and at English-speaking churches on Sundays, which puts them in contact with other minority groups and foreigners, including FDWs. I counted more than fifty African men, some with Asian partners and babies, at an English mass at a Roman Catholic church in Yuen Long one Sunday.

Given their small numbers, Africans may be overrepresented as fathers of domestic worker's children. If South Asians, who have a long history in Hong Kong, continue to feel discriminated against by Chinese and prefer to socialize with "friendlier" Southeast Asian women, it is no wonder that Africans do, too. Many African asylum seekers spoke warmly about FDWs. Ali, a Muslim asylum seeker, was very supportive of "domestic helpers." When his Somali refugee friend, now settled in North America, wrote and said, "Thank goodness, I never have to go to Kowloon Park to see another Indonesian domestic helper again!" Ali was incensed. "Domestic helpers are kind and generous" to asylum seekers. "When we need food they give it to us. When we need clothing they take us shopping. When we need money they give it to us. They take care of us!" he said emphatically. "So how can he say this?" If "he was here and I had an AK47" he said, dramatically, "I would have shot him!" He was openly envious of his friend's resettlement but furious that, as soon as the friend moved up, he criticized those "beneath him." Like others, Ali was impressed by the generosity and kindness of Indonesian and Filipino women toward asylum seekers who have no source of income and are dependent on meager aid for survival. "If someone is your friend when you don't have a penny, then it is a true friend," he said. Not all men were as positive or complementary toward domestic workers.

I knew seven African fathers through the mothers in this study, knew two others through other contacts, and was acquainted with several men who had FDW partners but no children. Six of the fathers were asylum seekers/torture claimants, and two were traders on visitor visas. Angela's father (chapter 3) was presumably "African," but Ara did not know him.

Two African men had babies with Filipinas, and seven with Indonesians. Four of the men were Christian, like their partners, and met in church, including a Roman Catholic African-Filipino couple. Four men and women were Muslim. In addition to men who fathered children with the mothers in this study, I heard many stories about other couples, and I knew of two Filipinas who had taken their babies to the Philippines against the African fathers' wishes.

Two Indonesian-African couples and their children lived in tiny Kowloon flats I visited. The flats were paid for by the ISS, since parents both were asylum/torture claimants. One couple was Christian and called each other "husband and wife," but they were not officially married because of the cost and complication of divorcing the woman's long-estranged Indonesian husband. The Muslim couple had "married" with a *nikah* ceremony. In several other cases I knew well, and many I heard about, mothers complained about partners who were not monogamous and had moved on long ago.

NGO staff said African men often express great pride at fathering children but have little or nothing to offer the mother or child in terms of economic or emotional support. Their lack of financial contributions is not surprising, since asylum seekers/torture claimants are prohibited from working. Moreover, as noted, those who seek asylum for "political" as opposed to "economic" reasons are often unwilling to risk undermining their claims as "real" asylum seekers by working illegally (see Mathews 2011, 173). Even if they are among the small percentage of asylum seekers who are recognized as refugees, however, they will not be resettled in Hong Kong. Given the indeterminate state of their lives and the long duration and arbitrariness of the asylum process, especially for those who have suffered severe emotional stress or physical torture in their home countries, it is not surprising that enduring or economically responsible relationships with women and their children are evasive. Some asylum seekers I knew were chronically angry or distraught from years of waiting and anxiety about their futures. Many were formerly productive individuals who would prefer to work than live off charity, which can be frustrating and humiliating. Given how closely "providing" is linked to male pride in many African (and other) cultures, it is not surprising that the prohibition against work is emasculating. Under such circumstances, sexual relations or fathering children may provide some reassurance of their masculinity.

One African father was said to have slept with three women I knew, and he had fathered children with two Indonesians and a Chinese woman. He left his pregnant Indonesian girlfriend to marry a Chinese permanent resident who was also pregnant and willing to sponsor him as a dependent. Men used the term "trading up" to describe asylum seekers who dropped their FDW girlfriends in favor of local Chinese permanent residents. There was little sugarcoating. Men bluntly said that they like Indonesians and Filipinos better, "but relationships with helpers have no future." The goal of many asylum seekers is to trade up and "meet and marry a Chinese woman" who can provide what he desires most. "She can give us a future in Hong Kong and the helpers cannot."

CHINESE MEN

Chinese men were only the third most common category of fathers in my study (eight men, roughly 14 percent), but, as noted in chapter 3, there are probably many more Chinese men who have fathered children with FDWs than this figure suggests. Many factors "promote" relationships between Chinese men and FDWs. Ninety-five percent of Hong Kong's population is Chinese, and most FDWs work for Chinese employers. Unlike Singapore, which prohibits women who enter as domestic workers from ever being granted residence as a wife, Hong Kong has no such prohibition. In Hong Kong, marrying a Southeast Asian requires a much shorter wait and less complicated bureaucratic procedure than marrying a Chinese mainlander. According to the Immigration Department, between 2008 and 2011 approximately 2,180 registered marriages of Filipinas and Indonesian women took place, averaging 545 per year (personal communication, March 12, 2012). Few registered marriages (as opposed to religious marriages) took place between the mothers in this study and South Asian or African men, so most "official" marriages probably involve Chinese or other Hong Kong permanent residents. Hong Kong Chinese men likely have other sources of assistance to turn to for problems involving immigration, dependent visas, marriage registration, or birth certificates, so there are likely to be fewer of such couples—married or unmarried—who went to PathFinders for help.

The Chinese men who fathered children with FDWs fell into several categories. Some men officially married the mother and took responsibility for the child. Some men were already married and had a consensual relationship with the mother that got more complicated when she got pregnant. In some cases, men pressured women to have abortions. In cases I knew of where domestic workers were raped by employers, the pregnancies were terminated.[4] Several women who came to PathFinders had problems with Chinese men who denied paternity or refused responsibility for the child. Three such men were already married. One man was the woman's former employer; unbeknownst to his wife, he and the FDW had a consensual relationship. He took the child to live with a relative in China, and the mother was in the process of trying to legally reclaim the child. Another married man had met the woman when she worked for his neighbor. When the neighbor learned the FDW was pregnant, she terminated her contract. The man then signed her new contract and brought her to live with him and his wife. This was intolerable for both women, and eventually the FDW returned to the Philippines with the baby. In another case, the man arranged for the woman and child to go to Macau, where he initially hoped to maintain the relationship with her and with his wife.

Some former FDWs I knew (several who were not among the fifty-five interviewees) were officially married to Hong Kong Chinese men and were Hong Kong residents or en route to becoming residents. Yip and Caroline considered themselves very fortunate. Yip was a Hong Kong Chinese Christian whose parents had come from the mainland. He worked as a chef in an upscale Chinese restaurant. He was introduced by a friend to Caroline, a never-married Indonesian Christian domestic worker in her early thirties who worked in another restaurant. Caroline had overstayed her visa in order to avoid agency fees, and she was working illegally. They developed a relationship, and Caroline got pregnant and needed prenatal care but, without a valid Hong Kong identity card, was afraid of being arrested for overstaying if she went to the hospital. Yip wanted to marry Caroline but was unsure what to do since she was an overstayer. Afraid to approach immigration officials and unable to afford an immigration lawyer, the couple turned to PathFinders. Caroline was advised to surrender to the Immigration Department, which she did. The advanced state of her pregnancy was cited as the reason to give her a suspended sentence for overstaying, but Yip's status, his desire to marry her, and the assistance of a pro bono lawyer also helped. Eventually, Caroline and Yip were married, and in 2013 she applied for permanent residency.

Chinese fathers' socioeconomic status was, on the whole, much better than that of African or South Asian illegal workers. Chinese men I knew who married former FDWs were mostly middle or working class. They all owned or rented reasonable housing (often government housing) and were literate in Chinese. Their jobs ranged from working class (like Yip) to those who had small businesses or managerial positions. Women sometimes expressed ambivalence toward Chinese men, considering them less physically attractive than men of other nationalities but potentially providing greater financial security and better futures. The women's views were likely influenced by wider attitudes in both the Philippines and Indonesia, where Chinese minorities control a disproportionate amount of the wealth. The children that result from relationships with Chinese men are sometimes complimented for their "lighter skin" and are often said to "look Chinese"—the former being a compliment and the latter expressing some ambivalence. In Hong Kong, a child's Chinese appearance makes it easier to fit in at school but also more likely that the mother will be mistaken for "the helper" rather than mother or wife. Because of the discrimination that such couples face, some choose to socialize only with other "mixed" couples in which the women are all former FDWs. At various social occasions, I met Hong Kong Chinese and other resident men married to former FDWs. Two Chinese men had been married close to two decades, and their former FDW wives ran small businesses, one that catered to Filipinos and the other to Indonesians. I knew of one Chinese man who signed the same Filipina FDW's contract for over a decade. They lived together "as husband and wife." He never paid her; she cooked, cleaned, and willingly slept with him. As her friend recounted, she expected to marry him as promised, but, when he retired, he wanted to travel and just left. When the woman's contract expired, she expected she would have little choice but to return to the Philippines with nothing to show for a decade of unpaid intimate labor.

SOUTHEAST ASIAN MEN

Southeast Asian fathers included five Filipinos and three Indonesians who, unlike the other men discussed above, all fathered children with women of the same nationality. Most such couples were legally married to each other in their home countries. Three Filipino couples were married in the Philippines and worked together in Hong Kong as FDWs. There are hundreds of Filipino FDW married couples in Hong Kong.[5] Two Filipino couples worked together for the same employer and raised children in Hong Kong. One couple worked for different employers. When Dom's pregnant wife, Caitrin, ran into him on a bus with a pretty young woman, he pretended not to know her (they later separated). Two Filipino men were Hong Kong permanent residents. Nellie and Cesar (chapter 3) married in Hong Kong, and Melinda and Niko (chapter 2) lived together but were not married since neither was divorced. Cesar had worked for a migrant NGO for many years, and Niko arrived as a child when his mother married a local resident.

Two of the three Indonesian fathers lived in Indonesia and were married to the child's mother. Both women got pregnant when they went home to visit, one intentionally and one accidentally. Both women gave birth in Hong Kong and returned home with the baby afterward. There was no doubt about either child's paternity, but one father claimed the child was not his until the resemblance became unmistakable. The third Indonesian man went to Hong Kong as a tourist and was described as a handsome, charming "bad boy" who went to Hong Kong regularly to take advantage of Indonesian domestic workers who are lonely and have unfulfilled sexual needs and money in their pockets.

OTHER MEN

Many other nationalities of men have relationships and children with domestic workers. Three Indonesian mothers in this study met the child's father at bars in Wanchai that catered especially to Western expatriates, servicemen, and tourists.

Juan was a married man in his thirties from Mexico who was in Hong Kong for several months on business. He met his Indonesian girlfriend at a bar, and they saw each other for several months. When he learned that she was pregnant, he left her and soon after returned to Mexico. She had no contact with him and gave the baby for adoption. Gerry was white, around fifty, from the United States, and worked and had permanent residency in Hong Kong. He met Rose at bar, and they spent many nights together at his flat. When she told him she was pregnant, he gave her money for an abortion, and they did not see each other again until she found a lawyer with the help of an NGO, was awarded legal aid, and filed a paternity claim against him (see chapter 7).

Wilhelm was from the Netherlands. A middle-class businessman who came to Hong Kong every month for several days, he met Wahyu at a Wanchai bar. Wahyu had originally come to Hong Kong from Indonesia with a FDW contract, but she worked at bars, overstayed, and was later arrested for selling drugs. For six months, each time Wilhelm was in town, Wahyu stayed with him in his hotel room. She knew he was married but thought they had a steady relationship, and she called him her "boyfriend." When Wilhelm learned Wahyu was pregnant, they had a final sexual encounter which she described as uncharacteristically violent, intended to cause a miscarriage. Wilhelm left and never contacted her again. Wahyu had amassed significant information about him, however, including contact information for his employer and his wife in the Netherlands. Last I heard, Wahyu had contacted a lawyer who was exploring the possibility of filing a paternity claim in the Netherlands.

Western expats are easily seen flirting with domestic workers in certain neighborhoods and bars. I knew of several such relationships that did not result in pregnancy because the men used condoms. In the course of my research, I met two other Western men (one from the United Kingdom and one from Germany) in their fifties or sixties who were married to former FDWs (one Filipina and one Indonesian). I did not formally interview them but chatted with them about my research. Both couples originally met in Wanchai bars, married, and had children together. Both men were previously divorced, had adult children, good jobs, and were twenty or more years older than their wives. The couples lived in upscale New Territories flats. Both women had obtained Hong Kong permanent residency. I also heard about Western university students who fathered children with domestic workers (see also Sim 2009).

MEN'S VIEWS OF WOMEN

Over the course of eighteen months, I attended a dozen or more English classes for asylum seekers and refugees. Ten to twenty students showed up each week; all were men, most were African, and a few were South Asian. Since most of them were highly fluent in English and very articulate and knowledgeable about current events, the class was more of a discussion/ debate session than an English class. Aware of my research interests, the class often discussed topics related to women, especially domestic workers. It soon became clear that all of the men knew men who were (or had been) involved with domestic workers, including some of the students themselves, several of whom shared their opinions and experiences with me in private. In general, men's views ranged from highly appreciative of the "kindness" and "generosity" of domestic workers (as noted above) to highly critical of their loose morals and sexual aggressiveness, including doubts that Indonesians are "really Muslim."

Asylum seekers often expressed pragmatic views about women. They all knew men who had "traded up" from domestic workers to Chinese permanent residents and thus achieved the goal of becoming a dependent and gaining the privilege to work and live in Hong Kong. Such men were spoken of with envy, as though they had won the lottery, regardless of possible negative qualities of their wives. One Muslim asylum seeker had spoken of his Indonesian ex-girlfriend as his "soul mate," so I asked how he felt about his Chinese wife. He answered, "If you live with a dog for fifteen months, you learn to love the dog." His answer was especially telling, since Muslims consider dogs *haram*.

When October 2011 headlines announced that a Filipina domestic worker had won her court case, which would allow FDWs to apply for permanent residence, it became a heated topic of class discussion.[6] At first the men were very excited about the ruling because they thought, mistakenly, that it meant that Filipina domestic workers *would* have right of abode in Hong Kong (as opposed to the possible right to apply). They enthusiastically applauded the decision because "they are much nicer than Chinese women" and "they like us better than Chinese women." The men agreed that, if Filipinas had residency, they would prefer to marry Filipinas than Chinese women. This led to a discussion with a smaller group of African men after class about the relative merits of different nationalities of women. Filipinas, they said, are confident and better educated than Indonesians, "they are good" but "not flexible" and "bossier than Indonesians," and they always think they are right. Indonesians are less educated but "have curiosity and interest." Indonesians are more naive but "very kind." The most serious criticisms were reserved for Chinese women. "They whiten their skin; they don't like it that nice golden-brown color." "They are spoiled" and "never bring you food or cook for you." "They expect you to do everything for them." "They can only do two things: shop and get take out." As one man put it, "Indonesian women bring you food; Filipinas will cook for you; and Chinese women will say either 'What are you cooking for me?' or 'Where are you taking me for dinner?'"

Some of the class conversations I found most disturbing were about homosexuality. Men expressed extreme condemnation of homosexual relationships. They recounted fear of prison and detention because of the "terrifying" sounds of men having sex with other men at night, including men who otherwise appeared to be pious Muslims. No opposing views were voiced amid the outspoken vehemence. When a local newspaper announced in 2012 that a wealthy Hong Kong tycoon's daughter had married her same-sex partner in France and that her father sought a husband for her, the teacher asked what they, as fathers, would do in such a case. The students were unanimous in their condemnation. Several agreed they would kill her; the less vehement said they would give her the choice of leaving the community or be killed. One African Christian said he would pray, then talk to her about renouncing her lesbian ways. He was severely chastised by the others for "sounding like a Swiss white man."

In other conversations, men expressed curiosity about "all the Indonesian tomboys and lesbians" in Hong Kong. One African Muslim asked, "Why do so many beautiful Indonesians go with tomboys?" and another asked, "Why do tomboys make themselves look so ugly?" One speculated that "ugly women become tomboys." When I said that some women prefer women and have sexual relationships, but that *some* dress like boys or have relationships with other women in Hong Kong in order to avoid unwanted male attention—including male employers or men who harass them on the street—some of the men seemed thoughtful. One nodded and said, "I hadn't thought of that." Since "good women" stay away from men, the idea that some do so by making themselves unattractive seemed surprising and interesting. He and others were especially disturbed by the idea of lesbian sex, and one man retorted, "It is better that we have sex with them so that they will not become lesbians!"

Whereas the mothers I knew often criticized men who did not take responsibility for their babies, some men, like George and his friends, complained that women, like his former girlfriend, "take our babies away from us," not allowing them to play a role in their children's lives. His ex-girlfriend recently returned to work in Hong Kong after taking their son to the Philippines to stay with her parents. He complained that, if the child was a girl he would not mind, but a boy should be with his father. "We Africans think a boy needs to be raised by his father or else he might grow up to be gay," he explained. In contrast to women's complaints of learning belatedly that men are already married back home, George and his friend criticized women who tell men they are "single" and turn out to be married in Indonesia or the Philippines. Some women, they said (I also knew of such cases), harbor the hope or possibility of returning to their husbands back home.

When I asked about violence against women, George's friend said that African men would never do that but that perhaps Pakistanis would. He then thought for a minute and said that Indonesian women think that "if men beat them it means they love them."[7] When I expressed skepticism, he said, "Sometimes women are the violent ones" and "they ask for it." Women shout at them, pull at their shirt collars, and scream and hit them. He cited one case—witnessed by many men—where the woman threw a cleaver at the man, who was African, and "of course then the man may beat her because he cannot shout at her." In his view, shouting would only serve to make him look weak in the eyes of other men, and the woman's violence demanded a violent response.

Given that most South Asian and many African men are Muslim, they echo some of the same gendered value judgments as Muslim women, but they are even more adamant about "good women" who are wives and mothers and "bad women" who are *haram*—prohibited—and are aggressive and sexually motivated to sleep with men who are not their husbands. The women they meet in Hong Kong often do not seem to fit the ideal. Many do not dress modestly, and they are obviously unprotected by male family members, so they are viewed as "fair game." But beyond these culturally and religiously based generalizations are more complex and conflicting views.

Some men adamantly argue that women are often the aggressors and that, by having sex with them, they simply give them what they ask for. As one man said, given "men's needs" and "how aggressive women are," men have little choice but to sleep with them. In class, however, men who had been in Hong Kong several years warned newcomers that "laws are different here" and that what they may think is normal male behavior can get them into trouble in Hong Kong. One new arrival, a young African, was surprised to learn that being drunk does not absolve you of responsibility for sexual assault. He was also surprised to learn that elevators often have security cameras and that molesting a woman alone in an elevator at night could get him arrested.

One day I was introduced to a tall, well-dressed, Nigerian Hong Kong resident who worked as a translator. It was mid-afternoon, and he stood in the Tsim Sha Tsui 7-Eleven store drinking beer with two domestic workers. The women had apparently approached him; one was very upset. He bought one a beer and the other a coke. This air-conditioned store, open all day and night, where beer costs much less than in pubs, was known as an African hang out. After finishing their drinks, his companions left, and we talked. He was interested in my research and offered to accompany me to Victoria Park on Sunday—where Indonesians congregate in the thousands on their day off—to demonstrate to me "how aggressive Indonesians are" regardless of men's passivity. He described his "experiment" as follows: I would sit on a park bench. He would stand a few yards away, within view. He was certain that, within minutes, an Indonesian woman would approach him. He would start to walk away with her and I would get up. He would act flustered and introduce me as his wife, and she would quickly leave. He said all he had to do was stand there and within a few hours dozens of women would approach him. I did not take him up on the offer, but his point was clear: women often pursue men. When they do so, many men feel little compunction—and some obligation—to "give them what they want."

George, the African asylum seeker who had a son with his Filipina ex-girlfriend, and his friend Tom talked to me one day about FDWs. Although the worst George could say about his ex-girlfriend was that she was "too strong," he and Tom were highly critical of domestic workers they called "prostitutes." By this they referred not only to women who have sex for money but also to women who sleep with more than one man or who have had multiple boyfriends.[8] A common source of conflict, George said, is that "women think there is love because they have slept together, but sex doesn't necessarily have anything to do with love. Men have a need, and sleep with people they do not love. The women, as soon as they enter the man's room, are fair game." He and his friend stressed that women do not understand that "having sex does not mean people love each other!" However, George believes that people "should love each other"—as he did his ex—if they have sex.

Whereas men and women both talked about sex as a "basic physical need," especially for men, some men also spoke of it as a necessity for women, especially for once-married "experienced women" who develop "a need for sex." African and South Asian asylum seekers talked about prostitutes of many nationalities (including South Asians, Southeast Asians, Chinese, and Africans) in and around Chungking Mansions and other areas who serve the needs of migrant men who can pay for sex, and contrasted them with domestic workers who "have sex for free." One story I heard from different sources was about a well-known Indian prostitute who was away from Chungking Mansions for several years. Upon returning, she asked, "Where have all the men gone?" only to be told "they all have domestic helper girlfriends."

Some men in the English class spoke openly about their relationships with women, while others only listened or alluded subtly to them. One African Muslim asylum seeker said that sexual relationships with women other than your wife are wrong according to Islam but that the greater sin is if one openly admits it and then continues. Another man tried to pin him down, "Does that mean you do or you don't then?" but he refused to answer, and his classmates were left to wonder how to interpret his silence, which they continued to do even when the class was over. Many men seemed to think it was impossible for men to go without sex.

Based on what Hakim knew from Dini, his Indonesian ex-girlfriend, he offered his perspective on Indonesian women who "become prostitutes":

> These Indonesian girls [who are prostitutes] most are married in Indonesia. For those who are married, prostitution is the last degree [the final stage] after they are married. Why these girls go to this last degree? Because they are married in Indonesia and they think if they have a boyfriend here it will be useless [i.e. the relationship will go nowhere]. At the same time, they find boys for their own sexual requirements and after that it starts. So most of the girls in these types of situations as prostitutes, I think most of them are married in Indonesia. Because unmarried girls are very immature here; the eighteen to twenty-one year olds, when they fall in love at that age it is very hard to forget your first boyfriend, so they stay with the first one or two boyfriends. If they quit with one boyfriend, they go to the other. There is this dependency in the early years, but when they get mature, in their thirties, they have been married in Indonesia and they know all about sex. They are the ones who are prostitutes.

To close this chapter, I recount two strikingly similar stories involving domestic workers and asylum seekers that were told to me by two different men in the course of one day. One of them described a Filipina who came to Chungking Mansions every Sunday, meeting one boyfriend at 8 A.M. for sex, then another at 10 A.M., one at noon, another at 2 P.M., and another at 4 P.M. before she headed back home to her employer's place. "She's just a prostitute," he said with disgust. The same day, another man told me about a man he knew who, each Sunday, met with one domestic worker girlfriend at 8 A.M., another at noon, another at 3 P.M., and another at 6 P.M. The first brought him breakfast and they had sex; the next brought him lunch and they had sex; the next brought him tea and they had sex; and the last one would brought him dinner and they had sex. "It's amazing!" he said with clear admiration of the man's resourcefulness. I was struck by the blatant gendered double standards. The woman with multiple sex partners is considered a whore; the man with multiple sex partners is a hero. Could the opposite interpretation of the gendered sexual exchange also be true, since he was the one who provided sex and received food?

5 Sex and Babies

> You'll be faced with loneliness, worry, anxiety, and homesick-
> ness. Given all these challenges, ask yourself if you can han-
> dle it physically, emotionally, and spiritually. Through it all,
> remember your family. Some people deal with these prob-
> lems with sex, but you need to remember what our role is
> with God. Sex is supposed to be for procreation in a family.
>
> — A nun, speaking to a group of women at a Philippine
> predeparture seminar (quoted in Rodriguez 2010, 114)

LONELINESS, FREEDOM, AND DESIRE

Many, if not most, migrant women follow the predeparture seminar advice expressed in the epigraph above, and they avoid sexual relationships in Hong Kong. Some, despite the warnings, have relationships with men or develop same-sex relationships that do not carry the risk of pregnancy. As Amy Sim writes, "Many young, attractive and single Indonesian women are frequently caught in the ambivalence of desiring and rejecting men at the same time. They fear the consequences of indiscretion with men that lead to the loss of reputation, chastity and to unwanted pregnancies" (2009, 20).

For men and women who are temporary migrant workers or asylum seekers with little hope of remaining in Hong Kong "for good," far away from home and from the surveillance of partners, kin, community, and the state, Hong Kong is a liminal place where social rules and expectations are relaxed or put on hold. As one Indonesian woman said to Salim (whose family is described below), "This is Hong Kong! In Hong Kong everything can do. Don't care if you have a husband; don't matter if you have wife."

Ideas about acceptable sexual and gendered behavior in Hong Kong are far less conservative than at home. Of course, rules are flexible or can be broken even at home, and some do adhere to those rules in Hong Kong, but social pressure to follow them is weaker. In Hong Kong, too, there is gossip and criticism, and those who preach and moralize, but few to impose sanctions. Away from the usual pressures of respectability and shame, men and women are in some ways freer to act on temptation and desires.

On any given Sunday, near the Star Ferry terminal in Tsim Sha Tsui, behind the Kowloon mosque in Kowloon Park, in Statue Square or along the raised walkways in Central, in Victoria Park, near the MTR station in Sham Shui Po, and in many small parks and shopping areas throughout more remote parts of the New Territories, one can easily see men of different nationalities, young and middle-aged, standing around or sitting and eating, talking or flirting with female FDWs. Each region of Hong Kong, Kowloon, and the New Territories has parks, public spaces, shops, pubs, and restaurants where migrant workers are known to congregate. A common scenario is that a couple—a South Asian or African man and a Filipina or Indonesian woman—will introduce their groups of friends to each other; they will mingle in the park or at some other location where they congregate on Sundays. Churches with English-language services or programs for migrants are also meeting grounds for men and women of different nationalities. Some meet at fast food restaurants, when one asks to share a table in the crowded place. Some meet at bars that cater to different ethnic groups: Western and European men—mostly white—at certain Wanchai and Lan Kwai Fong bars, and Nepalese men in the Jordan/Yaumatei area. Women are often approached on the MTR or while waiting for a bus. Sometimes an acquaintance gives a man a woman's number. In two cases I knew, the man borrowed the woman's phone to make a call, dialed his own phone, got her number, and persistently sent messages until she agreed to meet.

Besides socializing and flirting in public spaces and bars and restaurants that often cater to men of a particular class and race, couples also meet in subdivided rooms in tiny flats or in crowded guesthouses where men live, or domestic workers pool resources to rent a place to relax away from their employers on Sundays, and where they sometimes have parties.

Such rooms are often crowded and occupied, but there are other places where couples can rendezvous more intimately. They can be seen entering and leaving Chungking Mansions on Sundays—where cheap rooms can be borrowed or rented. When women heard that I walked through Kowloon Park at night to avoid the roadside crowds, they warned me to avoid the side paths where couples sometimes go for sexual encounters.

As this chapter illustrates, women often struggle with freedom and desire and notions of being good women, especially in relation to their seemingly conflicting roles as migrants, wives, and mothers. They are faced with whether or not to meet men, have sex, use contraception, consider abortion or adoption, or have a child. Ratna's story below—and that of her partner and her baby—is about love, jealousy, sex, desire, and her dreams.

RATNA, SALIM, AND BABY AMAL

Ratna is from East Java. After a year of college studying Economics, she went to work in Singapore, then in Hong Kong, where she has worked for over six years. As we talked, her seven-month-old baby, Amal, sat smiling and gurgling in a baby seat that gently rocked back and forth. Each time I spoke, he laughed uncontrollably. When Ratna spoke, he listened intently:

> I came to Hong Kong because I want to earn more money for my family. I also came to Hong Kong because I don't want to get married so soon. In my country if a girl does not leave, she gets married very quickly. When I was working in Singapore, somebody was already coming to my house wanting to marry me. I said to my mother, "I need more time. I don't want to get married yet. Let me leave for two years." But in Hong Kong—I'm here just two years and then I get a boyfriend and then I don't want to go back. Salim is my first and only boyfriend and is now my husband and the father of my baby.
>
> First time I get to know him, I feel he is very good for me. I feel he is very much in love with me. I was married in 2008 at the Wanchai mosque. We got married first and then come together, and then I sleep with him. It is my first time. First time I love. First time everything.
>
> We met at the beach. He bumped into me and then I took his mobile [phone] and he took my mobile by accident. His friend called and I answered. Then we become friend, friend, friend, and he is very—I cannot

say—very handsome, very nice to talk to and is very emotional. And then like—ah how to say? Looking, looking [at each other], and I can say I have a feeling I like when we are becoming friends. And then he is talking about his story in his country [Sri Lanka] and then I think I find this one and he is good.

And then when we are friends for eight months he said, "I want you to become my girlfriend, and if you love me okay, good, but if you don't love me, no problem." I think he is different because other people when looking will say, "Hi girls. I love you!" and those ones are very different from him. Then when we are together for nine months we get married. We married without his parents or my parents here. That was not good for me. But his parents know and I shared it with my family. I showed them his picture. I talked with my mother. At that time my father was still alive and my father and my mother say, "If you like him we cannot stop you." And then we got married.

But after we marry, I see he also has another girl so I fight her. I had to go to jail because I beat someone—the girl—because I love him. This is my crazy love and so I need to beat someone. So I go to jail for one day until my employer came to get me out. When I got out I found that girl and I beat her again. She is Indonesian and has a husband and a child at home. But she is in love with my husband. At that time we are married already. That is why I am so pained at that time. I never felt anything this way. When I beat her I said, "If you come to my house and my husband stays with you, I will leave. But if my husband loves me, I will kill you. Do not disturb me!" And then that girl says, "You think you are very beautiful, just more and more talking" and that's why I cannot control myself.

At that time I was just married one month. But the bigger problem was in 2009. That's when I cannot control myself. I know my husband is with that other person; I am very pained. He said, "Girls in Hong Kong are the same as VCDs [many counterfeits]. I need to look and see which one is the original and which is not. That is why I try the other girl. I don't love her but I want to try another person." I said, "This is very painful. Just leave me." But my husband said, "I don't want to leave you. If you don't love me I need to choose the other person. So many boys in Hong Kong do not only have one girlfriend. So many have many girlfriends! Why do I need to choose one? So let me try and I will come back for you." I said, "There is no need for you to come back for me. You can leave me. Please do not disturb me." But my husband said, "No, you must be with me. You only [need to] give me time, I want to look for other girls . . . ."

That answer gave me more and more pain, that's why I cannot control myself. I cannot do anything except cry. It was very bad time for me. I just did my job and I went to Macau and changed my employer there. I tried to forget my husband. But it was useless and I cannot forget him. That's why I came back to him. And then he says, "I won't do again. I won't do again." That I believe. One day he is looking at a girl and he said, "I was only looking at the Indonesian girl and she gives me her number. She said she is in love with me." "Um hmm, and then what?" "No-wah! I said, 'I have a wife.'" And the girl said, "No problem. This is Hong Kong and in Hong Kong everything can do. Don't care if you have a husband; don't matter if you have wife."

Then I am worried about what I can do. That answer, until now I still can remember that. And then I say, "Okay, you choose one. If you, darling—my husband—I don't want you to have another person or to sleep with another person. If not choose, then we are divorced and I don't want this life" I say. And then my husband said, "No, Ratna, I want to be with you." "If you want really me, I want you to change everything!" I say. He says, "Okay I will try. I don't know, but I will try. I cannot change everything very fast." "Okay, I will give you time to try." And then in October 2009 it all stopped already and everything is good and is different. I see he is very good, and that's why I make sure I can make the baby with him.

He changed because I always look after him. Because now he very, very in love with me, like before we were married. Now everything is changed. Only smoking; no drink, no anything. Before he drinks and everything. I cannot say that everything about my husband is good, but now better than before. Now I live with him and the baby. Some weeks I work four days and other weeks seven days. I pay someone HK$2,500 to take care of my baby every month, but my work only pays HK$3,000 something. I pay the rest for transportation. My husband he works operating a machine. I cannot say much about his work, but it is very dangerous. He can get more money than me, so he pays rent and everything else. I don't earn enough to pay except transport and the babysitter. But I am lucky my employer is understanding. They don't mind that I live out.

Somebody told me, "You take your baby fulltime to Indonesia and come here for work." But my feelings tell me I cannot do it. I need to see him every day. I would miss him. Everything I do with my baby here with me. I know my baby is very naughty but I love him more than anything. I can throw my husband away, but I cannot throw my baby! I tell my husband that! My friend tells me, "Send your baby home and you can stay here and no need to spend more money." I say, "If I spend more money it is not a problem, but I want to live with my baby here." This one is my power. This one is my everything. I don't care what people say. I don't care if people tell me I am stupid, I say I just need to keep my baby. Very naughty baby! I have dreams for his education. My son will be a pilot one day. My husband says after his torture claim he will come back here as a businessman with another passport. I say okay.

GOOD WOMEN

Whereas men, as we have seen, often depict women as the aggressors, Filipinas and Indonesian women frequently complain about unwanted attention and harassment they receive from men in public, especially if they are alone. South Asian and African men follow them, make remarks about their bodies, and sometimes touch their breasts, legs, and bottoms in crowded places. Such men are considered rude, aggressive, and sometimes frightening. A woman with a baby is somewhat immune from such attention, but men still stare or utter insults if the child appears to be of mixed race. Julie, an attractive Javanese woman in her early thirties, demonstrated how she holds up her phone and shouts, "Do you want me to call the police?" when she is harassed. Sim describes a similar situation in Kowloon Park:

> [Walking with] two Indonesian migrant women in their early twenties, we were followed so closely by three African males that we felt their knees knock into the backs of our legs as we were hurrying out of the emptying park. They, too, had wanted to be "friends" and their aggression stopped only when I demanded their identification papers, to report them for sexual harassment. My respondents confirm that phenomena of this nature "happen all the time." (2009, 23–24)

Even when women welcome male attention—at bars or parties—women make a point of depicting men as the aggressors. This is less important as a factual statement of who expressed interest first than a claim by women that they followed "proper" gender roles and are good women. Men are supposed to be the aggressors; the same behavior in women is considered immodest. Some women stressed that they had "no interest in meeting men" and came to Hong Kong "only to work" but that a persistent man broke her resolve and won her heart. Whether sex took place early in a relationship or after a prolonged courtship or marriage, women often said the man's good qualities made her "fall in love," as Ratna did. As in her case, only "other women" were described as aggressive and predatory toward men, thus lacking morals. Fighting to keep a man was defensible. Women distance themselves from the immorality or immodesty of aggressive women who blurred into categories of "bad women" or prostitutes. This was often expressed by younger women like Ratna who were not previously married, and also among women I did not know well. Once I got to know them and it was clear I was not judging their morals, a few women, including some who were married in Indonesia or the Philippines, and some whose relationships had ended badly, expressed a greater sense of their female agency. They described getting dressed up and going to bars or other places where men congregate, sometimes after church or mosque, actively trying to meet men. One Filipina Muslim showed me photographs of her and her friends covered up at the mosque, and photos of the same women in stylish, sexy clothing afterward, going to meet their partners at a bar. When I asked what the religious teacher would say if she saw them, she said, "No problem, she wouldn't recognize us!"

Women often reasoned that men need sex and that it is a natural and necessary part of a committed relationship (like marriage). Few women seemed okay saying they just wanted casual sex with few strings attached. Many, like Ratna, insist on marriage and hope and expect that the relationship will be ongoing and exclusive. Some fear that, if they withhold sex, a man will easily find "other women." The constant threat of other women, including former "friends," was a recurring theme. Some couples, like Ratna and Salim, considered it important to have the *nikah* marriage blessing before sleeping together, but marriage is no guarantee of fidelity. Some couples marry later, under pressure from the man's friends or family members who reminded him that such a relationship or children born of it are *haram*. Some non-Muslim or mixed couples marry legally if the man is single and a Hong Kong resident, but the majority of mothers I knew— whether they had experienced the Muslim *nikah* blessing or not—ended up as single mothers.

George's observation (chapter 4) that Filipinas and Indonesians often mistake sex for love—that they think if a man sleeps with them he must love them—helps explain some women's false expectations and misunderstandings. Young and inexperienced women's comments sometimes reflected the naive belief that, if they had sex, even with a man they hardly knew, he would be committed and responsible. In their hopes for marriage, women often did not understand that some men were already married and had no intent or desire to "marry" again. They did not understand that a man might be working in Hong Kong but have no legal right to stay there, let alone sponsor a dependent.

Three mothers, including two very young ones, said their pregnancies resulted from rape. One was raped by a stranger in an elevator of the building where she lived and worked. The other two women said they were under the influence of alcohol when date-rape drugs were slipped into their drinks. Ara (chapter 3) said she remembered almost nothing about that night. Analie said she went with a group of friends to a birthday party in a white man's hotel room and had hazy memories of drunken white men having sex with her, but she was unable to move or resist. All three women planned to give the child for adoption in Hong Kong. Ultimately, Ara kept Angela.

Some social workers expressed doubt about rape claims. One social worker said she never believes it. "Never. They just say so, so you won't blame them and say it is their fault." Despite how troubling it is hear a social worker mistrust her clients and deny the possibility of rape, it is not entirely surprising that women who are raised to believe that sex outside of marriage is wrong should express their pregnancies either as a result of violence and force (which they could not resist) or as a result of marriage (even a failed marriage) so as to absolve themselves of some sense of blame. Especially if they choose to keep the baby and return home as single mothers, the idea that they were married, but the marriage failed, is more acceptable than the idea that they simply had sex with a man.[1]

MEANINGFUL TERMINOLOGY

Many women spoke of men as "the father" or "his/her father." When asked about their relationships, most Indonesian mothers spoke of their partners as "husbands," which implied a long-term commitment and exclusivity (whether or not this was actually the case), or as "boyfriends," to imply something more ongoing than a one-night stand, with some hope of commitment, even if they later understood that the man viewed the relationship very differently. When I asked an Indonesian woman about the sort of relationship she had with the man she slept with, she answered simply, "In my country, if married, sleep together; if sleep together, married." In other words, her sexual relationship was by definition marriage. Like many others, she normally referred to a woman's partner as her "husband." Describing a sexual partner as a husband can retroactively be a claim to respectability. The majority of mothers spoke of sex as if it were inseparable from hopes or expectations of a committed and ongoing relationship with the father, ideally a "marriage."

More of the Indonesian women who had white or Chinese partners—as opposed to African or South Asian ones—spoke of them as "boyfriends." In some cases, they knew the man was married and unlikely to divorce his wife, but they still hoped for a long-term relationship. As my research progressed, it became clear that, for Indonesian women, "boyfriend" blurred into a sort of customer, client, or benefactor relationship. In response to my question about terminology, Riana—a former FDW now married to a Chinese man—once said, "husband is really boyfriend and boyfriend is really customer."

Soliciting for prostitution is illegal in Hong Kong but prostitution itself is not, which helps fuel ambiguities. Men ("boyfriends") like Wilhelm (chapter 4) took Wahyu out, bought her drinks and a meal, brought her home or to his hotel room, and usually gave her "gifts" or money. Although he and other men might have seen this as a variation of the money-for-sex "girlfriend experience," without the hassle of finding a new woman each time he came to town, women like Wahyu depict this as something qualitatively different from more blatant forms of "prostitution" (Bernstein 2007). As a "boyfriend" he was not a client but someone who cared about her and gave her gifts or money because he wanted to and liked her. Women explained that prostitutes exchange specific sexual acts for defined sums of money (a price). Meeting men at bars, going out with them, sleeping with them for gifts or money, and leaving open the possibility of a long-term relationship was understood or justified as different from prostitution. As one woman explained, "At certain bars men know there are bad girls. If I need money, I say to him 'I like you and I am a bad girl. But I'm not a prostitute. You just give me what you want to give me.'" A few women, like Wahyu, entered Hong Kong with FDH contracts but freelanced at bars. Some couples later married, which reinforced the blur between customers or clients and "boyfriends" and the fantasy of marriage.

Hamish, a British expatriate who frequents Wanchai pubs, is described as follows:

> With his canny nose for a bargain, Hamish knows that "working girls" fall
> into two categories. There are professionals, prostitutes who are "very, very

expensive" and Filipino or Indonesian maids freelancing on the side. The latter will "fuck your brains out for the price of a gin and tonic." Alternatively they may want to form intimate alliances of various kinds with (Chinese and Western) men of financial substance who can buy them presents or give them small amounts of money. Hamish astutely connects the labor force around what he calls the "girlie bars" and the maids he sees in Statue Square on Sundays in what he dismissively calls the "birdcage" because of its concentration of women chattering. Some of them freelance in a variety of ways in Wanchai. He identifies a spectrum of Southeast Asian female migration circumstances in which "gweilo" [foreign] men are a resource for accumulating money and opportunities. Intimate relationships with wealthier men supplement low wages. Marriage offers a route out to another kind of life altogether. . . . The emotional and the financial are interconnected. It is easy, Hamish says wistfully, for men of his age to fall in love with younger women: especially when they are beautiful. Love, sex, and money form a powerful matrix in the Wanchai night. (Knowles and Harper 2009, 188–89)

The International Sex Guide and the World Sex Guide, two websites for English-speaking men who seek advice or share experiences about their sexual "hobby" in different parts of the world, include comments by locals and tourists about having sex with "DHs" (domestic helpers) in Hong Kong.[2] Some men online, like Hamish, consider sex with domestic workers a variation on sex with a professional prostitute or "working girl" (WG). They share advice on where and how to meet "helpers" and how to treat them nicely so they will think they are your girlfriend and have sex for "free" or at little cost. One man bragged about his sexual experience with a Filipina virgin who considered him her "boyfriend" rather than a tourist looking for free sex. Although he bragged about his DH conquest and thought he suavely manipulated a virgin into having sex with him, some women I talked to suggested that he might be the one who was fooled. Some women convince men that they are domestic workers (not WGs) and that they are virgins. One type of *jamu* (Javanese traditional medicine) involves a drying agent in stick or powder form that is inserted into the vagina, causing it to dry and close up. Puzzled about why "dryness" was desirable, I was told it increases a man's pleasure and can be used to make a man "think she is a virgin," making penetration difficult. Recalling the man's online post, we might wonder whether the woman was a virgin and the victim of his manipulations, or whether she had manipulated him. One Filipina mother I knew well was concerned about an Indonesian woman who was "chasing" her boyfriend. An Indonesian friend helped her buy that *jamu* from an Indonesian shop. Her partner's reaction was not what she expected: "He shouted at me to throw it away and never use that again!"

CONTRACEPTION

Contraceptives that require prescriptions in other countries can often be bought over the counter in Hong Kong, and contraceptives are available at subsidized low-cost government clinics for those with Hong Kong identity cards (including FDWs). We might wonder, then: Why didn't the mothers use them to avoid pregnancy? The answer is more complicated than it seems. Cost and availability may be factors, but they are not the main reasons for FDW pregnancy. In keeping with the normative view of good girls who become wives and mothers, some women associated contraception with immorality or feared the side effects, and some wanted a child. Others lacked adequate knowledge of contraceptive use or simply "trusted the man" to take precautions or bear the consequences.

Studies of married women in Indonesia and the Philippines show that contraceptive use is much higher and more effective in Indonesia, where a strong, government-promoted family planning program has existed since the 1970s and advocates reliable "modern contraceptives," including hormonal methods (pills and injections), longer-term methods (IUDs and sterilization), and barrier methods (condoms and vaginal methods). However, contraception in Indonesia is mainly available to *married* women (Schoemaker 2005; Sim 2009).[3] The level of "unmet contraceptive need" in the Philippines is roughly double that of Indonesia, reflecting Philippine church and state opposition to the sale and government subsidy of "modern" forms of contraception (Guttmacher Institute 2010a, 2010b, 2010c). Many Filipina mothers I knew practiced withdrawal or had ideas about their "safe time," utilizing methods that are condoned as "natural" and thus approved by the Roman Catholic Church and the Philippine state, methods that are free and less morally problematic.

When I asked a Filipina staff member at an NGO about barriers to Filipinas using contraception and having a child, she answered:

> I was trying to figure that out myself because I was also a young single mother so I try to figure out where did I go wrong? Why didn't I use condoms? I thought back and the sex education we had in school was mostly about puberty and human anatomy. Even the use of condoms is still not officially promoted in the Philippines. In that sense it is mostly religious [reasons]; it wasn't introduced, so people are just not aware of contraception. An average Filipina is faced with a dilemma. She is not empowered with enough information to make decisions or alternate decisions because she doesn't know. . . . And of course we are Catholic and we like very large families.

Domestic workers may not know where to go to get reliable information about contraceptives in Hong Kong, or they may lack the time to find out, since they work six days a week and most clinics are closed on Sundays. They may be reluctant to spend money on contraceptives, which are sometimes associated with immorality and frivolity, as opposed to money remitted home for living expenses, for school fees, or to repay debts. Some women think that only married women can get contraceptives and are shy or embarrassed purchasing them or asking for them, especially if it means interacting with a Chinese clerk, doctor, or pharmacist. To avoid pregnancy, many women opt for the less reliable rhythm method or withdrawal, methods that are more familiar to Filipinas and poorer rural Indonesian women (Guttmacher Institute 2010a, 2010b, 2010c; Schoemaker 2005).

A Chinese social worker who had worked at a Hong Kong government-funded welfare organization whose clients were asylum seekers and torture claimants told me that many former FDW clients are pregnant or are single mothers, but, instead of figuring out how to help them avoid unwanted pregnancy, the staff members' attitude (and her own at the time) was one of condescension and blame: "'How come they are pregnant?' I admit to thinking that myself. . . . There were times when we . . . blamed it on former domestic workers that they don't use protection and have another child." Later on, after getting to know some of the mothers well, she came to see things differently:

Now I hear more of the girls' stories and I know it is not that they *don't want to protect*, but there are other reasons for not having contraception. The man may not want to use the condoms—or the woman does not know that there are other methods. Then, if they know they worry about the fee and they don't know there is a medical waiver to cover the cost. But [we] can give them instructions like: "You can do this to protect yourself and to prevent yourself from being pregnant." "You are strong enough and there are things you can do on your own. You are strong enough to make this decision!" In [my old job] I did not have this perspective. I was stuck in "Why are you doing this? Why are you doing that?" [There] they discouraged distributing condoms. They think that distributing condoms encourages them to have more sex! And they don't think they should. But they are couples and are having sex anyway! They may not be husband and wife legally but they are boyfriend and girlfriend and they are not just sitting at home and watching TV all the time! Here we just let them take condoms if they need them. There they give them only if a couple asks for them, and then they hand over the condoms to them. Usually they are much too embarrassed to ask for them.

Referring to the mothers she knew, the same social worker said that their main problems are "lack of knowledge of contraception and lack of confidence. They are too worried and afraid to seek help." Chinese, including employers, she said, often describe Indonesians as *hou teng wah*, meaning they listen very well: "They know what you want from them; they listen to instructions; they do what you say and do not say 'no.' But it can also be a bad thing. They also cannot say 'no' to their boyfriends too. The Filipinos say 'no.' Or they say 'yes' and then they give you attitude!"

Not using contraception is another clear example of "cruel optimism" (Berlant 2011). A woman conveys her trust in the man by not using contraception, in the hope of establishing a good life with a committed relationship. Not using contraception is associated with trust, hope, and intimacy. Mothers said men did not want to use contraception, or they were in love and did not worry about getting pregnant. It is "God's will." Rarely does this lead to the desired results. Men often felt little responsibility toward such women and children, and, even if they do, they may have little to offer in terms of material support or a future together. Thus, romantic dreams of establishing a better life are doomed to failure.

Using contraception was not associated with being a responsible, careful, strong, liberated, or self-empowered woman, except among a few women who were older, had "enough" children (including those at home), and did not place much faith in male partners. According to Sim, Indonesian women "did not know or think that they could insist on contraception. By inference, a woman who asked that male contraception like condoms be used, indicated that she was sexually experienced and quite possibly, of loose morals" (2009, 27). Several women said that prostitutes (bad girls) may know how to prevent conception, implying that contraception is antithetical to committed relationships. Ironically, good girls get pregnant and are then seen as bad. Many men and women do use contraception, but for a woman to initiate it can indicate to that she is promiscuous or immoral.

Even women who took birth-control pills sometimes misunderstood how they work. Megawati became pregnant when she returned to Indonesia to see her husband, but she said it was an accident because she was on the pill. When I asked how long she had taken it, she said she had taken it the day before she had sex. She did not know that she had to take it for at least a month before it became effective. Taking pills in Hong Kong seemed illogical, wasteful, and embarrassing to her. Endri, who had two children with an Indian man, insisted that "the pill doesn't work," pointing to her one-year-old as proof. It turned out Endri was referring to the "morning after pill" that she had taken twenty-four hours before having sex. The instructions said to take it "within forty-eight hours of intercourse," so by taking it ahead of time she thought she would be okay.

Given the very different backgrounds of the men, it stands to reason that their views regarding women, sex, and contraception also vary greatly. African and South Asian men I spoke to who had relationships with domestic workers were adamant that men must take responsibility for contraception. In contrast, in one English class, some men admitted to "never" or "not always" using condoms because "it is the woman's responsibility." One man said he takes precautions, mostly withdrawal, about 80 percent of the time. Several men shouted all at once and chastised their classmates, calling them fools, not only for the risk of pregnancy but also because of possible HIV infection.

George once talked about African men's reluctance to have children. He recounted the story of a young African man who was "not ready for a relationship" but was having sex with an Indonesian woman who told him she was taking the pill. To be safe, he used a condom anyway, but she removed it at the last moment and got pregnant. Despite his friends' criticism and stern warnings, he stayed with her "because of the child. And then, she did the same thing again! She tricked him into having a second child with her." George said, "Once, okay. But how could you let her do that to you twice?!"

ABORTION

Filipina and Indonesian women are largely opposed to abortion on religious and moral grounds, but, when it comes to practical matters and everyday concerns, their views are more complex. Abortion is officially prohibited in their countries and by their dominant religions. According to the Guttmacher Institute, abortion is permitted in Indonesia only with "confirmation from a doctor that her pregnancy is life threatening, a letter of consent from her husband or a family member, a positive pregnancy test result and a statement guaranteeing that she will practice contraception afterwards" (2008, 1). Religious leaders oppose abortion, but some Muslim religious leaders are more tolerant than Christians, and a few sects permit abortions before 40 days or up to 120 days after conception (4). As many as four out of five women in rural Indonesia use "traditional birth attendants, traditional healers or masseurs to terminate their pregnancy" (4). Philippine law prohibits abortion, but illegal abortion is "widely practiced" with a third of women obtaining abortions from medical professionals and two-thirds who "consult traditional practitioners or attempt to induce the abortion themselves" (Juarez et al. 2005, 140).

In Hong Kong, abortions are legally available up to the twenty-fourth week of pregnancy, but it is against the law to obtain an abortion or attempt to have one outside of official channels. In 2012, according to the Hong Kong Family Planning Association, an abortion cost HK$3,000 (US$400) in the first twelve weeks, more for later-term abortions. The procedure requires "two registered medical practitioners" to agree that the pregnancy poses a risk to the "physical or mental health of the pregnant woman" that is "greater than if the pregnancy were terminated" or that there is a substantial risk of "physical or mental abnormality" of the child, the woman is under age sixteen, or she was the victim of forced sex, rape, or incest and reported it to the police within six months of the event. It takes two weeks from the initial consultation to undergo an abortion.[4] In practice, Hong Kong medical practitioners as well as local women who obtained legal abortions say it is easy and routine to obtain the required medical approval, but migrant women are mistrustful of the process.

Arida and her long-term boyfriend agreed than an abortion was the best option, and he paid for it. Arida's employer was also supportive. I met her with a friend at the family planning clinic in Wanchai when she was five weeks pregnant, and I accompanied her out because she was not permitted to leave the clinic alone after the procedure. Her East Asian boyfriend of five years worked in Hong Kong in a mid-level position at his country's embassy and had a wife and children in his home country. Arida was married and committed to her husband and children in Indonesia, though she had been away for over five years. She and her boyfriend had tried to end their relationship several times because of their families, but it was difficult because "we rarely see them and," she explained with a sigh, "we love each other."

In 2012, I accompanied a former domestic worker (who was married to a local resident) to the family planning clinic. She had missed a monthly contraceptive shot and took a "morning after pill," but her period was late and her home pregnancy test was positive. According to her calculations, she was eight weeks pregnant. She and her husband agreed an abortion was best. The clinicians estimated she was already more than eleven weeks pregnant. They could not schedule her next appointment for two weeks, by which time it would be too late for the cheaper and less risky abortion at the clinic. She would need to go to the hospital for the procedure where the cost was several thousand dollars more. The earliest public hospital appointment was a month away. By then, the pregnancy would be fifteen weeks along. The clinician apologized for the delay and recommended she try for an earlier (and far more expensive) appointment at a private hospital. Given the stage of her pregnancy, she and her husband decided to have the child. Later, it turned out that the clinic had been wrong; her pregnancy was less advanced. Because she was married, not working, and in Hong Kong legally, she was happy with the outcome, but for a working

FDW, torture claimant, or overstayer it would have been a far more diffi-cult situation.

In 2010, a presenter was scheduled to speak at a migrant mothers' dis-cussion group about contraception, but she emphasized her opposition to abortion. As she quizzed the women about fetal development, she tossed out dozens of tiny little plastic fetus dolls as prizes to those who answered correctly. She stressed that, immediately after conception, the fetus is "already a little person" and should not be "thrown away." The women seemed very receptive to her message and echoed her antiabortion mes-sage. As one Filipina said in a later interview, the Philippines is a Catholic country so when a Filipina gets pregnant "all she is thinking is 'this is a life and I cannot take this life' that's all. And so regardless if she thinks her family will kill her for doing that, she doesn't take it upon herself to take a life (the one inside her). It is that mentality." Yet, despite Filipina and Indonesian women's vocal opposition to abortion, given the lack—or inef-fective use—of contraceptives, abortion is in fact frequently treated as a valid alternative to pregnancy. Once it was clear I was not judging them for it, I was told dozens of firsthand stories of attempted, effective, and also failed abortions.

At another mothers' discussion group in 2012, the topic was family plan-ning and termination. The tone was remarkably different from the meeting in 2010. The presenter was a Chinese social worker who many women knew. She began by asking, "How many of you know people who have ter-minated a pregnancy?" The women (mostly Indonesians) all raised their hands and spoke at once. One pregnant young woman who was planning to give her child for adoption said she had friends who took pills and miscar-ried: "You can take five pills by mouth and put five pills inside the vagina." Others bought pills illegally from the pharmacy; the salesperson said, "don't tell anybody you bought it here." Gina had referred friends to a Chinese Indonesian doctor in Mongkok; her friend was the "doctor's helper." Gina accompanied one woman there for an abortion at six months and said that the doctor used something that "looked like a water hose." One woman said that "If a woman is six months pregnant it costs HK$9,000–9,500; HK$2500 is the cheapest for earlier around five weeks." The presenter asked about the risks of illegal abortion. Women mentioned infection, odor, bleeding, pain, sterility, and failed procedures. The speaker said that, if they are caught, they can be charged with an offense. Only the Family Planning Association or public or private hospitals can legally provide terminations in Hong Kong. She described the risks of illegal termination, including poor hygiene, faulty and unsanitary equipment, wrong doses of anesthesia and pain killers, and the possibility of contracting HIV or other sexually transmitted diseases. Illegal facilities cannot handle emergencies such as heavy bleeding or pelvic and uterine infections. She showed a picture of an illegal clinic, but the response was unexpected: "Wow," they said, "it is much better" than the clinics they had seen.

Despite the availability of legal abortions and subsidized contraception, women are deterred for a number of reasons: the staff are condescending and ask too many questions; medical practitioners do not speak their language; the services require identification; they mistrust Hong Kong's bureaucracy; and their employers might find out. Those who have overstayed are afraid that their "illegal" status will be discovered and reported or, if they are on recognizance papers, that they might be treated badly or turned away. Required forms and bureaucratic procedures, cost, time invested in repeated visits, and restrictions surrounding the procedure also deter them. As one Indonesian woman who had overstayed and later filed a torture claim put it:

> I don't go to family planning for the same reason I don't like to go to MCHC [Maternal and Child Health Clinic]—I go and they talk too much. They ask too many questions. They disapprove of us because we are on welfare; they don't like me if I use welfare to pay. The doctors are okay, but the nurses just talk, talk, talk.

If the illegal methods are effective, they can be easier, faster, less visible, and cheaper. If they do not work, at best they do nothing, at worst they are life-threatening or damaging to mother or child. Herbal remedies (*jamu*) that are used for "menstrual regulation" in Indonesia are unavailable in Hong Kong. The most common abortive methods are pharmaceuticals. Vicky, a Filipina, said she took about thirty tablets "of an abortion medicine called Provera" and that she bled but did not lose the baby. Provera, a variant of the hormone progesterone, is a contraceptive pill that prevents ovulation and can cause some spotting when first taken. It is not an abortive medicine but is mistakenly believed to have abortive effects. It can also have ill effects on the fetus. More often, women took Cytotek (Misoprostol), a drug that is used to treat gastric ulcers, for early abortions and to induce labor. This drug has been used since at least the 1990s for illegal, cheap, and effective abortions in the Philippines.

Ara (chapter 3), took around fifty tablets of Cytotek (more than double the recommended dose) costing HK$1,500, with no effect. Ronni, a thirty-five-year-old Indonesian mother of a two-year-old, took "many pills" and then bled and thought she had miscarried. A month and a half later, she bled heavily but was still pregnant. At the hospital, she was told the fetus was not viable, and she was scheduled for an abortion. Her friend—whom I encountered in the subway returning from the hospital—had scolded her for waiting so long and reminded her she could have been arrested for trying to abort illegally.

When Lolli, a Filipina in her mid-thirties, thought she was two months pregnant, she discussed the pregnancy with her Pakistani boyfriend, who said, "Do what you want." She told him she would abort, then "took many, many pills to throw away the baby." Two months later she went to the doctor, had an ultrasound, and discovered she was over seven months pregnant. Fearing the child might be damaged from the pills, she said nothing to her partner, but simply called him from the hospital and, when he arrived, she surprised him with a healthy son. As she described it, he "cried out of shock" because he thought she had aborted. He shed "tears of joy because he had no children and now has a son." Lolli's partner then concocted a story for his parents about why he could not marry in Pakistan. He said he had a son in Hong Kong whose mother died. He then introduced Lolli as "the Filipino auntie" who looks after his child.

Few men shared the "you decide" attitude of Lolli's partner. When I asked women whether they talked to partners about contraceptives or pregnancy, several said no, others said men simply told them, "Don't worry, we'll deal with it if it happens." Some women understood this as a vague promise about the future: "I thought he meant it would be okay if we have a baby." But what he really meant was, "I don't want to think about it now. If you get pregnant, you can have an abortion." When the time came, men encouraged or pressured women to abort, or they disappeared.

Hakim (chapter 4) explained that his former Indonesian girlfriend, Dini, was very kind to other Indonesian women who were in trouble and who came to them—as a respected couple—for help and advice:

> One girl was around nineteen and was pregnant about five months and she asked the boyfriend to marry her. The boy said "No, I don't think the baby is mine." The girl is very disturbed and my girlfriend took her to our home and we sat together and discussed the problem. I contacted that Pakistani and talked to him and he says, "This girl, she goes with so many boyfriends! So how can I tell that this is my child? So please don't force me to marry this girl like this." So it was very complicated. The ultimate result was that we decided that she should abort the baby. I just told her, "What are you going to do? He is not willing to marry you. So this is difficult for you to have a baby. So my advice is to abort it." This was her problem and I don't know how she solved it.

In another case, the woman wanted an abortion and the man did not. Rohan was an Indian Hong Kong permanent resident who was married to an Indian woman for ten years with no children. Her family blamed him, and his blamed her. Tensions mounted, and the couple divorced. Yanti and Rohan had only known each other a few weeks when she learned she was pregnant. She wanted an abortion because her relationship with Rohan was casual and she planned to return to her husband and child in Indonesia. Rohan begged her not to. When she showed no sign of changing her mind, he threatened to call the police and take her to court for "murdering" his child. He viewed her pregnancy as a "gift from God" and proof that he was "blameless" in his ex-wife's failed conception. When I met Yanti, she had succumbed to Rohan's pressure. She overstayed and gave birth, but she was afraid that Rohan would take their son and send her back to Indonesia. When I spoke to Rohan, he was desperate to keep the child. He said that if marrying Yanti was the necessary "cost" of keeping his son, he would "pay the price."

Letty was a well-educated Filipina FDW. She developed a serious relationship with an elegant and well-educated Nigerian man who told her he was a "businessman." She trusted him and willingly took out a HK$20,000 loan, as he requested, to invest in his business. Shortly afterward, she learned he was an asylum seeker and that she was pregnant. Upset about his lies and devastated that she had been "taken in" by a nonexistent business, she broke up with him and had an abortion.

When Delia, a Roman Catholic Filipina, learned she was pregnant, her married Chinese boyfriend pressured her to abort. She refused, and when he later learned the baby was a boy, he became very kind, declaring his love for her and his desire to leave his wife. When the baby was just a few months old and Delia had to go back to work, he offered to take the child to live with a relative. Instead, she took the baby to the Philippines, and her boyfriend refused to see her again.

Eka met her daughter's Nepalese father, Vikram, at a bar. They broke up when she was six months pregnant because she refused to have an abortion. She told me that, when Vikram learned she was pregnant,

> he and his family asked me to have an abortion. He gave me a choice: me or the baby. He said "What will you do when you have a baby? Will you have enough time for me? How can we have this [our relationship] with a baby?" He said, "Do you think if you have my baby you can hold me like this? If you have my baby you cannot do everything for me." He arranged for me to get an abortion, but I ran away from him. I told him it was six months already and that I cannot abort because it is too dangerous for me and the baby. The doctor we went to said it is okay though, if we have HK$10,000. My boyfriend had the money and I had a ten o'clock appointment for the abortion. But before ten, I woke up, and while he was still in the bathroom, I ran out. I chose my baby and not him. After that day he never called me anymore. He said, "You chose your baby, not me." I hope her father will open his heart to her, but so far his heart is like a stone. Like that. He chose. He wanted all the attention. He is jealous and selfish.

In the asylum-seeker English class, when the topic of abortion was in the news, the teacher asked the men what they would do if their girlfriends became pregnant. A few men said they would want her to have the baby; others, assuming the girlfriend was a domestic worker, said that "she is in Hong Kong to support her family so she should not have a baby." One man, referring to his asylum-seeker status, said, "I am enough of a problem already, so she doesn't need another problem [a baby]." "How can we support her?" "How can we be responsible?" One man said that "if it is a fling thing" he would encourage her to have an abortion, but if it is serious they should have the child, and she would have to go home and take care of it. Several men said abortion is never justified. "If a child is unwanted, the mother should give it away since so many people don't have children who want them." One man said he had a Chinese girlfriend and an American girlfriend and hoped one of them would get pregnant and have to marry him. Another, referring to Hong Kong's low birthrate, retorted, "Chinese women don't get pregnant." The teacher commented on African men's directness with women, "going up to them and saying 'I love you, come with me.'" Without missing a beat, another said, "I would never go up and say 'I love you' to a Chinese woman, only to an Indonesian or a Filipina!"

MATERNITY POLICY

In theory, an FDW is protected by the Maternity Provision of Hong Kong's Employment Ordinance. She is entitled to ten weeks' paid maternity leave if she has worked for forty weeks "immediately before the commencement of scheduled maternity leave; she has given notice of pregnancy confirmed by a medical certificate to her employer; and she has produced a medical certificate specifying the expected date of confinement if so required by the employer" (Labour Department 2012, 17). Maternity leave pay is four-fifths of her average daily wages. Employers cannot legally dismiss a pregnant domestic worker from the date she presents the medical certification of pregnancy until she is due to return to work except for "serious misconduct." An employer "who contravenes the provision is liable to prosecution and, on conviction, a fine of HK$100,000." The employer is required to pay the worker "wages in lieu of notice; a further sum equivalent to one month's wages as compensation; and 10 weeks' maternity leave pay if, but for the dismissal, she would have been entitled to such payment." Domestic workers are also entitled to "claim remedies for unreasonable and unlawful dismissal" (ibid.).

Despite such a law, many factors obstruct its implementation, including the fundamental view that FDWs are in Hong Kong for the sole purpose of working. Many employers and workers are unaware of the law or, if they are, do not follow it. Workers who attempt to exert their reproductive rights by simply being or becoming pregnant are often considered disobedient, disloyal, promiscuous, and a serious problem for their employers. Domestic workers are discouraged from getting pregnant in Hong Kong because of the inconvenience it will cause their employer. Needless to say, becoming pregnant increases the precarity of migrant workers.

Most Indonesian domestic workers are subjected to pregnancy tests before departure or upon arrival in Hong Kong, and employment agencies and employers avoid employing pregnant workers. Some employers hire workers in their late thirties or older with the expectation that their child-bearing years are over. Some workers report being required by employers or agencies to sign agreements promising not to get pregnant. Some are accompanied by employers to the family planning clinic to get contraceptives before they go home on holiday. One domestic worker knew she was pregnant on arrival in Hong Kong and, afraid of dismissal, submitted her friend's urine in the hopes of working long enough to pay her agency fees. If a domestic worker becomes pregnant, some employers help them or require them to obtain abortions. Other employers, with the support of the agency, terminate them or get the worker to terminate the contract.

Hong Kong antidiscrimination law makes it illegal (in most cases) to discriminate in hiring based on pregnancy, but it is common knowledge that most employers do not want pregnant domestic workers. Despite the illegality of terminating a worker who has presented certification of pregnancy, pregnant workers are often fired, judging from the many cases I encountered and those reported by NGOs. I met several women like Wulan (below) who were required to sign a termination agreement and others who, unfamiliar with their rights, thought they had no choice but to resign. One woman believed her employer who said maternity benefits only apply to Hong Kong married women. Some women, who did not realize that presenting a certificate of pregnancy is intended to protect them from termination, delayed telling their employers and were terminated. Employers who can say they were never notified of the pregnancy (and did not know) cannot easily be charged with discrimination, even if the pregnancy seemed obvious.

Theoretically, the Employment Ordinance protections guarantee FDWs maternity benefits, but reality is often different. As one NGO employee put it:

> In most cases, the employers terminate the contract when they find out the helpers are pregnant. For so many reasons, despite the fact that it is against

the law. And then they call it—they say the helper told lies. Because when they are first taken in, helpers tell the employers that they are not married. When they are married back home they do not tell the employer because the employer prefers that they are unmarried, because they think that there will not be any other commitment. They think they will not be feeling homesick and they will not be wanting to go back home frequently for all the reasons. So the moment they get pregnant they tell them, "You told us lies in the beginning when you signed the contract! We wouldn't have signed if you told the truth!" and then they are terminated. In some cases they even get the helper to sign a document to say that they will not get married during the contract or they will not get pregnant. Of course that is not valid at all—anything signed outside the employment contract will not be valid—but some of these employers will resort to that kind of thing.

Lilik (chapters 2 and 4) won her claim but was awarded a fraction of the amount she was entitled to. Wulan was discouraged from pursuing her claim and felt intimidated by the agency, her employer, and the tribunal officer; she finally gave up and went home.

BABY KASIH AND WULAN

I got to know Kasih and her mother, Wulan, in 2011. They had a visible bond. Kasih was a few months old then, with a charming giggle, a constant smile, and her mother's dimples. Her tiny mother (who made me, at 5'1", feel tall) carried Kasih in a batik sarong snuggly tied over her chest and a large old backpack of infant supplies on her back. I first met them when I accompanied them to the Labour Tribunal with Liana. Wulan was there for an attempted reconciliation with the employer who she claimed had wrongfully terminated her when the employer learned she was pregnant. I was not allowed to attend the meeting, so I waited outside. Wulan and Liana, who was the translator, described it to me afterward.

Wulan's former employer, an elegantly dressed and bejeweled Chinese woman, arrived late and made a big entrance accompanied by her sister and the agency manager. The employer reportedly shook her head and said, "I am very disappointed in you, Wulan." Wulan stood her ground, looked her in the eye, and said, trembling, "I am very disappointed in you too, Ma'am." Wulan described how she looked after her employer's elderly mother and only occasionally saw her actual employer. She hid her pregnancy until the end because she feared termination. The old lady, with whom Wulan got along well, thought she had simply "gotten fat," but her employer confronted her a week before her due date, asking if she was pregnant. Out of fear, Wulan lied and denied it. Her employer took her to a doctor, who confirmed her pregnancy. Her employer then had her sign a letter accepting a ticket home and her pay up to that day. If she did not sign, her employer threatened to tell the employment agency. Wulan said she had signed under duress and claimed that her employer owed her maternity pay, a month's pay in lieu of notice, and compensation for illegal termination. Her employer's sister and the agent supported the employer's version of the story. According to the three Chinese women, Wulan was deceitful about her pregnancy, which was grounds for immediate termination without notice, and she had willingly signed the letter but now had changed her mind. The tribunal officer, whose job was to mediate, seemed to side with the employer, discouraging Wulan from pursuing her claims and warning her (erroneously) that, if she took the case further and lost, which he said was likely, she could be required to repay her employer's lost wages from missing work. Given her lack of evidence and her fear of going into greater debt, Wulan decided to give up, but she did not leave Hong Kong immediately. While contemplating what to do, she renewed her visitor visa and stayed for almost two months. During that time, I learned why she was so ambivalent about returning home.

Twelve months earlier, between contracts and waiting for her new job to start, she had met a good-looking Indonesian man who came to Hong Kong as a tourist. They met at an Indonesian shop in Causeway Bay. He made small talk, flirted, and asked her to meet him the next day. She agreed to help him buy a computer since she had a friend who was selling one. At first he seemed kind and attentive. She had free time before beginning her new contract. She was attracted to him but told him she was married and would not have intercourse. As she explained later, he forced himself on her and refused to use a condom. She subsequently learned that he had many girlfriends whom he treated as a source of income.

Wulan had initially planned to give her baby for adoption in Hong Kong. She met several times with an NGO social worker to discuss the process, and she secured her husband's required approval, even though he was not the child's father. After the baby was born, however, Wulan encountered opposition at almost every turn: the hospital staff, nurses, hospital social worker, and Social Welfare's Integrated Family Services Centre all pressured her to take the baby to Indonesia. A Social Welfare Department social worker had her in tears and made her write "I am willing to go back to Indonesia with my baby" and sign it. As Wulan and the NGO staff member who accompanied her recounted, the social worker said, "Your baby looks just like you. Why do you want to get rid of it?" and "How can you get rid of her to suit yourself? . . . You are an irresponsible mother. . . . Even if your husband does not support you, you should ask another family member." Wulan recalled how the immigration officer told her the baby was cute and smart and urged her to take her time, talk to her husband: "This is your baby. You need to think. You still have time. You are the mother. Where is your heart?" Guilt, pressure, and a growing bond with her child led her to change her mind.

When I met them, Wulan had begun the painful struggle of figuring out how to tell her husband she wanted to keep Kasih, and of exploring possibilities that might allow her to at least see Kasih in Indonesia. She said her husband was a very kind, hardworking farmer in an impoverished region of East Java. Their families were close growing up. He was like an older brother and helped look after her as a child. When she reached her teens and men began showing interest in her, he professed his love. With family approval, they were married and had a child. Soon after, she went to work in Singapore, sending money home. There she had a relationship with another man, told her husband, and he forgave her. Although her husband begged her to come home and stay, which she did for a while, she went to work in Hong Kong to earn money "because our place is so poor."

When she first told her husband about the baby, he was distraught. He said he forgave her once but would not suffer the humiliation of raising another man's baby. He told her to come home to him and their older child, be a good wife, and have another baby with him, or to keep the baby and not come home. Wulan already felt estranged from her older child who barely knew her, and she longed for closeness with Kasih. Once, while I was holding Kasih, Wulan asked, "Wouldn't you like to take her to

America, Nicole? You are so good with her. You are not too old!" She said it in a teasing tone, perhaps so that we could both pretend it was a joke. She struggled to figure out how to stay with her husband, who was good, kind, loved her, and never drank or gambled or cheated, and how to keep in touch with Kasih to whom she was deeply attached. She described the situation as follows:

> It is like if I carry two heavy things in each hand. In both hands it is too heavy and too hard to put them down. Both things are very equal. Two hands holding heavy things cannot put one down. You cannot choose one. You can carry both, but if you put one down you fall. I must choose one. If I choose my baby, I lose my husband. If I choose my husband, I lose my baby. [She shook her head.] Very painful.

Eventually a childless woman she knew in Yogjakarta (a former domestic worker she met in Hong Kong) was willing to take the child. Wulan's hope was that, when her husband saw the child, he would change his mind. But, even in the final hour when she left for the airport, he reminded her by phone of the shame that the family would face in the small *kampong* (village) if she returned home with a baby. As we parted, she sobbed at the thought of leaving Kasih.

In Indonesia, as Wulan later described, things did not go as hoped. Her husband refused to see Kasih, so she was forced to leave her with the woman in Yogjakarta and to take a bus home. The woman planned to get a new birth certificate, to change Kasih's name, and to introduce her as her own. Meanwhile, according to Wulan, the woman kept increasing demands for more money for Kasih's medical care, threatening to give the baby to a foreigner who would pay to adopt her if Wulan did not send more money. Two weeks after her arrival in Indonesia, distraught, Wulan came up with a new arrangement that met with her husband's approval. Her brother and sister-in-law, who lived in a *kampong* an hour away, agreed to raise Kasih as their son. Her brother accompanied Wulan to Yogjakarta to reclaim Kasih with none of the anticipated conflict. When I spoke to Wulan the day after Kasih's first birthday, she described her birthday party. Wulan saw her often; her husband and older child had come to love Kasih, who lived happily with her aunt and uncle. Wulan said she was "working side by side" with her husband, planting and farming.

Wulan had not told the women with whom she lived in the Hong Kong shelter about her situation, but they became suspicious when they learned that she had given them a fake phone number in Indonesia. They gossiped among themselves and wondered aloud whether she had really been raped, whether she had in fact terminated her own contract with the employer, whether she knew the woman in Indonesia, whether she had "sold" her child, and whether her actions were ever in the baby's interests. Regardless of the answers, it was clear that Wulan did not know her legal rights and had, as a result, made uninformed decisions. She was entitled to certain maternity benefits that she did not receive. She wanted to stay close to Kasih, so having her adopted in Hong Kong was unappealing. She was committed to her marriage and struggled with how to become "a good wife." She contrasted her relationships with Kasih and with her older child, who refused to talk to her. Working in Singapore and Hong Kong was exciting; she dreaded the boredom and poverty of the *kampong* and the ache and tedium of farm work.

ADOPTION

Despite many rumors to the contrary, and the controversy surrounding the topic, only a small number of babies of migrant mothers are given for adoption in Hong Kong.[5] The Indonesian government opposes the adoption of Indonesian children in Hong Kong, and the consulate encourages Indonesian women to take their babies home. If they cannot keep the child, they are told to "give it to someone [in Indonesia], such as a poor farmer who needs more help in the fields." Aside from private arrangements, adoptions are handled through the Hong Kong Social Welfare Department and related institutional processes. The latter type of adoptions of migrant workers' babies is small but has grown steadily over the past few years.

According to PathFinders, in 2011 eight babies of Indonesian clients were adopted locally (PathFinders 2012), and they reported a significant increase in the number of adoption referrals in 2012 and 2013. Mother's Choice, one of three "babies' homes" for children who are up for adoption, reported a noticeable increase in migrants' babies from 2010 to 2013.

Mother's Choice can house up to twenty-four healthy babies awaiting local adoption. When I visited in 2011, six out of the twenty-four resident babies were born of Indonesian migrant mothers. Two of the babies were thought to have African fathers, one had a South Asian father, and the other three looked East Asian, perhaps with Chinese or Nepalese fathers. The six babies were generally older than the Chinese babies. Whereas Chinese babies are usually released for adoption within one or two months, migrants' babies often take significantly longer to be released for adoption (often over a year) because of the "tracing process" required by the Social Welfare Department.

In most cases, birth mothers say they have no knowledge or contact with the child's biological father, and he is not on the birth certificate. If, in such cases, the mother is officially married in Indonesia, then even though the husband is not the father, his approval is required for adoption. If the mother cannot contact him (a common claim whether true or not), an attempt to locate him and obtain his approval is made through the ISS, which can take many months. Once the tracing process is finished, as I was told by several sources, visibly "mixed race" babies are usually adopted by expatriate parents, since most Chinese prefer Chinese-looking babies. The expatriate parents I met seemed to confirm this pattern.

Ultimately, giving a child for adoption in Hong Kong is not common, but many women initially contemplate this option, especially if they plan to return home to their husbands or have no contact with the baby's father (as in the case of rape or fathers who left Hong Kong) and thus had no hope of being "good wives and mothers." After the child is born, under much pressure to keep it, as in Wulan's case, many women change their minds. Stories of last-minute reversals are common, and mothers who did so spoke of it without regret. Some decide to keep the child and pursue a paternity claim if the father is a resident or has financial resources, seeing it as a possible avenue to staying in Hong Kong. Others see it as a chance to "do what is right" and take motherly responsibility.

One woman was unusually open about her decision to give her child for adoption in Hong Kong. Her boyfriend had left Hong Kong, and she already had children at home. She was convinced the child would have "a better future" with well-off expatriate parents in Hong Kong. She left a note with her contact information and photograph with the Social Welfare

Department, and she hoped her child would eventually find her. She also described the painful barrage of criticism she endured from other Indonesian women who thought this sort of adoption was terribly wrong. Finally, fed up with the criticism and pressure, she told them that PathFinders had paid her several thousand dollars for the child. "That finally shut them up," she said. "Was it true?" I asked. "Of course not!" she laughed. The commodified logic of giving a child up in exchange for money seemed to make better sense to other migrants who sold other forms of reproductive labor as FDWs than the logic of "giving the child a better life" (see Zelizer 2005; Constable 2009). Yet this story had the unfortunate result of fueling a lingering rumor that PathFinders "buys babies" and pressures women to give them for adoption.

Mother's Choice speculated that the reason they had few, if any, babies with Filipina mothers was because "they are Catholic and better educated." However, there are other possible explanations. As one South Asian community leader suggested, some adoptions are done privately within that community, sometimes by a relative of the father. Besides the possibility of private adoptions or adoptions through institutions in Hong Kong, fewer bureaucratic processes exist in Indonesia and the Philippines. A Filipina who worked for an NGO explained that, in the Philippines, formal "adoption is not as popular as in the U.S. or Europe. My aunt adopted someone, but not through an adoption agency, through a network, through family."

Children born "out of wedlock" are not uncommon in the Philippines, partly because of prohibitions against contraception and divorce. As a result, there are informal and institutionalized methods of dealing with the children of unwed mothers. In cases of "adulterous relationships," the family may hide the child's paternity. It is not uncommon for children to be raised by a relative, especially when mothers migrate. Children are often raised by a relative who treats the child as her own in a pattern of informal adoption. One Filipina domestic worker, the eldest daughter in a large family, said that her fiancé deserted her when she was pregnant in her teens. Her parents raised the child as though she was their own, and the child grew up thinking (as did all her relatives) that the birth mother was the sister and the grandparents were the parents. Another Filipina described going to a convent where single mothers (including returned migrant workers) gave birth and left their children in the adjoining orphanage for adoption. She had adopted a child from the orphanage because she had none of her own. Three Filipino domestic worker sisters—two of whom I met in Hong Kong in the early 1990s, and the third whom I met in Italy in 2011—jointly adopted a child from a married domestic worker who could not keep the baby because her husband was not the father. The three sisters jointly supported their daughter; two mainly financially with remittances they sent home, and one who raised the child. None of the sisters married, and they adamantly expressed no regret. The important thing was to have a child who could reciprocate and care for them in old age.

Adoption in Indonesia is also often done informally, as in the Philippines. If a couple has no children or want more, they may take in the child of a relative. One of the mothers I knew had been adopted as a child. She knew little of the circumstances, but, as she explained, her parents loved her and supported her post–high school education. Another Indonesian woman adopted a child who was left in the hospital immediately after birth; there was no formal adoption process. The adoptive parents' names were simply put on the birth certificate. One pregnant woman I met in Hong Kong went to live at a boarding house outside of Jakarta for pregnant women to stay (for a fee) until delivery. She told her Indonesian husband she was working in China and would be out of touch. She planned to leave the baby at the hospital and to return to her husband.

I met a few Filipina domestic workers who had adopted babies from other domestic workers. Some birth mothers wanted to avoid damaging relationships with husbands back home, whereas others aimed to keep working and sending remittances home without the burden of a child. One lesbian domestic worker adopted a child in the 1990s from a domestic worker who gave birth in Hong Kong. The adoptive mother said she brought the baby to the Philippine Consulate and had a birth certificate issued with her own name as the mother, and then obtained a travel document for the baby. Another woman recounted how she arranged to keep the child of another domestic worker who did not want it; she concealed her own identity from the woman to prevent her from later taking the child back or demanding money. She did not share the details of how she arranged for the child's documents but said it would be harder today, given that the consulate now requires a Hong Kong birth certificate accompanied by hospital documentation of the birth or a DNA test if the birth is not in a hospital. Two very young Indonesian overstayers I visited had taken in the abandoned baby of a nineteen-year-old FDW. They had naively imagined raising her themselves until the infant became seriously ill and needed emergency care. Eventually the birth mother was located and agreed to give her for adoption in Hong Kong.

THE AMBULANCE RIDE

I was going to meet Suparmi, her son Wahid, and some other mothers and babies for dinner at their place in Sham Shui Po. The dinner had been postponed once because of a sick child and a friend's labor. I was planning to pick up chicken curry and spend a leisurely evening with them, but, in the middle of the afternoon, as I was transcribing an interview, Suparmi phoned in a panic, sobbing. Her voice trembled: "I am sitting on the toilet and I think I had a baby. . . . I think I lost the baby. There is a lot blood and pain. I think I saw a tiny baby in the toilet. What should I do?" I told her whom to call. An ambulance was ordered, and I rushed to catch a taxi to meet her at the hospital, while her friends agreed to babysit her son.

I lived farther from the hospital than Suparmi and, when the ambulance arrived at her place, I had just caught a taxi, so I expected she would arrive first. But when I got to the hospital she was not there. Alarmed, I phoned her roommate and was told the police were there, the ambulance had not left, and they were treating it as a "crime scene." The ambulance drivers told Suparmi's roommates not to touch anything and not to clean up the blood, because they suspected an illegal abortion.

An hour later, Suparmi arrived in the ambulance and was wheeled in on a gurney. A bag with the fetus in it had been placed on her stomach. I held her hand as she was transported into an examination room. She was required to provide blood and urine specimens. A doctor came into the room, asked who I was, and said, "You know what happened?" I replied, "She had a miscarriage." "She had an abortion," he said. "She didn't even know she was pregnant," I insisted. "She had an abortion," he repeated, laughing. A well-meaning ambulance attendant came in and saw Suparmi pale and crying, and he said, "Don't worry. You are very beautiful and can have more babies." This only made Suparmi cry more. Her relationship had recently ended, she did not know she was pregnant, and she had not wanted more children. After her blood and urine tests confirmed that no abortive drugs were used, they escorted us both into the ambulance and drove to a different hospital, where Suparmi was told she would stay for several days. At the thought of being separated from her son for days, Suparmi became agitated and asked me to talk to a nurse or social worker. I explained to the nurse that Suparmi's baby was still nursing and could stay with friends overnight, but if she stayed in the hospital longer, the baby would need to come too. The nurse explained that the baby could only be "admitted" to the pediatric ward for a fee. When I said that Suparmi could not afford to pay, since she had no work or income, the nurse said nothing could be done. I stayed with Suparmi until I was told I had to leave, and I promised to come back the next morning after checking on Wahid, who had been separated from his mother for the first time two days earlier and had cried the whole time.

When I arrived at the flat in the morning, Wahid was in bed between two "aunties." I gave him a bottle, which he happily drank and then gurgled away, smiling as we played. I snapped a photo and dashed out to buy diapers, then headed to the hospital. In Suparmi's ward were several other women, including a very young mainland Chinese woman who was literally chained to the bed and was being watched by two policewomen. In the night, while the guards slept, Suparmi had lent the woman her phone. She was apparently charged with having an illegal abortion, and they were afraid she would run away. Much reassured that Wahid was well (with evidence from the photo I took that morning), Suparmi waited impatiently as they considered whether to let her leave. After assuring them that she would rest and signing a promissory note for the bill, we headed out.

This chapter has illustrated the complexity of ideas and practical factors that make sex and babies both problematic and promising. As the following chapters show, babies can serve as an anchor, offering women (and sometimes couples) a sense of stability, opportunity, and fulfillment amid the instability. Sex, intimacy, pregnancy, and babies offer the promise of family, belonging, and rootedness. Alternatively, babies can weigh mothers down and cut them off. Their partners leave them. Their reputations suffer. Children expose the cruel paradoxes of migration and reveal the difficulties of being good migrant mothers in the face of bare, stripped-down lives.

6 Wives and Workers

> [O]ne of the main aims and purposes of having immigra-
> tion controls in the first place is to enable society to control
> and regulate who can, and who cannot, immediately or in
> due course, become a national citizen or, as the case may
> be, permanent resident with the right of abode, of that
> society.
>
> — High Court Chief Justice Andrew Cheung (2012, 21)

CITIZENSHIP AND BELONGING

When it comes to citizenship and belonging in Hong Kong, mothers' and children's situations are highly varied. On one end of the spectrum are those considered most fortunate because they have a claim to remain in Hong Kong and a legal path to becoming permanent residents or "citizens." This includes former domestic workers, like Riana and Nora (both described below), who are legally married to local residents. Their marriages are officially recognized as legitimate, and their husbands can afford to sponsor them as dependents. They show how citizenship privileges certain types of heteronormative family formations and excludes others, including migrant workers and single mothers (Oswin 2010, 2012). These women receive "dependent" status, and their children obtain permanent residency. After fulfilling the seven-year residency requirement, women normally qualify to apply for permanent residence, allowing them to escape the precarious status of temporary migrant workers. Slightly more complicated and less assured is the situation of women whose marriages to local residents end before fulfilling the seven-year requirement, but, as we see below in Putri's case, some can successfully assert their right to remain in Hong Kong.

On the opposite end of the spectrum are mothers and children whose situations are most precarious. Most have children born "out of wedlock." This includes Melinda, Hope, Indah, and many others who overstayed their FDH visas—for anywhere from a day to many years—and are literally "outside the law" until they either surrender or are caught and detained or imprisoned. They have breached their "conditions of stay" in Hong Kong and are thus undocumented or "illegal" overstayers (De Genova 2002). Most mothers do not remain in this category. When they become pregnant, they often "surrender" so as to get medical care; some file torture or asylum claims in the hopes of staying longer.

Between these two extremes are several other categories. Toward the relatively more privileged side of the spectrum are mothers who continue to work as foreign domestic workers with two-year renewable employment contracts and corresponding FDH visas (see Figure 2). These FDW mothers can be further subdivided into those, like Ratna and Irene Domingo (described below), who give birth to a child or children in Hong Kong and manage to keep their babies in Hong Kong with them, despite the odds. In some truly exceptional cases, the children of FDWs have obtained permanent residency. As discussed below, a fierce legal battle took place from 2011 to 2013 over the right of FDWs to apply for right of abode. Unlike Ratna and Irene Domingo, many women go home to give birth or, if they do give birth in Hong Kong, take the baby home soon after. Some, like Megawati, go home for good, whereas others, like Caitrin, take the baby home to be cared for by a relative and then return to work in Hong Kong when their maternity leave ends.

Toward the more vulnerable and precarious end of the spectrum, as will be discussed further in chapter 7, are a large number of the mothers I knew whose contracts were terminated either by themselves or their employers and who overstayed for a period of time and then filed torture or asylum claims through the Hong Kong government or the UNHCR, or who filed claims right away when their domestic worker visas expired. This category includes some women who filed torture claims while in prison, and women like Mia and Bethany (chapter 7) who filed claims when they were pregnant and were terminated. They do so not because they necessarily expect to win such claims, since no domestic workers have ever done so, but because filing a torture claim allows them to remain

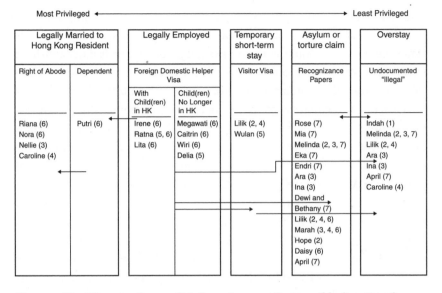

Most Privileged ←————————————————————————→ Least Privileged

Legally Married to Hong Kong Resident		Legally Employed		Temporary short-term stay	Asylum or torture claim	Overstay
Right of Abode	Dependent	Foreign Domestic Helper Visa		Visitor Visa	Recognizance Papers	Undocumented "Illegal"
		With Child(ren) in HK	Child(ren) No Longer in HK			
Riana (6)	Putri (6)	Irene (6)	Megawati (6)	Lilik (2, 4)	Rose (7)	Indah (1)
Nora (6)		Ratna (5, 6)	Caitrin (6)	Wulan (5)	Mia (7)	Melinda (2, 3, 7)
Nellie (3)		Lita (6)	Wiri (6)		Melinda (2, 3, 7)	Lilik (2, 4)
Caroline (4)			Delia (5)		Eka (7)	Ara (3)
					Endri (7)	Ina (3)
					Ara (3)	April (7)
					Ina (3)	Caroline (4)
					Dewi and Bethany (7)	
					Lilik (2, 4, 6)	
					Marah (3, 4, 6)	
					Hope (2)	
					Daisy (6)	
					April (7)	

Figure 2. The Migratory Status of Mothers. Arrows reflect possible directions for change of status. Numbers in parentheses refer to chapters in which the mother's migratory circumstances are described in some detail.

in Hong Kong while the case is being processed (Constable forthcoming *b*). As such, the Immigration Department provides them with "recognizance papers" (popularly known as "immigration papers" or "recognition papers") permitting them to stay in Hong Kong and receive medical care, but not to work, while the claim is pending.

This chapter focuses on the privileged end of the spectrum of citizenship and belonging: mothers who are married to locals, and foreign domestic workers who are far less privileged than married women, and still vulnerable as workers, but who hold FDH visas and thus have certain rights and benefits. This includes domestic workers who fought legal battles for right of abode for themselves and their children. Chapter 7 turns to the less privileged, most marginal mothers, such as asylum seekers, torture claimants, and overstayers. The spectrum of privilege and precarity—corresponding with citizenship on one end and exclusion on the other—are not fixed or absolute. The division of these two chapters is organizational; it does not indicate any sort of permanent, fixed divide. These juridical categories may unintentionally imply fixity, but it is clear, as the

arrows in figure 2 are meant to suggest, that mothers move along the spectrum in different directions and take on different statuses at different
times. One day a woman is in one category, and the next day, month, or
year is in another one. Moreover, despite the relative "privilege" of mothers
in this chapter, their situations are not easy or guaranteed. For a variety of
reasons, including marriages that do not last or are not legally recognized,
employment contracts that end abruptly or illegally, or abusive husbands
or employers, mothers can be quickly propelled to another place along the
spectrum. If women are divorced or their jobs terminated, they may temporarily enter the liminal position of "visitor" or the less privileged purga-
tory of "recognizance paper" holder, or they may become undocumented.
Some women, like Lilik (chapters 2 and 4), traverse the spectrum from
FDW to temporary visitor pursuing legal claims, to overstayer, to torture
claimant, and to asylum seeker over the course of several months, pointing
to the impermanence and fluidity of these categories and the vulnerability
of the women who inhabit them.

MARRIAGE AND PRIVILEGE

Many FDWs want to earn money for one or more contracts and then go
back home, but others imagine additional possibilities. Some mothers spoke
of their youthful hopes and envy of women who had "made it"—escaping
their domestic worker lives by meeting and marrying men in Hong Kong
who could provide financial security, the stability of marriage, and residence
in a desirable location. The dream of staying in Hong Kong or a "better"
location, escaping rural poverty, social constraints, bad marriages, and bitter
divorces or separations back home, is well known. However, whereas most
migrant men (asylum seekers and overstayers) I knew understood that
domestic workers cannot offer them the possibility of citizenship or legal
residency in Hong Kong through marriage, and some men were strategic
about finding a resident to marry (see chapter 4), most migrant women,
especially Indonesians, seemed less clear about the status of the men they
met and much less savvy and strategic about their partner choices.

Even women with relatively long-term, monogamous relationships
described how they had very little understanding at first of their South

Asian or African partners' residential (or marital) status and of the realistic possibilities for a future together in Hong Kong. In some cases, the man lied or neglected to explain his situation or simply allowed her to "assume" he was a resident. In other cases, women simply did not understand the implications when a man said he has "immigration papers" (recognizance papers). As Wiri, an Indonesian domestic worker mother with a Pakistani husband, explained, Abu told her he had "immigration papers." She knew he worked, and she assumed that he did so legally, but she never thought much about it. She later learned that his older brothers were all legal residents (dependents), but Abu's father had died before sponsoring him. Abu came to Hong Kong and filed an asylum claim after he was caught working illegally. Only after Wiri became pregnant, and Abu was in prison a second time for illegal work, did she fully understand that he was not a resident, likely never would be, and that he could not offer her and the baby that status. She stayed with him "because I love him," and she visited him in prison as often as allowed, bringing him food and news of the baby, whom she had taken to live with her parents in Java while she continued to work as a domestic worker.

In other cases, women complained bitterly that their partners (mostly South Asian men) said they were residents and would sponsor them but never did. In one case, the man had simply lied to her and to many others, pretending to be a resident. In another case, the man was a resident but had already sponsored a wife and could not sponsor another one. Fatimah's case was similar. A Filipina FDW, she had married an older Muslim Pakistani widower and converted to Islam. For six years, she continued to work because he said he could not yet afford to sponsor her. When I met her sister one Sunday and asked how Fatimah was doing, she said angrily, "Pakistani men are just trouble." Fatimah's husband had traveled to Pakistan for Ramadan and, upon his return, told Fatimah he had married. Fatimah was very upset, having thought he would eventually sponsor her as his dependent. Now she feared that this was never his plan and that he might sponsor the new wife instead. Fatimah's sister was relieved she had kept working, was still on an FDH visa, and that the couple had no children. Fatimah was, from her sister's point of view, free to end the marriage and return to the Philippines.

The domestic worker mothers—perhaps because they were already mothers—were rarely as explicitly strategic and opportunistic about partners as the men I knew. Most emphasized "feelings" for men and the fact that they had children together as more important than pragmatic and opportunistic considerations of residency or the future. Yet "lucky women" who married locals and had the opportunity to stay were much envied and gossiped about. Daisy, a young and attractive Indonesian single mother who was "born Christian" and was unusually explicit about her strategies for meeting white men, was also one of the most opinionated women I knew when it came to expressing her sense of the hierarchy of men in relation to race and the different socioeconomic opportunities and futures they might afford. She was also not shy about expressing her views on women who take up with different sorts of men.

Daisy's harshest criticism was reserved for women with African partners, including Dewi and Bethany, Indonesian women with unusually long-lasting relationships with their asylum-seeker partners. Echoing a common racist view, Daisy considered these men "as ugly as monkeys" and "frightening." Most African men, in her eyes, had "immigration papers" (that is, were asylum seekers and torture claimants) like her, with no future and no resources to offer. Her hierarchy had no room for wealthy or successful African traders, nor did she acknowledge or respond positively to the African fathers who were responsible and supported their families or to the many well-educated and well-dressed Africans, including asylum seekers.

Condescending toward Muslims in general, Daisy criticized women who had children with South Asian men as well. She agreed that those men are sometimes handsome (and their children might have lovely eyes), but she complained that "they are poor" and "Muslims always have other wives" and are "usually here illegally" and thus they "cheat women." They offer no likely means for women to remain in Hong Kong and no permanence, she said. "You are better off working as a helper and saving money" than taking up with "useless men" who "have no future." She criticized Indonesian women who adopt South Asian clothing styles, such as *salwar kameez* (loose pants and thigh-length blouses) and *hijabs*, and speak of settling in Pakistan with their partners. "What will they do there? . . . How will they survive the mother-in-law?" she asked, pointing to what she understood as a place where women are confined, veiled, secluded, and treated like unpaid maids.

At the top of her list were white men whom she associated with financial security. "I really like white, rich, bald, middle-aged men," she laughed. Although she knew a few cases of Indonesian women who married Westerners (and were no longer part of her social circles) and a few more Indonesian women who were supported by Western men who did not marry them, such men nonetheless epitomized the opportunity of escape from small-town Indonesian poverty and narrow-mindedness. They also fit with her sense of being Christian. Although she no longer attended church, she preferred to be around people she assumed were Christian. Daisy and her friends met white men in pubs and nightclubs. She met the white man who fathered her child in a bar; he disappeared from her life before she was aware of her pregnancy. Yet her experience did not cause her to rethink the validity of her model. She simply reasoned aloud that "all men are bad" but some offer better opportunities, and a few women are smart, lucky, and sexy enough to get them.

Daisy's greatest ambivalence was reserved for Chinese men. She vaguely traced her dislike of Chinese men to being in Indonesia where "in my place, we hated the Chinese; they did so many bad things in Indonesia." In Hong Kong, she mistrusted them. "It is very easy to meet Chinese men," she claimed, but "most of them are already married" and they easily take advantage of domestic workers. Nonetheless, she envied one former domestic worker we knew who had married a local Chinese man—not for the man, but because "she is clever and lucky enough to become a Hong Kong resident."

Admittedly jaded by her experience, which fueled her sense that "all men are bad," Daisy adhered to a utilitarian and opportunistic use of men and marriage in relation to upward mobility and residence rights. Only some marriages are legally recognized in Hong Kong, and, of those, only some locals can actually afford to sponsor their spouses to stay in Hong Kong as dependents. The problem with undocumented overstayers and asylum seekers—most of whom are South Asian or African—is that they might marry domestic workers in Muslim religious ceremonies or come to a mutual agreement that they are married, but they cannot remain in Hong Kong or sponsor spouses as dependents. Moreover, these marriages provide little prospect for mobility if the man (or woman) is already legally married elsewhere or if—as is often the case—he has no desire to return home or go home with her. Local residents can provide a path to residency for their partners, but they must be otherwise unmarried and have the resources to support her as a dependent.

One dramatic story illustrates the anxiety over marriages to local Chinese men who might make promises but turn out to be unmarriage-able. Lara, a caseworker, was invited to serve as a witness at the wedding of a very pregnant former domestic worker to her long-term Chinese boy-friend. Although Lara did not know her well, she agreed to go as a favor to the eager bride. As she described a few hours afterward, it was a fiasco. The bride appeared at the marriage registry in Tsim Sha Tsui in her wed-ding best and the groom in his suit, along with the witnesses and others milling around. Before anyone knew what was happening, the groom was surrounded by plain-clothed immigration officers, arrested, and taken away. The bride collapsed, fainting on the floor. Lara shouted at the immi-gration officer in charge and insisted that he call an ambulance. Needless to say, the marriage did not take place. Unsubstantiated speculations about the various immigration-related crimes the groom might have com-mitted included previous marriages or trafficking of women to Hong Kong through marriage. Such stories serve as cautionary tales. The pregnant bride's future hopes—and the promise of an optimal position along the spectrum of privilege—literally disappeared before her eyes. While such tales warn women against men who plan or promise to marry them and never do, other stories fuel migrant workers' hopes and envy.[1]

RIANA AND NORA'S LUCK AND FATE

Riana said that, when she was young, she dreamed she would marry a "European," but she is now married to a Chinese man twenty years her senior. They have a child and a comfortable middle-class existence. He works hard and is a good provider. They rent a three-bedroom flat in Sheung Shui and can afford occasional vacations outside of Hong Kong. Riana admits that she is very lucky. Many Indonesian women envy her—as do her kin, neighbors, and friends in East Java—who think she is rich and lucky. In Hong Kong, she mainly avoids Indonesian women whose situations are different from her own. When she takes her lighter-skinned child to school, she is often mistaken for a "helper" but tries to distinguish herself from them by dressing stylishly and elegantly. She maintains a professional, not close, relationship with her own Indonesian "helper" because she fears the expectations that come with friendship. It is difficult to be envied; those who are less fortunate often want and expect her help. Although she has helped many Indonesian women in need, she tries to steer clear of friendships with women who are still domestic workers or are overstayers because she finds it too difficult to turn down their requests for loans, money, or work. Although she acknowledges her good fortune, she also feels that their envy is misplaced as there are aspects of her life that are not quite the "fairy tale" some expect. She is lucky, but life is not easy. Her best friends are women in similar situations: one is a Filipina former domestic worker married to a Filipino engineer who is a Hong Kong resident, and the other is an Indonesian former domestic worker whose husband is a European Hong Kong resident and runs a business. All three women have young children, and all three are on the way to becoming Hong Kong permanent residents.

Nora is a Filipina; like Riana, she came to Hong Kong as a domestic worker and later married a local. At twenty, newly arrived and ready for adventure, she met a handsome young Chinese man while shopping at the market. She described their romantic courtship, how she "fell in love" and believed their feelings were mutual. She lost her virginity to him and naively believed his promises of marriage. After some time, and with a deep and growing sense of disappointment, shame, and regret, she came to see his faults. He repeatedly borrowed money from her and never repaid it. He had other domestic worker girlfriends as well. Eventually, Nora could no longer pretend they had a future together. Soon after ending their relationship, she met another local man who energetically pursued her and quickly proposed marriage. Still broken-hearted, she agreed to marry him. She gave a month's notice and collected the required paperwork from the Philippines, including her birth certificate and proof she was unmarried. Shortly after giving notice, she discovered she was pregnant. The child was undoubtedly fathered by her husband-to-be, but, as her pregnancy advanced, he became uncontrollably jealous and angry, accusing her of infidelity, perhaps to cover up his own. As she told me, the birth of her child should have been a joyful occasion, but it was the saddest time of her life. She wept as she described it:

> I called my husband at work when I am in labor but he sent me to the hospital alone. I just gave birth to the baby in Queen Elizabeth Hospital and I call my husband, but he doesn't come. After my delivery, a few minutes after I give birth the nurse just gives me the phone and says, "You let your husband know." But when I call him, he doesn't answer. After I give birth I am very, very sad. That's why I cry when I remember that day. May 10 I give birth to my baby and May 11 when I call him and I ask him to come and he didn't come. There's this visiting time in the evening and my neighbor was a Chinese girl and during visiting time her family comes, but there was not even one person for me. At the time I just called my Mom. I told her that I just gave birth to the baby and I am very sad right now. And my Mom wants me to bring the baby back. And the next day he still didn't come. When I call he says, "Why do I need to get the baby? It is not my baby."

Eventually, the child's resemblance to his father was unmistakable, and their relationship slowly improved. Today, Nora looks back on her decisions with a sense of fate: she married a man and established a life that many of her friends envy, but it is far less romantic than her youthful imaginings. Her husband and son recently traveled with her to meet her family. Over the years, ever since she began working as a domestic worker more than a decade ago, she has continued to send remittances home. She bought some land and built a small house in Northern Luzon. She provides money from a part-time job she recently took at a Filipino market to support her sick and elderly parents and to send her nieces and nephews to school.

PUTRI'S CLOSE CALL

I first met Putri through a friend who came from the same region of Central Java. She was depressed, panicked, and fearful of losing her right to remain in Hong Kong because the Chinese man she had married several years earlier had divorced her without her knowledge. He would no longer sponsor her dependent visa, nor did he want anything to do with their child. Putri was, at the time, only a year short of the seven years of residency that would entitle her to apply for right of abode.

Around thirty when I met her, Putri had come to Hong Kong a decade earlier as a domestic worker. She met Lo, her future husband, who was divorced and worked in maintenance and security. She gave up her work and her domestic worker visa. They were legally married, and Lo sponsored her as his dependent. After five years together, during which time they became increasingly distant, Putri informed him she was pregnant. Shortly after, he moved out and went to live with another Indonesian woman. Nonetheless, he signed the required form for Putri to renew her dependent visa that year, but he pressured her to have an abortion. He did not want more children; he already had them with his Chinese ex-wife. Putri—who was otherwise childless—decided to have the baby.

By virtue of her marriage certificate and Hong Kong identity card, and the fact that she had kept Lo's Hong Kong SAR passport when he moved out, Putri was able to register the child's birth on her own and to obtain a birth certificate listing both parents' names. Because of Lo's residency, the birth certificate indicated that the child's "right of residency" in Hong Kong was established. After notifying Lo of the baby's birth, Putri tried to contact him to sign the form for her visa renewal. He reluctantly agreed to meet her at a train station, whereupon he refused to sign the form and presented her with a finalized divorce decree.

At that point, Putri's visa was about to expire, so she approached an NGO for help. Shortly after, I accompanied her and her child to the office of the lawyer who was working on her case (pro bono at first, until legal aid was approved). The fact that the divorce was processed without Putri's knowledge seemed of less concern to the lawyer than the fact that Lo had denied his knowledge of the child's existence, possibly perjuring himself and failing to establish material support in the course of obtaining the divorce. Whereas divorce is fairly easy to obtain in Hong Kong, especially for couples who have lived apart for a year or more, it nonetheless requires at least an effort to contact the spouse and, most important, for the petitioner to establish arrangements for the support of any children. Without contact information, the petitioner is permitted to post the notice and to obtain a divorce without directly communicating with the spouse. Lo may have claimed he did not know Putri's whereabouts and was thus permitted to post the notice in local newspapers. Putri, in turn, would not have been likely to see or read English or Chinese newspapers.

At first, Putri's main problem was that, since she was divorced and no longer recognized as her husband's "dependent," she had no legal right to remain in Hong Kong. She had approached the Immigration Department for a renewal and explained the circumstances well over a month before her visa expired, but, when several months passed and she had not heard back, she grew increasingly anxious. Shortly after her visit to the lawyer and the posting of his letter to immigration officials requesting a response and reiterating the situation, Putri was granted the one-year visa renewal, after which time she would be free to apply for permanent residency.

In Putri's case, the Immigration Department, with its high degree of discretion in granting or denying visas, was willing to allow the mother of a permanent resident (or "citizen") child and a woman who had been married to a Hong Kong resident for almost six years to remain in Hong Kong without pressure to return home with the child. According to Putri's lawyer, this was not a "given." Legal records indicate that a Filipino former domestic worker named Maura Juliet Raquiza, whose status was also converted to dependent when she married a local Chinese resident but was divorced from him ten months short of seven years, was denied residency (Julve 2007; HCAL20 2006). One factor that might have influenced the different outcomes was that Raquiza had no children with recognized right of abode. However, in another recent legal case involving Comilang Milagro Tecson, also a Filipino former domestic worker who was for a time married to a resident and whose child was granted permanent residency (like Putri's child), she was only allowed a temporary visitor's visa and lost her legal challenge to convert it to a more regular status, despite her child's right of abode (Moy 2012; HCAL28 2011). As scholars of citizenship have noted, "a citizen child cannot generally use the fact of citizenship to block the removal of parents facing deportation," though the reverse—a parent's ability to block the deportation of a child—is possible (Bhabha 2009, 194).

FOREIGN DOMESTIC WORKER MOTHERS

FDWs whose contracts and visas are valid do not have nearly the same privileges as women who marry locals, but they have some legal rights and benefits. Those who give birth in Hong Kong are, as discussed in the previous chapter, protected by the Maternity Provision of the Employment Ordinance. Workers whose employers follow the law are in a reasonable situation. Pregnant domestic workers are entitled to medical care at local subsidized rates (which makes it cheaper to give birth in Hong Kong than in a Jakarta or Manila hospital). They are—theoretically—protected against termination, and if they have worked for the employer for forty weeks, they are supposed to receive ten weeks of paid maternity leave at 80 percent of their regular salary. A major complication arises if the mother wants to keep her child with her in Hong Kong while continuing to work. All successful cases I knew had the support and understanding of the employer. Employers are under no obligation to allow workers to keep their children in Hong Kong or to provide the child with housing, and most are, understandably, opposed to the idea. A domestic worker is hired to work for them, and, if she is looking after her own infant, her attention and time will be divided. Moreover, space is usually a significant issue, because middle-class flats are often tiny and crowded. In a few noteworthy cases, however, including several cases involving wealthy employers with large homes and spacious servant quarters who employ multiple domestic workers, some of whom are married couples, the situation is not unheard of.

In one case, a domestic worker couple was employed for many years by a couple and their son. After the employers died, their adult bachelor son continued to employ the couple and allowed them to keep their Hong Kong–born child with them. As the FDW mother, Lita, explained, "He considered us his only family and wanted us to stay." Children, such as Lita's, who are born while the mother or father (or both) have a FDH visa are normally given a visa that corresponds with that of the domestic worker parent. As such, it becomes possible—but not common or well known—for the child to remain in Hong Kong and to make a case, after seven years of legal "ordinary residence," for right of abode.[2] Although a few children of FDWs have followed this route, for most of them it is impossible.

Most employers have little desire or space for an additional child, and the domestic worker's salary is insufficient to provide the child with outside care and housing. So, unless the employer is willing to allow the child to reside there as well or unless they are willing to condone alternative arrangements that would likely breach the contractual conditions of stay, keeping a child in Hong Kong is extremely difficult. In Kareem and Marah's case (chapters 3 and 4), he had the FDH contract, and their son Mohamed was given a visa with a matching permit of stay while Marah, a former FDW who had filed a torture claim, looked after him. A problem will likely arise if Marah's claim to stay in Hong Kong ends. At that point, Marah says she and Mohamed will have no choice but to go to the Philippines. In some cases, like Ratna's, the employer allows the domestic worker mother to live out, even though it is a breach of the employment contract. In most cases, as the following examples show, an FDW who wants to keep working has no choice but to return home and leave the baby with a caregiver.

TAKING BABIES HOME

I met Caitrin and Megawati, and they met each other, in 2011 when they moved into a shelter for pregnant domestic workers. They were an unlikely pair but became good friends. Caitrin is a stylish, elegant Christian Filipina who has strong religious convictions, often posts popular relationship slogans on Facebook, and enjoys the glamour and luxury of Hong Kong. She worked for a European employer who would have allowed her to stay in their large flat in the prestigious mid-levels region of Hong Kong during her maternity leave, but she preferred to stay in the shelter. Despite its curfew and prohibition against visitors, the shelter provided Caitrin with freedom from her employer. Had she stayed there, she would have felt obliged to keep working during her maternity leave. Caitrin's husband was also a domestic worker, but he was not supportive of the pregnancy. Caitrin's mother, who had been a domestic helper in Singapore when Caitrin was young, came from the Philippines to help with the birth and stayed at the shelter for three weeks.

Megawati is an Indonesian observant Muslim. In contrast to Caitrin's sophisticated elegance, Megawati wore no makeup or jewelry other than a dried herb that she pinned to her own and her baby's clothing to fend off evil spirits. She dressed in baggy T-shirts and loose pants. She saved her pennies and was uninterested in the city's distractions. Her single-minded purpose was to work and save money to invest in her home and family in Central Java, then to return home. She got along well with her working-class Chinese employer, whose authority she never questioned and whose instructions she followed carefully in the tiny flat in a crowded area of Kowloon. Her employer was law abiding but did not know about FDW maternity benefits. Not wanting to look like she knew more than her employer, Megawati asked a Chinese staff member at an NGO to explain to her employer her obligations with regard to Megawati's leave. The day after Megawati gave birth, I accompanied her and her baby to the shelter, where she cried from postpartum exhaustion and the loneliness of giving birth in Hong Kong, away from her mother, her family, and familiar Javanese birth practices.

Caitrin and Megawati shared a great—often trilingual—humor despite their privacy and reserve. Their babies were born within days of each other, and they joked that they were "brothers from different mothers." When Caitrin spoke of visiting Megawati in Indonesia one day, Megawati responded by saying she would sooner put up "wanted" photos of Caitrin all over her town, and Caitrin responded with the same image of Megawati's face on wanted posters in the Philippines. Megawati was what Lara called "very proper." She once criticized us for hungrily gobbling down our *lai wong bau* (egg custard buns) on the street, echoing the Indonesian view that "ladies" never eat in public. In sharp contrast, when she joked around at the shelter, she took on the comic persona of sexy seductress. She feigned a desperate crush on Justin Bieber, teased Caitrin that she would seduce her "rich husband," and warned me that she would seduce my "Justin Timberlake lookalike son." Together we celebrated the two babies' one-month birthdays as Megawati and Caitrin waited through the many weeks it took to obtain birth certificates and travel documents. For Caitrin, the process was faster because she had easy access to the required papers (including an original copy of her husband's Hong Kong identification card), and, after obtaining the baby's Hong Kong birth certificate, it was relatively fast and easy to get a Philippine one and her baby's travel documents. For Megawati and her baby, however, it was harder and took many weeks longer. She needed her husband's identity papers and her marriage certificate sent from Indonesia, and she had to get them translated for the Birth Registry; after that, the Indonesian Consulate took considerable time to produce the requisite papers. For the first weeks, while Caitrin's mother stayed in the shelter, she offered both new mothers reassuring tips on nursing, holding, bathing, and burping babies, as well as an extra pair of arms. After Caitrin's mother left, Caitrin and Megawati offered one another companionship and support at a stressful time. Both women had married despite their parents' misgivings, and both had children with husbands who were unsupportive. Both were knowledgeable enough to take advantage of their maternity benefits and to give birth in Hong Kong. As "married women" back home, whose children undoubtedly belonged to the husband, both would escape the worst stigma associated with out-of-wedlock children.

The main difference between Megawati's and Caitrin's situations had to do with their postpartum plans, symbolized perhaps by Caitrin's early efforts to train her baby to drink formula from a bottle versus Megawati's exclusively breast-fed baby. After she obtained her baby's travel documents, Caitrin returned home to the Philippines and left her child with her mother. She returned to work for her employer in Hong Kong, planning to stay for one more two-year contract. Megawati exclusively nursed her baby, and during her maternity leave she gave her employer a month's notice. She returned home with the baby, planning to stay. Her husband, who her mother said was "lazy and no good" (while Megawati carefully reserved her own judgment), lived in the wooden house Megawati had built in back of her parents' house. He made no effort to earn money and did not help care for their older child (who stayed with her parents while she was in Hong Kong). Megawati's mother urged her to divorce her good-for-nothing husband who drank and gambled away her earnings. Soon after Megawati and the baby returned home, her husband "ran away." One rumor was that he had gone to work abroad, but Megawati did not know.

RATNA, AMAL, AND THE VISITOR VISA

The story of Ratna, Salim (an asylum seeker), and baby Amal was recounted in chapter 5. Here I turn to Ratna's remarkable efforts to keep

Amal in Hong Kong, stay with Salim, and continue to work as a domestic worker. When I first met Ratna at an NGO office, her baby was not with her, and I mistakenly thought she worked there. She looked professional and spoke nearly fluent Cantonese and excellent English. As I soon learned, however, she was an Indonesian domestic worker who was struggling to keep her son in Hong Kong.

About two years earlier, when Ratna lived with her former employer, she and Salim had married, and Ratna had become pregnant. She presented her employer with an official certification of pregnancy and was promptly terminated. Knowing her rights, Ratna filed a case with the Labour Tribunal. In order to pursue her claim, she got a visitor visa and was not permitted to work. The reconciliation meeting was unsuccessful because her employer did not show up, so the case went to a hearing. The process took many months, during which time Ratna repeatedly paid to renew her visa (and later her baby's visitor's visa as well). Eventually, she won her case and was awarded over HK$10,000 for back pay, punitive damages, and maternity benefits. Unfortunately, as in many other cases, the employer refused to pay, and the Labour Tribunal did not have the power to enforce the judgment. Two years later, she had still not been paid.

Because Ratna had registered her pregnancy with the hospital before her domestic worker visa expired, her delivery and medical care were provided at subsidized local rates. The NGO that assisted Ratna during her pregnancy was impressed by her, so it helped her to find a new employer who supported her keeping the baby in Hong Kong. Shortly after Amal was born, Ratna's new contract began, and she received a new FDH visa. But because Ratna was on a visitor visa when Amal was born, he was only granted a visitor's visa for an initial period of two weeks. Each time Amal's visa was about to expire, Ratna had to take time off work, beg the Immigration Department for more time, and was told "this is the last renewal" and that she must take him to Indonesia.

Over the first nine months of his life, Amal was granted dozens of visitor visa extensions for anywhere from three days to two weeks, depending entirely on the whims of the immigration staff person behind the counter. The renewals were time-consuming (often taking half a day or more) and expensive, costing Ratna over US$30 in fees and transportation costs each time. She missed work, and her employer became increasingly impatient. An NGO staff member sometimes accompanied Ratna to the Immigration Tower to help her make the case to extend her baby's visa to the duration of her own visa. As they argued, this would have normally happened automatically if Ratna had been on a FDH visa (not a visitor visa) when Amal was born. With the support of a lawyer, introduced by the NGO, Ratna provided immigration officials with evidence that she had won her case in the Labour Tribunal. Were it not for the wrongful termination, she would have been on an FDH visa when Amal was born, and he would most likely have been granted a stay matching her FDH visa. After nine months and over twenty renewals, Ratna was running out of money and her employer was running out of patience. Her lawyer sent a letter to the Immigration Department asking that they give her a "yes or no" answer rather than keep stringing her along. Finally, Amal was granted a 160-day extension as a visitor, and Ratna's lawyer urged her to consider other options since further renewals would likely result, at best, in further visitor's visas that would never qualify Amal for residency.

Ratna had told me of her ambitions for Amal to be educated in Hong Kong and for his future career. She had patiently attempted to keep him with her and Salim through a legal channel. She resisted giving up her work and filing a torture or asylum claim because, she and Salim thought, "that has no future." Her goal was to continue to work legally and stay in Hong Kong "as a family" as long as they could. The alternative was to take Amal to Indonesia. Given Salim's asylum claim in progress and his ability to work there (illegally), he initially had no desire to go to Indonesia or return to Sri Lanka. When I spoke to Ratna a few months later, she was beginning to think that their Hong Kong dream was not to be. Instead, they were exploring plans for her and Amal to go to Indonesia and for Salim to join them there.

LILIK'S CHOICES

Lilik, whose relationship with Rashid was described in chapter 4, illustrates the complexity and fluidity of what might otherwise appear to be a neat spectrum of boxes and corresponding categories of more or less privileged status. Lilik first entered Hong Kong as a domestic worker and became pregnant when she was employed. When her employers discovered her pregnancy, her contract was terminated and her FDH visa expired. She filed a claim against her employer, and, because her case with the Labour Tribunal was in process, she was allowed to apply for a visitor visa. This visa was granted for a maximum of fourteen days at a time, and, like Ratna, she had to pay to renew it each time. Meanwhile, her baby was born, and she sought a new employer, unsuccessfully. When Lilik's case was finally settled and her former employers reluctantly paid her a few thousand Hong Kong dollars, her employment agent (who had sided with the employer) would not help her find a new job. Her visitor visa was about to expire and would not be renewed. Despite her attempts to try to find an employer through several agencies, she did not find one, and she decided to overstay rather than separate from Rashid. As she explained, she had two choices: she could leave Hong Kong with Husain, or she could remain there illegally, despite pressure from the NGO staff not to do so. Soon after, she surrendered to the Immigration Department and filed a torture claim, hoping it would allow her to stay with Rashid and Husain while they lived together and Rashid worked and saved money for the future.

It is important to note that, had Husain and Amal been born while their mothers—Lilik and Ratna—were still on FDH visas, they most likely would have been awarded the same length of stay as their mothers. Instead, they were seriously disadvantaged by illegal job termination. For children born to mothers (or fathers) who have valid FDH visas when they are born and manage to keep them, as we see below, the situation can be very different.

FIGHTING FOR THE RIGHT OF ABODE

In 2011 and 2012, Irene and Daniel Domingo made headlines in Hong Kong as two of the plaintiffs among five Filipinos who went to the High Court to fight for the right of FDWs to apply for right of abode. The case of the Domingo family, which I read about in newspapers, observed in court, and learned more about through many hours of interview and conversation with Irene, is important and unique, in part because it shows how the Hong Kong–born children of FDWs might become permanent residents—but not their parents. It also illustrates how laws can protect the citizenship rights of locals and elites but can nonetheless be used by the non-elite to claim their rights (Constable forthcoming *a*). As Marxist historian E. P. Thompson famously argued, unless the law is seen as just, it loses its power to mask and legitimize class hegemony, and it cannot seem just "without upholding its own logic and criteria of equity; indeed, on occasion, by actually *being* just" (1975, 263). Laws can thus serve as "tactics" that, as described by Michel de Certeau, "make use of the cracks that particular conjunctions open in the surveillance of the proprietary powers. It poaches them. It creates surprises in them. It can be where it is least expected. . . . In short, a tactic is an art of the weak" (1984, 37).

Irene first came to Hong Kong from Ilocos Sur, the Philippines, in 1982, and Daniel arrived from the same region in 1985. They met in 1986 at a Filipino club on their day off. Later, they were engaged and returned briefly to the Philippines to marry in 1988, then returned to Hong Kong, working for different employers and meeting on their day off. When Irene's employer left the then-colony for good the following year, Daniel's employer signed her contract, so in 1989 they began to live and work together in the same home. Irene worked for that employer for sixteen years, and Daniel for twenty-two.

Irene and Daniel's son Dariel was born in 1992 and their daughter, Darlene, in 1995. They lived together in Irene and Daniel's employer's large home. In 2003, when Dariel was eleven, the age at which most Hong Kong children get their first Hong Kong identity card, Daniel applied for the children's residency, but the application was rejected. In 2004, their son Dickson was born, and Irene returned to the Philippines with him to renew her visa. While she was there, her employment contract renewal with her employer of sixteen years was denied. She then returned to Hong Kong on a tourist visa, leaving Dickson with her mother.

Irene was eventually allowed to process a visa in Hong Kong to work as an FDW with a new employer, albeit on the opposite side of the city from her husband and two older children. Meanwhile, Daniel had reapplied for Dariel and Darlene's residency, which was granted, making headlines in 2006 as the first children of FDWs to be granted right of abode in post-colonial (post-1997) Hong Kong. When Irene's new employers read the headlines and learned that she had a family in Hong Kong, they promptly terminated her contract. That began an especially difficult time for Irene, separated from her youngest child, not permitted to reside with her husband and two older children, and with her visa status in question.

Following their children's success, Irene and Daniel applied for residency but were denied. Shortly after, with the help of the law firm Barnes and Daly, they were granted "unconditional stay" for seven years, beginning in 2007. With the granting of their unconditional stay, Daniel and Irene were no longer required to be domestic workers or to remain with one employer. The family visited the Philippines and brought Dickson back to Hong Kong. Dickson was also granted residency.

As one of three cases heard in court in 2011, the Domingos' lawyers argued that it was unconstitutional to deny FDWs the right to apply for permanent residency. They argued that the Immigration Ordinance, which explicitly excluded foreign domestic workers from applying, went against Hong Kong's Basic Law. The government's lawyers, on the other hand, argued that foreign domestic workers—like prisoners and asylum seekers or refugees—cannot ever be "ordinarily resident" in Hong Kong (a stipulated requirement for residency) regardless of their overall length of stay or the extent of their wider involvement in the community.

Irene and Daniel's hearing followed that of Evangeline Banao Vallejos. In Vallejos' case, too, barrister Gladys Li argued in the High Court that the Immigration Ordinance's exclusion of FDWs was unconstitutional as it went against Hong Kong's Basic Law. Stressing the distinction between the rule of law upon which he must base his ruling, on the one hand, and political, social, and practical considerations that were outside of his purview, on the other, Justice M. H. Lam of the High Court found that Vallejos indeed had the right to apply for right of abode. He ruled that the decision to deny her application on the basis that an FDW could not be "ordinarily resident" was wrong.

Justice Lam's judgment yielded vehement protests and criticism from citizens. Members of the pro-Beijing Democratic Alliance for the Betterment and Progress of Hong Kong party and a new group that was formed online and called itself "Caring Hong Kong Power" took part in angry demonstrations outside of the High Court. One protestor's sign read, "We Pay You for Your Work, No Need to Give You Right of Abode." Protestors hurled insults at people they assumed were Filipino domestic workers in Central District on Sundays. The Hong Kong Employer's Association asserted that "the helpers" are welcome to Hong Kong only when they "know their place," which is to provide labor to locals.

Given the initial decision in the Vallejos case that it was unconstitutional to categorically exclude FDWs from submitting applications for right of abode, the main question in the case of the Domingos, which took place shortly after, was, first, whether they had in fact been "ordinarily resident" for seven years, and, second, whether by accepting "unconditional stay" they had given up their right to apply for permanent residency until after that period expired. The discussion of "ordinary residence" in this hearing and the others was fascinating. The government's lawyers maintained that, among other things, FDWs who maintained a home in their country of citizenship or who still voted there could not be considered "ordinarily resident" in Hong Kong. However, expatriate "skilled professionals" whom I knew and informally queried told me they were never asked about such things, and many of them do indeed maintain homes and vote abroad despite having Hong Kong right of abode. Ultimately, the ruling in Daniel's case was that he could submit an application, but in Irene's case, given her brief absence from Hong Kong and the change in her visa status before unconditional stay was granted in 2007, the judge ruled otherwise. Irene then opted not to pursue her case further, since she was not assured of legal aid and could, in any case, apply for right of abode, based on her seven years of unconditional stay, in 2014.

Following Justice Lam's ruling and the initial victories for FDWs in 2011, the government immediately filed an appeal and refused in the meantime to process right-of-abode applications from domestic workers. In March 2012, the government won in the Court of Appeal; the Vallejos ruling by Justice Lam was overturned. Chief Justice Andrew Cheung ruled that it is not unconstitutional for the Immigration Ordinance to exclude FDWs since they can be legally disqualified from being "ordinarily resident." In his decision in favor of the government, Justice Cheung wrote that "foreign domestic helpers' stays in Hong Kong are highly regulated so as to ensure that they are here to fulfil the special, limited purpose for which they have been allowed to come here in the first place, and no more." In addition, he said:

> Whether compared with the abode of a local person or with the residence of a foreigner who has been given a work visa to come and take up employment here, a foreign domestic helper's stay is highly regulated, "out of the ordinary", exceptional or "far from regular", particularly from society's perspective. The central characteristic of the expression "ordinarily resident" as used in article 24(2)(4) of the Basic Law is therefore not infringed by the exclusion in section 2(4)(a)(vi). (Cheung 2012, 50)

He clearly expressed the primary—and, some would say, exclusive—government-regulated role of FDWs to provide the "good life" for their employers. Bringing their children or other family members with them would interfere with their "special and limited" role as solely workers.[3] In March 2013, the justices of the Court of Final Appeal upheld the government's position.

These rulings illustrated yet again that, though FDWs are essential to the prosperity, well-being, and "good life" of Hong Kong people, they are excluded from the rights and benefits of citizens. They are treated differently from other workers and other expatriates: their contractual minimum allowable wage is below the hourly minimum wage guaranteed to Hong Kong locals; they are required to "live in" with their employers, reinforcing the extent to which the employer's household is the focus of their time and energy; they are not permitted to bring family members to Hong Kong; they must leave Hong Kong within two weeks of the termination of their contracts (with a few exceptions); and they are excluded from applying for permanent residence after seven years. These exclusions offer protection of local resources for local citizens, since domestic workers do not qualify for educational, welfare, housing, retirement, or most other government subsidized benefits.

An especially striking aspect of the Domingo case was that their children, who were born and raised in Hong Kong, attended Chinese-language schools, and knew Hong Kong as their only home, were granted permanent residence, along with over a dozen other children of Filipino domestic workers, mainly couples (Benitez 2006a, 2006b), but in these cases, the parents, as in the general pattern discussed by Jacqueline Bhabha (2009), were denied residency. Daniel and Irene were awarded unconditional stay (a status that I am told is no longer awarded in this way) presumably to appease them and to deter them from pursuing claims for right of abode. Those familiar with the case have commented that, in retrospect, the Immigration Department is unlikely to think it was a good decision. No similar unconditional stays are known to have been granted to FDWs since then, at least as of this writing in late 2013.

The legal status of the two older Domingo children was fairly unique. They had a long uninterrupted stay in Hong Kong that was facilitated by having two parents who worked there legally and had an unusually sup-portive employer who sponsored them and allowed them to live together in his home. For Ratna and Amal, it was not so easy. Ratna's marriage was not legally recognized since it was a religious ceremony, and, as an asylum seeker, her husband had no right to remain in Hong Kong. Even if he were granted refugee status, which is highly unlikely, he would be resettled elsewhere. Meanwhile Ratna and her employer were both vul-nerable because they contravened the conditions of the domestic worker contract, since Ratna did not reside with her employer. She spent all her salary on a babysitter and Amal's visa renewals. Without Salim's ISS sup-port, supplemented by illegal earnings, they could not make ends meet. Ratna and Amal were at the mercy of the director of the Immigration Department, who had the power to deny Amal's visa renewals, which, as "visitor visas," would never qualify him for permanent residence anyway.

CITIZENSHIP AND HETERONORMATIVE PRIVILEGE

Blogs, editorials, and everyday conversations in Hong Kong from 2011 to 2013, during the legal battle for FDW right of abode, claimed that the Hong Kong government (like any government) has the right and obli-gation to exclude FDWs or anyone else from becoming permanent resi-dents. Domestic workers were said to know that they would have no right to remain when they came to Hong Kong in the first place. Many locals believe government must protect limited local resources (such as housing, welfare, and medical care) from outsiders who, given the opportunity to do so, would flock there. Tinged with undertones of "humanitarian reason," FDWs are considered fortunate—and should be grateful—to have temporary jobs.

Hong Kong's lifeboat mentality, colored by various waves of mainland migration and by the "flood" of Vietnamese refugees in the 1980s and 1990s, paired with the common view that it is the exclusive right and privilege of Hong Kong citizens to reproduce and form families there, shape local attitudes and fears regarding FDWs becoming residents and having babies in Hong Kong (Marshall 1998). Despite Hong Kong's low fertility rate and an anticipated future labor shortage, outsiders' and noncitizens' babies are unwelcome. Race is a factor in the case of FDWs and asylum seekers, but the issue cannot simply be reduced to racial and national difference since the most vehement popular opposition is voiced in relation to mainland Chinese.

In 2011 and 2012, mainland mothers who gave birth in Hong Kong, even those married to Hong Kong locals (Ornellas 2012), were blamed for the critical shortage of hospital beds and of pre- and post-natal medical care available for Hong Kong citizens. Locals held protests, and the Hong Kong government actively sought legal and other ways to exclude mainland mothers from giving birth in the city. Opposition to both mainlanders and FDWs, nonetheless, is linked to a fear of difference and minorities (Appadurai 2006). In the case of mainlanders, it is the fear of a flood of poor immigrants from across the border who are Chinese but have a different history and mentality from Hong Kong people. In the case of FDWs, the difference is understood in racial terms but also in terms of poverty and competition for resources of which many Hong Kong people (who are often mainland immigrants) only recently availed themselves.

Whereas the Hong Kong–born babies of mainlanders obtain right of abode by virtue of birth and Chinese parentage, the babies of FDWs have no such right unless the baby's father is a legal resident. Ironically, FDWs who are employed—that is, those whose FDH contracts have not been terminated when they give birth—receive prenatal care and are permitted to give birth in Hong Kong public hospitals at the subsidized local rate (less than US$50 for a normal vaginal birth and two nights in the hospital), whereas mainlanders are not. For those whose contracts have been terminated, legally or not, the process of giving birth in Hong Kong is much riskier and more complicated.

As we have seen, FDWs are subject to controls and regulations that do not apply to locals or more privileged immigrants. According to Hong Kong's Immigration Ordinance, they are "outsiders" in terms of citizenship and belonging, and, as the government barrister argued in the right-of-abode hearings, they are "exceptions" to the rule, comparable to "prisoners and refugees." The FDW employment contract thus creates a "zone of exception," excluding them from many of the everyday rights of local citizens and workers (Agamben 1998), or a "zone of social exclusion" (Biehl 2005), where they can be disregarded as "people." As workers, they are excluded from the right to form families or to choose where to live. For their employers, the home is a central site of the family where, as citizens, they are entitled to a "good life" made possible by the cheap and exploitable labor of noncitizen domestic workers. For those workers, the employer's home is a place where they are required to reside by law as a condition of stay. However, though laws often serve as a tool of the state— protecting its citizens from the threat of outsiders and controlling the flow of temporary migrants by denying them the right to remain there permanently with their families, thus protecting local and class interests—such laws, policies, and practices are not always consistent. Within the transnational context of Hong Kong, migrant mothers utilize various tactics (De Certeau 1984) to assert their own and their children's human and familial rights, thus escaping, expanding, or resisting the narrow construct of "FDH."

As the examples of Ratna, Putri, and the Domingos show, when migrants are aware of their rights, they utilize various legal means to assert those rights to remain in Hong Kong. To them, it is often a pleasant surprise to learn that the law can serve the interests of migrant mothers. In the cases described above, they did not do so as activists or out of a sense of righteousness but out of a commitment to their own future *with* their child, a sense that the option of "returning home" no longer seemed possible or desirable.

As scholars of U.S. immigration argue, family is a "key locus of state power and domination over immigrants," and government policies serve to "block or limit the formation" of *certain types* of immigrant families based on race, class, gender, and sexuality (Luibheid 2004b, 229; Pessar 1999). The power of the state to determine who has the right to form a family and what "family" means is illustrated in many other contexts as well. In the Netherlands, legal judgments are said to "display little or no awareness of the lived realities of the women" or of the meaning of family in the different cultural contexts of immigrants' lives (Van Walsum 2009, 233). In Hong Kong, state power is expressed in the prohibition against FDWs bringing family members with them, even in the rare cases when their employers might allow it. Migrant workers in Hong Kong, as in many other locations, face familial prohibitions that more elite and privileged classes of immigrants do not. In Hong Kong, much like in Singapore, FDWs are subject to "an exclusionary notion of reproductive futurity" that does not apply to "skilled workers" or those considered "foreign talent" (Oswin 2012, 1625; Oswin 2010). Foreign domestic workers' reproductive labor (in the broadest sense) is directed exclusively toward the interests of the household within which they work and reside. Their sexuality is subject to surveillance and control. They are prohibited or severely discouraged from getting pregnant, giving birth, or keeping a child in Hong Kong. Moreover, children born of FDWs—unlike those born in Hong Kong of mainland Chinese women—are not entitled to right of abode. These prohibitions are linked to the ill-defined notion that, for non-Chinese to claim permanent residence, they must be "ordinarily resident" in Hong Kong. A key element of ordinary residence is to live with and support a family there.

Some women manage to carve out unusual routes to motherhood in Hong Kong despite the odds. Those like Riana, Nora, and Putri who legally marry Hong Kong residents who are the fathers of their children can most easily gain residency for their children and, after seven years, for themselves. They are among the most privileged of outsiders. Others, such as the Domingos, who were legally married and both working as FDWs and had the support of a sympathetic employer, good lawyers, and their families in the Philippines, were able to establish residency for their children and will likely—in what may turn out to be a chain of exceptions that may not apply to other FDWs—obtain permanent residency themselves. It is probably no coincidence that these "success stories" involve legally married couples, in one case a Hong Kong local husband/father, and in the other a Filipino couple. For many others, such as single mothers or those with nonresident "other" men and religious (not legally recognized) marriages who cannot claim the heteronormative privilege of marriage—like Ratna and most of the women in the next chapter—the situation is far more precarious.

7 Asylum Seekers and Overstayers

> Maybe I can just stay put for a while. But I want to wait. It's
> not waiting, it's like you are making a puzzle one by one to
> make it whole.
>
> — Hope, a Filipino migrant mother, in 2011

PRECARIOUS LIFE AT THE MARGINS

The previous chapter examined the experiences and challenges faced by women who are in Hong Kong legally, either as recognized spouses or dependents of local residents or as foreign domestic workers who managed to retain their jobs and FDH visas in the course of pregnancy and childbirth. This chapter turns to asylum seekers and overstayers, women on the least privileged end of the spectrum, many of whom have spent time in prison and whose situations are more precarious and whose tactics are more desperate and more creative. Those tactics, in Michel de Certeau's provocative words, "are procedures that gain validity in relation to the pertinence they lend to time—to the circumstances which the precise instant of an intervention transforms into a favorable situation, to the rapidity of the movements that change the organization of a space, to the relations among successive moments in an action, to the possible intersections of durations" (1984, 38). Indeed, "time"—as also alluded to by Hope's words above—is central to mothers' tactics, which serve as interventions that transform a bad situation into a favorable one, change the organization of space, and fundamentally extend and transform their time in Hong Kong.

For former domestic workers who are mothers, time spent in Hong Kong is very different than it is for political refugees. Mary, a political asylum seeker from the Congo who was granted refugee status, had been waiting more than eighteen months for resettlement (and far longer for her claim to be processed before that); for her, Hong Kong was experienced as "a waste of time" and a form of institutionalized torture. However, for many of the Indonesian and Filipino mothers I knew, time spent in Hong Kong was anything but wasted. Despite the precariousness of their position, time in Hong Kong was widely viewed as the best solution to the many problems they face as parents. It provided time to come to terms with being a single parent and with the idea of return; time to potentially save money for the future; time to be with a partner and for children to have fathers; time to seek creative solutions to remain there longer or permanently; and, for a rare few, time to consider going somewhere else. Yet there is also a growing sense that what happens in Hong Kong is often bounded in time and space. The pleasures, independence, relationships, and resourcefulness cannot be packed up and taken home.

April, Endri, Mia, Dewi, Bethany, and Rose, the women described below, no longer have domestic worker contracts and visas that allow them to stay, and, for the few who still have partners or husbands, the men are not residents so cannot or will not sponsor them. These mothers have utilized a range of tactics to remain in Hong Kong with their children and to secure their subsistence, with or without male partners. The two overarching tactics are to overstay or to seek asylum. Those who overstay describe it as surprisingly simple. One day they have a visa, and the next day it has expired and they simply do not leave. Time goes on. No letter "O" suddenly appears on their foreheads, and no one notices them as overstayers. They do not suddenly feel "illegal" or like criminals. Overstaying may seem little different from any number of other common tactics, like getting a new name and age on one's first passport, which is so common in Indonesia that it is not experienced as "wrong" or "unlawful." This is especially true for women who unintentionally overstay.

Some women said they did not understand that the two-week rule kicks in when their contract is prematurely terminated and that it supersedes the length of time stamped in their passports. In such cases, by the time they figured out they had overstayed, some felt they might as well make the most of it and work.[1] Other women, like Ara (Angela's mother, chapter 3), overstay to avoid exorbitant agency fees and because they think they can find work and earn double, or more, what they earned as domestic workers. In Ara's case, being arrested for illegal work shortly after starting a new job was the worst imaginable luck. Although the juridical implications of being "legal" one day and an overstayer the next are significant, it is remarkably easy to become an "outlaw" and simply continue as though little has changed, especially for those who are single and without children. Becoming an overstayer happens not by doing something but by doing nothing, by simply staying put, like passive resistance or "foot dragging," which James Scott calls weapons of the weak (1985).

Several women I knew had worked as FDWs, then left Hong Kong while seeking a new employer, but the process took too long and was too expensive, so they returned on tourist visas (visitor visas) and then over-stayed for several years. Like most domestic workers, they became "illegal" by simply not leaving. Melinda (chapter 2) reentered Hong Kong on a tourist visa and overstayed for almost a decade. She had left Hong Kong with her fiancé at the time (a Hong Kong resident) so that he could meet her family in the Philippines, but they broke up and did not marry. When she reentered Hong Kong, her friends assumed it was as a dependent. That impression took no effort to maintain. Melinda had a steady job and sent money home. Not even her closest friends—or Niko, her new Filipino boyfriend of several years—knew she had overstayed. Her status only became a problem when she got pregnant and Niko (a resident) wanted to marry her. As an overstayer who was still married in the Philippines, Melinda could not get married, let alone go to the hospital to give birth. Her only option, other than giving birth outside a hospital or going to prison for overstaying, was to file an asylum or torture claim.

Besides overstaying, filing a claim under either the United Nations Convention Relating to the Status of Refugees (the "Refugee Convention" for short) or the United Nations Convention Against Torture and Other Cruel, Inhuman or Degrading Treatment or Punishment (the "Convention Against Torture"), discussed below, are the main tactics to remain in Hong Kong. Such claims mean that the Immigration Department must provide the claimant with "recognizance papers" that allow them to be in Hong Kong, but not to work, while their cases are being processed. They are also entitled to certain basic benefits from the ISS. In many cases, like Melinda's, women overstay and then file torture claims. Some do so after they are caught or arrested for doing illegal work, like Ara. Others simply surrender and begin the process as a means to buy time and obtain support. In Lilik's case, she could not locate a new employer so she overstayed briefly, then filed a torture claim so she could stay with Rashid. She considered overstaying to be riskier than filing a claim, but it was a tradeoff: overstaying provides no support but it has no time limit unless you are caught; an asylum claim provides a right to stay, some support, and health care, but it allows a limited (though variable) period of stay. In Melinda's case, having already overstayed for many years, she would have likely continued to do so were it not for her pregnancy, her need for medical care, and her child. In many cases, babies are the main consideration in a mother's decision to surrender and file a torture claim.

Asylum or torture claims are potentially useful to the state in an unintended way: they facilitate the "surrender" and "legibility" (Scott 1998) of pregnant overstayers, eventually leading to their processing and likely eventual voluntary departure from Hong Kong. Without the asylum claim option, many women might remain invisible, living out of sight until they are caught by a random immigration check on the street or at a market, or during a workplace raid in the areas of Yuen Long, Tuen Mun, Kam Tin, or parts of Sham Shui Po, Jordan, or Tsim Sha Tsui known for overstayers. Moreover, overstaying and filing torture or asylum claims may be fueled by Hong Kong's carceral approach to justice.

Despite its low crime rate, Hong Kong has one of the highest rates of imprisonment and the highest proportion of women prisoners in the world (Lee 2007, 847). Imprisonment in Hong Kong, as Maggy Lee contends, serves primarily as a "mechanism of migratory control," a means of warehousing and immobilizing "the unwanted and the undeserving poor" (2007, 857). She argues that, though this is partly meant to distinguish between welcome wealthy tourists from China and unwelcome illegal workers, especially prostitutes, it has an impact on other migrants as well. If, instead of incarceration for overstaying, migrant mothers knew they would be deported, some might well surrender sooner.

ASYLUM CLAIMS

In the generic sense, two sorts of claims for refuge can be made in Hong Kong. One involves seeking asylum through the Refugee Convention (often referred to as "refugee claims"); the other involves claims through the Convention Against Torture ("torture claims" or "CAT claims"). People who file either type of claim—regardless of the convention on which it is based—may use the terms "refugees" or "asylum seekers," and for some purposes the finer distinctions are not critical. However, for women and men who file claims and those who process them or advocate for them, the distinctions are important. Officially, "asylum seekers" are those who seek asylum under the Refugee Convention, and "refugees" are those—like Mary, the Congolese woman mentioned above—who have been recognized by the UNHCR.[2] In the Convention Against Torture, torture claimants are not called "asylum seekers" or "refugees," but, because of the similarities, many people refer to them generically as asylum seekers. Yet it is important to note that the two international conventions have different bases for granting claims, and in Hong Kong they are processed through two different bureaucracies. Therefore, people whose refugee claims are rejected by the UNHCR may subsequently file a torture claim with the Hong Kong government, or vice versa.

The 1951 Refugee Convention and its 1967 Protocol do not apply to Hong Kong; claims for refugee status are lodged and evaluated through the local UNHCR suboffice. The Refugee Convention (Article 1) defines a refugee as:

> Any person who . . . owing to a well-founded fear of being persecuted for reasons of race, religion, nationality, membership of a particular social group or political opinion, is outside the country of his nationality and is unable or, owing to such fear, is unwilling to avail himself of the protection of that country; or who, not having a nationality and being outside the country of his former habitual residence as a result of such events, is unable or, owing to such fear, is unwilling to return to it.[3]

Refugees should not be penalized for illegal entry or stay, nor be expelled (or "refouler") against their will to a place where they fear threats from persecution.

The Convention Against Torture, by contrast, was ratified by the United Kingdom and extended to Hong Kong in consultation with the Hong Kong government in 1992; the People's Republic of China's government notified the United Nations that the convention would continue to apply to Hong Kong after reunification with China in July 1997. Whereas the Refugee Convention is restricted to the "five categories" of persecution, the Convention Against Torture is not. Torture is defined (Article 1) as:

> Any act by which severe pain or suffering, whether physical or mental, is intentionally inflicted on a person for such purposes as obtaining from him or a third person information or a confession, punishing him for an act he or a third person has committed or is suspected of having committed, or intimidating or coercing him or a third person, or for any reason based on discrimination of any kind . . . when such pain or suffering is inflicted by or at the instigation of or with the consent or acquiescence of a public official or other person acting in official capacity.

Article 3 states that "No State Party shall expel, return ('refouler') or extradite a person to another State where there are substantial grounds for believing that he would be in danger of being subjected to torture" and "for the purpose of determining whether there are such grounds, the competent authorities shall take into account all relevant considerations including, where applicable, the existence in the State concerned of a consistent pattern of gross, flagrant or mass violations of human rights."[4] Especially given the prohibition against refouler, torture claimants are like asylum seekers.

In December 2009, the Hong Kong Immigration Department began a new "enhanced administrative screening mechanism" for processing torture claims.[5] The new mechanism resulted from several legal challenges. The initial challenge was the case of *Prabakar v. the Secretary of Security*.[6] Prabakar, a Sri Lankan who fled his country to seek asylum in Canada in January 1999, was stopped in Hong Kong, en route, then arrested and charged with having a false passport. He was sentenced to two years in prison and was notified that he would be deported to Sri Lanka after his sentence was served. While in prison, he applied to the UNHCR for asylum. His refugee claim was denied, and subsequently he filed a torture claim. That claim was rejected by the Hong Kong government's Secretary of Security solely on the basis of the UNHCR's rejection of his refugee claim. In court, represented by the law firm Barnes and Daly, Prabakar's representatives argued that the Hong Kong government was obligated to review his torture claim independently and could not rely solely on the UNHCR refugee assessment. Part of their argument was that the basis for granting asylum under the Refugee Convention is different from torture and that simply because a person is not approved as a refugee does not automatically mean he cannot be covered under the Convention Against Torture. Moreover, the UNHCR had not provided the Secretary of Security with its reasons for turning down Prabakar's refugee claim. Ultimately, the UNHCR reversed its decision regarding Prabakar's refugee status, but the government resisted rescinding the deportation order. In December 2002, Prabakar was resettled in Canada, but his case against the government went ahead, and in 2004 the justices of the Court of Final Appeal ruled that torture claims require a separate assessment and cannot rely solely on the UNHCR appraisal for refugee status. As a result, the Hong Kong government had to establish its own torture claim assessment process.

In the next several years after the ruling, the number of torture claims grew while the assessment process was slowly developed. From 2007 to 2011, the UNHCR received more than 4,400 asylum claims, and the Hong Kong government received more than 10,000 torture claims (see Table 1).

The opportunity to file torture claims caused a wave of South Asians to enter the territory, facilitated by agencies that charged them exorbitant fees and promised them work papers. Seeking asylum was never intended as a "work permit," so the government clamped down and prohibited asylum seekers from working.[7] According to one reporter, hundreds of South Asian torture claimants left Hong Kong after the policy prohibiting them to work was enacted in 2010 (South Asian Asylum Seekers 2010).

The fact that two different review and application processes are used for refugees and torture claimants has been criticized for inefficiency, redundancy, and the slow pace of processing claims. However, the fact that a person can submit one claim, let the process run its course, and then turn to the other is what allows people to use these claims as tactics to extend their stay and avoid deportation. Only one torture claim has been approved in Hong Kong (as of this writing), and legal experts claim

Table 1   Refugee Claims and Torture Claims, 2007–2011

	Year					
	2007	2008	2009	2010	2011	TOTAL
Refugee claims (submitted to the UNHCR)	1,624	735	815	457	790	4,421
Torture claims (submitted to Hong Kong government)	1,583	2,198	3,286	1,809	1,432	10,308

SOURCES: UNHCR (personal communication Sept. 11, 2012); Hong Kong Immigration Department, Year-End Briefings 2008, 2009, 2010, and 2011.

it is nearly impossible for FDWs to win torture or refugee claims. However, they have provided a way for more than 10,000 people to remain in Hong Kong with recognizance papers while their claims are under review. Although this was clearly not the purpose of the process, it is how it works for many claimants. I was told in 2010 that those who had filed torture claims in previous years were likely to face a five-year wait.[8] A year later, however, torture claimants were aware that some cases were being expedited and rejected. By the end of 2011, 6,477 of the over 10,000 torture claims were under review (Immigration Department 2011). By 2012, former FDWs had submitted 1,878 torture claims, 921 of which had been rejected (see table 2). The vast majority of former-FDW claims (80 percent) are from Indonesians, far fewer (16 percent) are from Filipinas (Immigration Department 2011).

In the course of my research, I met dozens of former FDW mothers who had filed torture claims during the past several years. At first, they harbored hope that the claim might allow them to remain in Hong Kong, but, by 2011, none of them expected to win their claims. Many had heard lawyers speak on the subject and had spoken to their own legal advisors. The odds of anyone winning a torture claim are extremely low. An impression also exists that "real political refugees" (as opposed to "economic migrants") file claims immediately upon entering the country; they do not enter Hong Kong as a tourist or a domestic worker and work for a period

Table 2   Foreign Domestic Worker Torture Claims and Removed Overstayers in
Hong Kong, 2005–2012

	Year								
	2005	2006	2007	2008	2009	2010	2011	2012	TOTAL
FDW torture claims submitted	0	2	22	105	472	600	433	244	1,878
FDW torture claims rejected	0	0	0	0	0	36	404	481	921
FDWs removed for overstaying		384	406	298	279	418	603	688	3,076

SOURCES: PathFinders, personal communication, Dec. 17, 2012; Immigration Department, personal communications, Aug. 9, 2012, and Aug. 21, 2013.

of time and then file a torture or refugee claim *after* they are caught overstaying or working illegally.[9] The claimant must provide evidence that she would face torture or persecution at home, as defined in the conventions. An Indonesian mother might claim that she fears her own or her child's mental or physical harm from family members, loan sharks, or others because the child was born "out of wedlock," because of the child's father's religious, national, racial, or ethnic identity, because of her religious conversion, or because of her massive unpaid debts, all of which are possible and credible. From the perspective of those evaluating the claim, however, this does not amount to "torture" defined as mental or physical violence that is condoned or perpetrated by a representative of the state or by others without an effort by the state to prevent it.

Despite knowing that they will likely "lose" the claim and eventually have to leave, former domestic workers continue to file torture claims to remain in Hong Kong. By mid-2011, however, it appeared to many NGO staff and to the women themselves that the heyday of FDWs filing torture claims was on the wane. Some women were rejected very quickly (within months) or were told they had no basis to apply. Others, who had filed years earlier, were beginning to receive final judgments. These rejections—several of which I was given to read or was told about—all followed a similar format, acknowledging that women might face difficulties back home but stating that those difficulties do not fit the definition of "torture" as set out in the convention. Some were told that their claims are not convincing or supported with evidence or that the Philippines and Indonesia have laws to protect them from domestic violence or persecution and that, given their experience in Hong Kong, they can find another place to live safely in their home countries.

Several women decided not to wait for rejection and withdrew their cases and returned home. Some, like Ara, left after a close friend's claim was rejected, or after being arrested and serving time for illegal work. Others, like Eka, left because they had been able to communicate with their families and were assured that their families were willing to allow them to come back.

Filing a torture claim is especially useful to women with children because they need time to figure out what to do next, to break it to their families, and possibly to earn more money before going home. A few women file torture claims after their refugee claims are rejected, and some file refugee claims after their torture claims are rejected. The longer that mothers delay their return, the better opportunity they have to exert control over the circumstances of their return. Torture claims are also useful to sympathetic staff at the Immigration Department, Social Welfare Department, and public hospital counters. When women say to an immigration official that "I don't want to go home" or "I can't go home" or "I am afraid of going home," they may be advised to file claims. Some women first learned about asylum and torture claims from social workers and hospital staff who told them to go to the ISS to learn how to file a claim so as to get prenatal care and deliver in the hospital. By promoting this option, the former domestic worker receives assistance, but she also leaves that counter and becomes someone else's problem, perhaps a strong motive for overworked civil servants.

Hong Kong's policies reflect ambivalence about asylum seekers and undocumented workers. Clearly some locals are afforded jobs in the bureaucracy that serves them; slumlords benefit from renting substandard housing to them; and local employers (and consumers) benefit from their precarious status. Since they are not legally permitted to work but must do so to survive, they can easily be underpaid, cheated, abused, and made to do dirty, dangerous work that locals shun. Hong Kong's economy undoubtedly benefits from the "illegal labor" of undocumented workers and those with immigration papers.

The following pages describe several mothers' paths to overstaying and filing asylum claims. They demonstrate a range of women's experiences, factors that influence their choices, the basis of their claims, and the tactics they utilize to subsist as overstayers and asylum seekers. These stories illustrate a spectrum of skill and savvy, naivete and vulnerability, and also chance and luck. They show how women try to put the life puzzle together, piece by piece, over time.

PRISON WITH A BABY

April was college educated, never married, and in her early thirties when she left Northern Luzon in 2000 to go to work in Hong Kong and escape what she called "my trouble in the Philippines." She worked as an FDW until 2006. Without a new contract, and averse to going back to the Philippines, she overstayed for the next five years until she became pregnant in her early forties. In 2011, she surrendered to immigration officials and filed an asylum claim from prison.

When she first overstayed, April worked at a warehouse where she sorted and packed used clothing for resale in the Philippines. Melinda, who was an excellent sorter (her boxes were popular and demanded the highest prices), had introduced April to the boss and owner of the warehouse, a Pakistani man in his forties who usually hired—and readily exploited the vulnerability of—illegal workers.

Soon after she was hired, April began a relationship with the boss and moved in with him. As she explained, he started out okay but never paid her and became increasingly jealous and abusive:

> Many years I worked there and he never paid me anything. . . . My boyfriend treated me very badly. Even then [at first] he is fighting me—he hits my face in front of Melinda. She sees it. She sees what is happening. But of course I have no place to go so I just stay there. . . . Since the day that I go to stay with him I feel that I am more of a slave. I work for him until 1:00 in the morning. I am alone from the first time I go until the last day that I got pregnant. I am always working, working. If I need money, he won't give [any]. But if

it's his friends who ask he can give. He is very generous to the other people. I worked so hard. He says, "You eat my food, you sleep in my house, what more do you expect?"

April's boyfriend was easily provoked, and when she stood up to him it fueled his anger. As an overstayer, she was vulnerable and, as he well knew, she could not report him without also putting herself at risk:

> Only a little simple thing and anger bursts . . . and if he wants to kill you he can kill you. And then if he says something and, for example, I try to reason it out, he doesn't like reason. He doesn't like it, for example, if he tells me something and I don't just obey. He says, "Just shut up your mouth, fucking bitch." Something like that. I am a human being. I respect him, actually, you know, from the time I begin to stay with him, I never go out. I just work for him. But I cannot call the police before because I am so afraid because I don't have papers.

When April became pregnant, her boyfriend pressured her to have an abortion, but as a Roman Catholic she strongly resisted the idea, and being in her early forties she reasoned that it would likely be her last chance to have a child:

> He wants me to abort but I really don't like that. But he is telling because I am not his wife and it seems to be *haram* with his religion to have a bastard. But I think it is more immoral if I take out [abort] my baby. . . . When I am pregnant he beat me and I ran away to Melinda's. I have so many bruises; they are already violet color. I really don't want to go back with him. But he says, "You go back or I will make trouble for your friends." My friends are also afraid.

Eventually, as her pregnancy advanced and she feared for the baby's safety, April managed to leave:

> I really want to go far away from him. But he is always still there at my back. I want to be free. I need freedom, you know. . . . Then I surrendered to immigration. They detain me and arrest me and then have two meetings and after that they bring me to Ma Tau Kok [prison], and then after Ma Tau Kok they give me an appointment in Shatin at the court. From there they bring me at once to Lowu [prison]. I stay Lowu since from September until December.

After she was in prison for a month and a half, April went into labor and was taken to the hospital to give birth. She returned to prison with the baby for the last two months of her sentence and was released early for good behavior. I asked her what prison was like and was surprised by her reply: "Lowu is a very nice place." "A nice place?" I repeated in disbelief.

Yes! In the morning they serve us food, they clean up the diapers, and the food. The people are all nice, especially the staff there. Very nice! The people who stay there too. Many of them are pregnant and also have babies, one-year-olds, two-year-olds staying there with the mother. . . . In one room you have three to five mothers with their children; in the other room maybe six mothers, something like that. It depends on the situation—some come and some go. It's not lonely. There is time for watching TV and listening to the radio. The babies are with you. And I also got a salary inside! Your salary can be used to buy biscuits. You get a salary for taking care of your own baby! When I get out I have HK$91. But the first and the second month I spent it to buy biscuits. The first time [I am paid] I am surprised. "Why? How come I have this salary?" They say, "Because you are taking care of your own baby."

Remarkably, compared with years of isolation, abuse, and unpaid labor at the warehouse, Lowu prison seemed to April like a welcome relief. There she had food, shelter, companionship, and support, she felt safe, and she was even paid. Her main problem was that her partner was expected to bring her baby supplies and he did not, so she had no diapers:

If they know the boyfriend has a Hong Kong ID, they will force you to call your friend or your boyfriend to bring diapers. When I take my baby out of the hospital, they just wrap the baby in very rough cloth. I don't have any diapers or baby clothes. It's terrible, and then for how many days he is very red from diaper rash from the rough cloth because I don't have diapers.

April reminisced about her friends in prison and their needs:

I still have a friend [at Lowu] who is from Indonesia.[10] She helped me. . . . She says, "Please, April, when you get out please come and help me." There are so many there who are in the same situation as me and need some help. Sometimes they don't have any friends and relatives to come and visit. They come from China and from Peru and no one can visit them.

In prison, April learned how to take care of the baby:

> I never expected that someone would care about my problems. . . . But they allowed an NGO from Singapore to go there to visit and teach us how to take care of the babies. Before, I really don't know how to take care of a baby. It was very important. . . . All the mothers there with children and the newborn babies all learn like this [about feeding and bathing, etc.]. But some babies don't have clothes, diapers, bottles, like this. They don't have and it is very hard.

To April's relief, her relationship with her boyfriend had ended when she surrendered and went to prison, but, when he heard she gave birth to a son, his attitude changed. On his own initiative, he registered the baby's birth, listed himself as the father on the birth certificate, and gave him a Muslim name, to April's chagrin. Later, after luring April back to his home when she was released early from prison and had nowhere else to go, he alternated between two opposing threats. One the one hand, he threatened to tell the Birth Registry that she had "fucked someone else" and that he is not the father, thus removing his name from the birth certificate and making the child a "bastard" with no right to remain in Hong Kong. On the other hand, he threatened to take the baby away from April, saying that as the father he had every right to send him to Pakistan to be raised by his wife.

After prison, the abuse resumed. When I met April, she was living with him again under constant fear. The few times she had gone out to buy baby supplies, he accused her of having an affair. He would not give her money to buy baby clothes, and she cried describing the shame of dressing her son in a friend's daughter's hand-me-downs. She was afraid to leave her partner, certain that he would find her if she stayed in Hong Kong—even at a protective shelter—and she thought it was impossible to return to the Philippines.[11]

In prison, April learned from fellow inmates how to file an asylum claim, and she wrote to the UNHCR. Her claim was later rejected, and she filed a torture claim. She said that she had not given the UNHCR the full story but was prepared to do so for her torture claim. Her story was strikingly similar to those I heard from other Filipina asylum seekers:

> I left the Philippines because of these problems. In the Philippines I had a small business and I borrowed some money from the bank. My aunty is the

guarantor. We put up the family land, my grandmother's. She didn't know. When she found out, she had a stroke and died. I could never pay anything [back] to the bank and the business failed. It was not good. My aunty, who was the guarantor, worked for the municipal government, so they [the family] were ashamed because of what I did to our family. They disowned me and don't want me as their relative anymore. Our family was very popular there, but then my grandmother died and we have no land anymore. . . . Their salaries are not high, and my uncle is only a jeepney driver in Manila. That is the problem. . . . The interest rate was very high already, and my aunty has twin boys and one girl going to college, so how can they support them? Then my uncle was found dead in the fields. They think the NPA [New People's Army] killed him because they blamed him for letting the bank take the land. The most important thing was my grandmother who died of a stroke. They said they blame me. . . . I said, "It's okay if you don't like me as your relative already. It's my fault. If you want to kill me, it's okay. I deserve to be killed."

April's mother forgave her, but other family members still blame her for the loss of their land and her grandmother's and uncle's deaths. "They will not forgive me. That's why, if I go to our place with a baby and not married, it's just another problem again. It's my life. It's a very hard life to have a baby like this."

The veracity of her particular story aside, the sort of political violence and familial ostracism that April describes—linked to forfeited high-interest loans and loss of family land and the NPA—is plausible. Nonetheless, it is unlikely to meet the official definition of torture—in which the government condones or does nothing to stop the violence. Moreover, such claims require evidence, which April does not have. The odds are poor for anyone, but especially for former domestic workers like April.

HONG KONG HAPPY

Endri, a torture claimant in her late twenties when I met her in 2011, first arrived in Hong Kong from East Java to work as a domestic worker in 2002. Like many other Indonesians who wanted to work abroad after middle school at the age of fifteen, she was below the Indonesian minimum age of eighteen, so her recruiter found her someone else's papers (a school certificate) to use as the basis for her new identity. Her new name and birth date added three years to her age and allowed her to go to work in Singapore. After two years there, she returned to Indonesia briefly, spent three months in a training camp where she learned to speak Cantonese, then went to work in Hong Kong.

She went to Hong Kong to "earn more money" and because her friends said that "Hong Kong is a good place." However, unlike many other Indonesian women whose families were poor farmers, Endri said her family was "not rich or poor." They had a shop and were involved in small entrepreneurial activities. The opportunity to help her family economically and also the adventure and independence attracted her. She was not eager to follow the inevitable path to early marriage and motherhood at home.

Over the years, Endri worked for five Hong Kong employers. She got along very well with the first three. She worked for the first two for one contract each, or a total of four years. While working for her second employer she met her first boyfriend, a Pakistani asylum seeker. She was very young and lonely when she met him at a party of Indonesian women and South Asian men on a Sunday. He was kind and handsome and swept her off her feet. She "loved him a lot" and planned to be with him forever, but he had many girlfriends. After a year, they split up.

For the next year or so, "broken hearted," she ignored attention from men and encouragement from friends to move on, have fun, and be "Hong Kong happy." She worked for her third employer for four years and during that time met Prakash, an Indian watch trader who was an asylum seeker who eventually became the father of her two children. They originally met on the MTR when, using a common ploy, Prakash borrowed her phone, used her phone to call his, thereby got her number, and began contacting her. At first she "kept away from him and was afraid of him." Then, as he persisted, she told him "that I just want to be friends and that I had been badly hurt." But Prakash kept calling and texting and met her on Sundays, "trying to convince me to be his girlfriend." He said "five fingers are not alike—not all men are like my Pakistani boyfriend" and he "promised to love and care for me forever." Although she "did not believe him at first," he persisted and said "he will make me forget." At first "he calls me every day. On Sundays we eat together and play; then later I love and trust him."

While working for her third employer, Endri became pregnant and took advantage of her maternity benefits to give birth in Hong Kong. With her Hong Kong identity card, her delivery cost about HK$300 (less than US$40), including three days in the hospital. When her baby was several weeks old, she returned to Indonesia, having finished her maternity leave, and forfeited her job. She remained there for a few months, then sought another employer and returned to Hong Kong to work, leaving her baby with her sister. To her pleasure, Prakash "waited" for her to return to Hong Kong. After she worked for her fourth employer for ten months, she terminated her contract, giving the requisite one-month notice. The work, which included looking after an incontinent dog that slept on her bed, was intolerable. She found another employer.

During that time, Prakash's asylum claim was rejected. He broke up with Endri and, under pressure from his family, returned to India to marry. Unbeknownst to Endri or Prakash, she was already pregnant again. Soon afterward, as she and others who knew her described, Endri was "wrongly accused of theft" and was convicted and sentenced to eight months in prison. When she began her sentence, she was several months pregnant. The baby was born during her sentence. When she was in labor, she was taken to a public hospital to deliver, and baby Nisha spent the first few months of her life in prison with her mother (an experience Endri remembered with far less fondness than had April).

At the beginning of the second pregnancy, given her boyfriend's departure, Endri considered having an abortion but ultimately decided not to. She also considered giving Nisha for adoption in Hong Kong. After the baby was born, a friend in Indonesia who had been married for years but had no children asked if she could have Nisha, but by then Endri wanted to keep her, partly because she was still "dreaming of being reunited as a family with the father." When we talked, Endri was adamant that she must devote herself to being a good mother. She did not want to be seduced by the cruel optimism of romance; she refused to be hurt again and no longer trusts men. After Prakash left, she fantasized about having "a family life" with him, but by then he was in China with his new Indian wife, a woman his parents approved of but who, his friends assured her, is thin and ugly. At some point, Prakash offered to marry her as well, but she did not think he meant it. As she explained:

I can't be like friends who are Hong Kong happy even when they know a relationship will not last beyond Hong Kong. I can't lie and just love them and be Hong Kong happy. I don't want a broken heart. Lonely is okay. I have children to think about. [In Hong Kong] men are not serious. Maybe one in a thousand men are good ones. My friends meet other boys. I cannot because my heart was very broken. Sometimes I dream that Prakash is back and we have a happy family. But I need to work to take care of my babies, and it will work only in the dreams.

After prison, Endri filed a torture claim. She vaguely knew about such claims from her boyfriend but, like April, learned more about them from other women she met in prison. When she first told me about her claim in 2011, she seemed to dismiss the claim's content. She quickly said she knew she would not ultimately win it but simply having filed her claim meant she could not be removed or deported. In 2013, she was still in Hong Kong, her claim still in progress.

SUBSISTENCE

While an asylum/torture claim is pending, some women make ends meet by locating low-paying illegal work that places them in vulnerable positions. After they have filed their claims with the Immigration Department or the UNHCR, they are also eligible for meager "in kind" social support from the ISS, which coordinates distribution of food to torture or asylum seekers every ten days. Basic food supplies, such as rice, oil, and milk, are provided. According to its website, the ISS also provides donated clothing when available, but no one I knew had ever received clothing. ISS provides housing in flats for eleven people or a housing allowance paid directly to the landlord.[12] According to the women I spoke to, the ISS provides an adult with around HK$1,200 per month in rent and up to HK$600 more if they register a child. The rent is paid directly to the landlord, and the landlord and the rental space must be "approved" by the ISS caseworker. The ISS apparently also provides allowance for transportation to hearings and medical appointments (but most women were unaware of this), and it supplies a monthly allocation of basic toiletries such as shampoo, soap, and toothpaste. Many ISS clients (not only former domestic workers) said that what the ISS provides does not fully cover rent, utilities, or required rental deposits. Some landlords who rent out rooms in subdivided flats or old houses with makeshift rooms and illegal extensions in the New Territories are flexible and will negotiate with tenants so they can creatively cover the costs that the ISS does not cover. ISS clients also devise other solutions.[13]

One strategy for piecing the puzzle together is to find roommates who are not ISS clients to share the bed and contribute to the rent or provide babysitting, as in Mia and Annie's case below. Tenants are not difficult to find among overstayers or women on visitor visas awaiting their cases with no place to live. Some ISS clients sublet their rooms and stay with their boyfriends. One African asylum seeker rented out his geographically well-situated room by the night to African traders and businessmen who traveled between Hong Kong and China, and he stayed in a cheaper place. Among the arrangements I observed were employed FDWs who paid ISS recipients for a place to cook, rest, or socialize on Sundays. Some employers paid for a share of a "boarding house," perhaps to give themselves greater privacy on the weekend. ISS caseworkers check on their clients' housing arrangements and make surprise visits to ensure they live where they say they do and that the place is appropriate. Some mothers had to relocate when the flat was suspected of "being a brothel" or deemed unsafe, including an illegal rooftop structure. ISS surveillance, however, is rarely effective at deterring creative tenant arrangements that can be easily explained as guests who are "just visiting."

With the money obtained by the creative use of space, some torture claimants are able to buy necessities they cannot get from charities, including highly valued disposable diapers. As Endri said, "Pampers" are one of their biggest monthly expenses and cost up to HK$400 a month. She and others complained vehemently about inequality, discrimination, and favoritism at certain NGOs and religious charity organizations. From their perspective, diapers are given by some churches or religious charities only to Christian asylum seekers and not to Muslims. Others complained that few NGOs give out diapers anymore, and those that do might exclude former FDWs and only give out diapers if the child's father is considered a "legitimate" asylum seeker and is a client of that organization. When I asked about such complaints, one organization explained that they make no such distinctions but that they draw the line when they have filled the quota of asylum seekers they can afford to help.

Tenants and roommates also pool their resources and facilitate other means of earning money. One popular way to get money "without working" or with minimal risk of getting caught involved being hired to wait in line for high-demand consumer goods—anything from concert tickets, to sneakers, to limited edition commemorative currency, to new iPhones. The November 2011 lines outside the Apple Store in Hong Kong for the iPhone 4S, newly released in Asia, provided an excellent source of income for Endri, Ara, Ina, and several mothers they knew who spent three nights camping in line (some with their children) amid crowds of people and clusters of South Asian men who had also been hired by "bosses" to buy the limit of five phones per person. The basic model cost HK$5,080 and could be resold by the bosses for at least HK$1,000 more in Hong Kong shops. Several groups of mainland Chinese also joined the line, planning to resell the phones in China. Endri recruited a team of Indonesian women for her South Asian boss (who preferred to hire women, especially mothers, because they are "less trouble" than men). She received HK$2,000 (and Nisha got another HK$200) while the women on her team received HK$1,500 (approximately US$200) for the three nights, almost half the monthly FDW salary. This income was very welcome, especially to Ara and Ina, who were about to leave for Indonesia and were otherwise penniless, to Endri, who considered a roommate as a last resort and needed money to cover rent, and to Mia (below), who was saving money for her and Annie's eventual return home.

One attraction of this type of money-making scheme is that it is difficult for the police to "prove" people are "working." Although the women were unlikely owners of such expensive phones, they nonetheless participated in and benefited from the global market in luxury goods. If police asked them to show the money with which they would purchase the phones, they said "a friend will bring the money when I reach the front of the line," which was true. Ara and Ina joked about how many buses it would take to hold all the South and Southeast Asians if the Immigration Department were to crack down. Despite police attempts to break up the crowd, they persistently returned throughout the night and defended their places in line so as to enter the Apple Store before the phones ran out. When it was all over and the women I knew had earned their pay, they chatted nostalgically about the great fun of it: free McDonalds food from their bosses, good pay, the festival atmosphere, and being surrounded by friends all night and day. Following numerous complaints from locals who claimed they were prevented from purchasing iPhones directly from Apple, the company switched to an online pre-ordering system, doing away with one opportunity for "queuers." However, I was told, "no problem," there were still plenty of opportunities for queuing since concert tickets, limited edition currency, and luxury goods are always desired by those too busy and wealthy to wait in line themselves. Moreover, when goods are reserved online, someone has to pick them up.

Another source of cash in 2011 came from reselling food provided by the ISS. Women could chose from a list of products. Some ordered the most expensive foods (such as basmati rice) and products that could easily be resold (such as oil and milk powder). At their appointment at the Pakistani or Nepalese-run shop or distribution point, some women would leave their goods and receive cash from the distributors instead. The cash was used to buy fresh produce and other goods at more competitive local markets. I once accompanied Rose and another mother to the ISS-designated distributor that was very far from their flats. Instead of lugging two babies plus their heavy bags of rice and sugar back to their places, they simply "resold" to the storekeeper. That time, my presence raised concerns, and the distributor told the mothers to return the next day, without me. It turned out that the ISS was investigating charges of "reselling"—which financially benefited the distributors as well as ISS clients—and they cracked down on it in the coming months. During the crackdown, Eka bought heavy products like rice and oil, loaded them onto the stroller, and resold them to people she knew with small shops or restaurants. Eka's customers got a better deal than in retail shops, and she got cash to spend.

Although food and rentals could be used to generate cash—working around the ISS in-kind assistance restrictions—many women who were overstayers or asylum/torture claimants also worked illegally. Some cooked Indonesian or Filipino food and sold it to FDWs on Sundays; some women babysat for those who went out to work. As Ina (chapter 3) put it:

[Overstayers] can do anything if they want to get money. They can even prostitute. If they don't want to do hard work, they can just go to Wanchai or the Nepal part of Jordan [and get paid for sex]. There are many Nepalese in Jordan. Some of my friends do this. Some do it to survive in Hong Kong because they get no rent or help from ISS. So that is why, if we have no work and no job, maybe they sell their bodies. In my old place, some of us are washing dishes in restaurant; some of us are doing part time same as a domestic helper; some of us are washing cars every night; some of us go for pick up [waiting in lines] to buy cell phones. One Chinese boss will pay us when we wait and pick up things for him. Some of us sell food. Some of us prostitute [ourselves]. Some are stealing money in the airport; she will dress like she is travelling and when someone is not careful she will just pickpocket.

Mia, below, was very cautious in her approach to making and saving money. Dewi and Bethany did not work but relied in different ways on their partners.

MIA AND ANNIE'S ROOM

Mia was never arrested, but she overstayed and then filed an asylum claim. I visited Mia and her daughter Annie's room several times in 2011 and 2012. Located on an upper floor of an old, run-down building on the border of Tai Kok Tsui and Sham Shui Po, their place is unlike most other mothers' urban flats I visited. Rose, Endri, Bethany, and Lilik's flats were all on higher floors of seven- to ten-story old buildings without elevators, which made it very difficult to maneuver a child, a stroller, and groceries but also assured them lower rent. To enter Mia and Annie's place, you went through a locked entrance, past a watchman, up a short dingy flight of stairs, up a small elevator, down an open hallway, and through another locked door. You entered a subdivided flat through a narrow hallway—wide enough for one person— piled with strollers, a child's bicycle, several pairs of old shoes, buckets, and umbrellas before arriving at the door. The room was about the size of a queen-sized bed (but twice the size of Endri's). At the entrance was a counter with a burner and rice cooker; a minuscule toilet cum shower was in back. The rest of the floor was covered with a foam mattress on which were a bedcover, pillows, stuffed animals, and dolls—serving conveniently as playroom, living room, bedroom, and dining room all in one. Two small windows allowed in some light and air and provided a tiny space to hang laundry; sounds of traffic entered from the expressway overpass that I could almost touch from the window. Annie's toddler-clothing hung above our heads like decorations, and every inch of space was utilized. All along the walls were children's vocabulary pictures, such as body parts that Annie could recite in English before she was two: "nose, hand, mouth" and so on. One was the alphabet in raised letters that you could trace with your fingers, and another displayed numbers, most of which Annie could precociously and effortlessly recite. On one uncovered bit of wall space, Annie had drawn in crayon, and I made a mental note to give her large sheets of drawing paper.

Despite the tight quarters, during one visit four adults and two-year-old Annie squeezed comfortably onto the mattress cross-legged for lunch. Mia placed ingredients for Laksa noodles on a plastic tablecloth at the center of the mattress. Annie was calmer than in the playgroup run by an NGO where she competes for attention, sometimes shouting and biting. In her room, she politely offered prawn chips and fruit slices. One of Mia's guests told me she is often mistaken for Annie's mother. Her father was from Irian Jaya so she has darker skin and frizzier hair than most Javanese; at first glance, she resembled Annie more than Mia does. She and another woman were temporarily boarding there. One of them had a labor case against her employer and the other was an overstayer. Mia's rent was about HK$2,600 per month (including electricity and water). The ISS paid HK$1,800, so Mia had to make up the difference.

Like other asylum seekers registered with the ISS, Mia and Annie received a food allotment every ten days. Mia told me that the handouts from the ISS and another NGO were not enough. She needed money for "Pampers" and other things. Annie was beginning to be potty trained, and Mia got some diapers from an NGO, but she still spent over HK$200 a month on them. She knew she was lucky because others, including her neighbor Eka, did not receive diapers. Seeing Mia's room, I understood why she would not use cloth diapers offered free by one charity group: her laundry is hand-washed, and there is no room to hang diapers to dry.

Annie's father, I had learned earlier, was an asylum seeker from Africa. Although he occasionally attended church, Mia insisted that he was not a "true Christian." By the time I met them, Annie was almost two and her father had married a Chinese Hong Kong resident with whom he had a child. He also had another child with an Indonesian woman. Mia had met him when her contract was terminated and she was kicked out of the house by her employer and had nowhere to go. According to Mia, her employer's mother never liked her and constantly criticized her, but ultimately she was terminated because she had cosigned a bank loan for a friend and the friend defaulted on the loan. The collector repeatedly phoned her and her employer in an effort to locate the friend or pressure them to pay. Fed up with the harassment and afraid of trouble from the collector, Mia's employer fired her.

Mia slept in Kowloon Park one night and spent the next few nights at the Star Ferry McDonald's. A man she met there kindly offered her food and shelter. At first he was kind, and she stayed with him while she pursued a case against her employer with the Labor Tribunal. When the case was finished, she was awarded one month's pay, far less than she owed the agency, and she felt she had no choice but to overstay and work illegally, doing part-time domestic work. She stayed with her boyfriend, got pregnant, and became aware of his other girlfriends. During her pregnancy, their relationship became violent. She told me, "He is quite bad-tempered, slapped me when I am pregnant, kicked me out when it is midnight. It is too much already. I decided to stay on my own."

Mia surrendered to immigration officials and filed an asylum claim with the UNHCR in 2009. Her claim was quickly rejected, and she continued to work part-time through her seventh month. As she explained in 2011:

> Now I have recognizance papers. I filed a CAT [torture] claim in 2009, before Annie was born. Before that I did a UN [refugee] claim—and was rejected already before Annie was born. After that the social welfare officer [at the hospital] recommended me to apply for torture claim. She said, "If you don't have UN or anything you cannot have help." At first my immigration officer at CIC [Castle Peak Bay Immigration Centre] says I have to go to my country. Immigration tried to force me to go home. I asked the officer to please give me chance and I explained my parents don't want me or the baby. He said, "Okay, okay." But when I go again, they do not agree. Then, after that, a good officer she said, "Okay, better your baby is born here." The

good officer also asked me to get the recognizance papers [i.e. file a torture claim] because if I go to hospital it is better. But I used my ID in the hospital; everything is okay because they do not know it is expired. After Annie is born, she got her recognizance [paper] too. Now I'm still waiting for them to call because I have not yet done the interview for the torture claim.

Mia managed her life in Hong Kong fairly well compared with many others. She and Annie had food, clothing, and shelter. Before Annie was born and when she was very small, it was much easier to earn money. Besides the help from her temporary roommates, another mother occasionally babysat while Mia did part-time domestic work. Even when Annie became a toddler, Mia managed to work and give some money to her pastor to save for her (since she had no bank account). Like Endri, Mia was paid to line up overnight to buy iPhones for resellers, but unlike Endri, who had brought Nisha with her for forty-eight hours, Mia left Annie with a babysitter and had to pay her.

Unlike some women who fended off questions about their future even before I had the chance to ask, saying that they refuse to think about it, Mia told me that she would be prepared to leave Hong Kong one day when she has to. It had been over three years since she filed her torture claim. It was clear that immigration was rejecting some more recent claims first—possibly to deter future applicants—and they were also processing older claims at a faster rate. Mia knew she would soon have to go back to Indonesia. In preparation, she had told her parents about Annie. It was difficult, but they gradually began to accept the idea. Mia often advised Eka (whose parents constantly complained about her lack of remittances because they did not know she was no longer working or that she had a baby) to do the same for the relief and peace of mind it would bring. Mia "prayed" about the future and "put my trust in God." One day she hopes her parents will look after Annie and she can go and work somewhere else, perhaps Taiwan.

TEMPORARY MARRIAGES

In contrast to the "lucky" wives of local Hong Kong residents, relationships between domestic workers and asylum seekers are known to be risky, and most such relationships do not last beyond Hong Kong. Even male asylum seekers who spoke highly of domestic worker girlfriends were frank that these relationships have no long-term prospects, in contrast to (far less common) relationships with local resident women. "Economic" asylum seekers like Rashid or Prakash, who are in Hong Kong mainly to earn money, may eventually go home to their country where they already have a wife, and they do not plan to bring their Hong Kong partners with them. "Political" asylum seekers like Annie's father, who are afraid or unable to go home, must pin their hopes on local women or on being granted asylum and resettlement. Many mothers eventually realize that relationships with asylum seekers are "temporary marriages." It is rare to hear of men who would even consider living in the Philippines or Indonesia. The rhetorical question is, "How can I earn money there?" I have met a few mothers who said they would "consider" going elsewhere when the time comes, including two who went to Pakistan.

Dewi and Bethany are both Indonesian former FDWs, and both applied for asylum through the UNHCR and subsequently filed torture claims through the Hong Kong government in order to stay in Hong Kong with their African asylum-seeker husbands and their Hong Kong–born children. Dewi and her husband, Mo, are both Muslim, and they had a Muslim marriage blessing. At Mo's request, Dewi began to wear more modest dress, covering up what others called "her sexy body" when she went out, in order to avoid male attention. Bethany and her husband, Christophe, are both Christian; he was born Christian and she converted from Islam in Taiwan, several years before they met. Bethany and Christophe were not officially married, partly because she was not yet divorced in Indonesia though she had been separated for more than a decade. Bethany nonetheless referred to Christophe, with whom she had lived for five years and had two children, as her "husband."

In both cases, the men did not want their wives to work. In Dewi's case, despite the fact that Mo was an asylum seeker and could not work legally, he took great pride in supporting his family—by selling clothing—and he would have it no other way. "He is too proud," Dewi said, to want her to work, and he did not want help from charities or organizations other than the ISS. Christophe also did not want Bethany to work, but he was adamant that he should not do so either because of the illegality and the risks involved. On various occasions, Bethany and Christophe each told me that he was a refugee who had been awaiting resettlement for several years. As a "legitimate" political refugee, he did not want to risk getting caught working illegally.[14] He adhered to the view that "real" political refugees must distinguish themselves from economic asylum seekers, who are said to come to Hong Kong only to work illegally for as long as they can until they are caught, imprisoned, and then deported.

During the time I knew Bethany in Hong Kong, her future plans shifted. When I first met her, she was committed to winning her torture claim and seemed to rehearse her claim story with me. It involved her religious conversion and persecution, family violence, and excommunication. She prayed to win her claim or be resettled with Christophe. Later, as her claims and appeals were rejected, she was frank about simply buying time. By then it was clear that her family in Indonesia had not rejected her, and, when I asked about their attitude toward her conversion, she laughed and said it was fine and that her paternal uncle was Christian. As her appeals were rejected, her second pregnancy advanced, and a doctor certified that she was not fit to travel. After the child's birth, she said she might have to go back to Indonesia. Instead of securing a divorce in Indonesia, getting married to Christophe, and joining his claim, the new plan was for Christophe to resettle in North America or Europe, then to send for her and the children. A year later, in 2013, her plans had changed again. With the help of a lawyer, Bethany was obtaining a divorce in Indonesia, after which she and Christophe would legally marry and she would, they hoped, be added to his claim. Meanwhile, Bethany, Christophe, and their children pooled their ISS benefits, lived together, and had an occasional boarder in their minuscule flat. They received assistance from a church that regularly gave asylum seekers a small amount of cash and from other religious and secular organizations that gave them diapers and "gifts" (not pay) in exchange for cleaning offices and doing odd jobs that were not considered "work." Toward the end of Bethany's second pregnancy, when she could barely move, Christophe took their child to various playgroups and NGO activities. Bethany's child was well dressed, and at one point she carried a much-envied iPad. Christophe had received a sizable government settlement from a lawsuit he filed over "illegal detention." I had heard of several such cases, and a few such settlements, mostly among asylum-seeker men who were detained for many months after filing for asylum. Mo filed a similar lawsuit later, but the outcome of his case depended on another one that was under appeal and had put the others on hold. Dewi worried that Mo's case might take years; she planned to buy a cow in Indonesia for each of her children with the anticipated settlement.

Both Dewi and Bethany regularly attended self-improvement and educational activities for migrant mothers and children. They took advantage of as many opportunities as possible to learn about health, mothering, legal issues, and child rearing. Both enrolled their younger children in playgroups and kindergartens. Both also hoped to learn skills (such as hair dressing, sewing, and baking) that could be useful for making a living in Indonesia. Dewi especially enjoyed the social side of these activities. She complained about how difficult and boring it is to look after two small children alone in a tiny one-room flat without air conditioning. One NGO meeting room was spacious and had plenty of toys and other children to play with and other mothers to chat with. Dewi often left with one or more mothers afterward to go to the park or to her place. She was friendly and supportive to other mothers and kept in touch by phone with several who had left Hong Kong. She sympathized with their troubles, offered counsel, and quietly thought about her inevitable departure. I rarely knew Dewi to be the subject of gossip or criticism, perhaps because she was warm, generous, and forthright about her current and future difficulties.

Bethany was also an advocate for other mothers, but she was envied by some who resented her financial windfall when Christophe won his claim. Guesses about the amount of the settlement spiraled, and later, when Bethany faced financial pressures and had to sell the iPad, others expressed some satisfaction. Bethany was the only mother whose partner sometimes met her at the NGO office, a space that was otherwise conspicuously and almost exclusively for women and children. That Christophe was involved in Bethany's life might have been cause for envy, but it also provoked criticism of Christophe's real or imagined flaws: his appearance, his bad habits (drinking and womanizing), and his unwillingness to work. That Bethany was Christian might also have contributed to the way she was regarded by Muslim Indonesians.

I asked Bethany why her relationship with her husband had lasted so long, compared with others. Christophe, she said, "says I'm very strong."

Bethany said she knows "how to talk to him nicely and to explain to him what he must do to be a better man." She reminds him "that you are Christian, but you are not behaving the way God would want you to behave, and God knows." He then shows remorse and tells her that she has made him a better person. "African men like to have many girlfriends, but I tell him he has to be a good father and a better person." Once, when they lived in the New Territories, Christophe came home late and was about to go out again. Because he had been out all day, she said, "Okay, but I will go with you." Bethany had been lying down, and he grabbed her by the hair. She jumped up and punched him. "He was so shocked. I said, 'I am not a man, but if you hit me again you are the one who will be hurt!'" She made it clear she would not put up with his nonsense. "Other women do not know how to talk to them. They just cry and act jealous." Instead, she appeals to his better self, his maturity, and his sense of responsibility. She is also tough.

Bethany was one of two lucky mothers (both Christian) who received diapers from one NGO, whereas most other mothers did not. She was older than most Indonesian mothers and conveyed a rare aura of confidence. She and her husband were appreciated and well liked by staff at several NGOs because they were helpful, grateful, and did not complain or make trouble. Bethany did her best to ignore gossip, jealousy, and competition and to focus on her family. But women who "establish boundaries and say no" (as they were taught in an NGO workshop) and who do not often share, lend money, or reciprocate, as well as those who are deemed to "think they are better than others" because of their religion, money, or partners, are easy targets of gossip and envy.

PATERNITY CLAIMS

As described above, mothers like Dewi and Bethany filed asylum claims in order to remain in Hong Kong with their children and their partners, which they had successfully done for over five years. In contrast, Rose filed a torture claim while also pursuing a paternity claim against her child's father, who is a Hong Kong permanent resident, in the hopes that she and her child could remain there, even after her asylum claim ran its course.

Rose is a slim and attractive Indonesian woman who, following a youthful heartbreak in Indonesia, went to work as a maid in Singapore in her mid-teens and then to Hong Kong as an FDW. After her last contract ended, she was unable to find a new employer within the stipulated two-week period, so she opted to overstay rather than return home and pay more agency fees to get another job. While overstaying, she met Gerry, an American who is a Hong Kong resident, in a Wanchai bar. They went out for a brief time, and she became pregnant. When she told Gerry, he gave her money for an abortion. Given that she had overstayed her visa (unbeknownst to him) and that this would likely become obvious if she registered at the family planning office, she opted for an illegal abortion instead.

Despite undergoing the procedure, the abortion was unsuccessful. Since her pregnancy had not ended, she reasoned that "the baby must really love me" and that it "was meant to be." She decided to keep the baby. Gerry knew about the pregnancy but refused to see her because, as Rose surmised, her former friend who was seeing Gerry told him it was not his child. Rose then filed a torture claim on the recommendation of some friends. She knew this would allow her to stay in Hong Kong for a while and, more important, would give her access to a medical waiver for prenatal and maternity care in a public hospital (Constable forthcoming a).

After Barney was born, Rose learned from an NGO about paternity claims and Barney's possible claim to Hong Kong residency. She consulted with a lawyer who encouraged her to apply for legal aid, which was granted, and then the lawyer helped her pursue a paternity claim against Barney's father. Rose provided the lawyer with everything she knew about Gerry: where he lived, his occupation, and other evidence of their relationship. Gerry was served with a legal notice and given the opportunity to prove by way of DNA testing that he was not Barney's father. Alleged fathers can refuse DNA testing, but the judge can then "draw inferences" from the refusal (Parent and Child Ordinance, CAP 429). As a social worker and a lawyer explained, it is up to the man to prove that he is *not* the father. Refusing the DNA test may well be interpreted by the judge as evidence against him.[15]

Rose hoped that, when Barney's paternity was legally established, not only would he be entitled to residency but that she, too, by virtue of being his mother, would have a chance to remain in Hong Kong. Like others, she was repeatedly told by immigration officials, hospital staff, and social workers to "take responsibility" and "take your child home." More assertive than many, and highly averse to returning home as a single mother ("I would rather they kill me here" she told her immigration officer), Rose ignored the pressure to go home and remained committed to utilizing any means possible to stay. If Barney's paternity was recognized, Gerry could then be pursued for child maintenance—or, if Gerry was financially unable to support a child, then Barney would qualify for government welfare assistance (like Putri's child), which would be enough for basic survival. To Rose (and as expressed by many others) that would be infinitely preferable to returning to what she described as small village life, the boredom and poverty she fled as a teenager, and the shame it would bring to her family as well as the stigma, criticism, and gossip from neighbors were she to return home with a child, no husband, and no money.

Meanwhile, the "in kind" support Rose received from the ISS as a torture claimant—in the form of rent paid directly to her landlord for the small room she shared in a boarding house with Barney and a roommate (an overstayer), and food supplies every ten days—was not enough. She needed to buy diapers and medicine and still tried to remit money to her parents when she could. Although torture claimants are prohibited from working, Rose nonetheless had to work.

As NGO staff have noted, the Immigration Department wants mothers like Rose to willingly leave Hong Kong with the baby, and some do. But it is difficult to deport the mother of a permanent resident child (even once their asylum/torture claims have been rejected). Hong Kong government policies, an NGO staff member explained, seem to prohibit them from purchasing an air ticket to send a Hong Kong resident child away. As long as the mother asserts her wish to remain with her child and not to leave, it appears that she cannot be forced to go. As of 2012, I had not heard of a single case of a mother being forced to leave, with or without her Hong Kong resident child, without her consent.[16] Rose was eagerly counting on this pattern in the hopes of raising Barney in Hong Kong. Should the judge uphold the paternity claim, Rose might be given a renewable visitor visa like Comilang (chapter 6). In Comilang's case, despite her lawyers' contrary assertion, the judge claimed the father and his new wife could take care of the child in Hong Kong, so there was no need for Comilang to be given the right to stay as other than a visitor. Assuming Barney's father would not want custody (a reasonable assumption), Rose would likely be granted at least a visitor visa to facilitate Barney's right to residency. April's case (above) could turn out differently because her child's father did express interest in taking the child, which could undermine her argument to remain in Hong Kong.

The stories in this chapter—of April, Rose, Bethany, and many others— have pointed to some of the legal and economic tactics used by migrant mothers in an attempt to stretch out their time in Hong Kong while they slowly try to put the puzzle pieces together, testing out relationships or exploring possible futures. In the course of discovering the impermanence of being "Hong Kong happy," they overstay, file torture or asylum claims, work, pursue strategies for material assistance, and file legal claims. In such instances, filing claims offers ISS support and "time" as a tactic and a source of future possibilities. For other migrant mothers, like Indah (chapter 1) and Ara and Ina (chapter 3), Hong Kong no longer holds any promise; life there is a prison stripped of all hope.

Domestic workers (in contrast to many African and South Asian asylum seekers) are often remarkably grateful for ISS assistance. Early on in my research, when I asked Dewi, "Why do so many women file torture claims?" she replied, "That's easy, it's because you get free rent and free food! In Indonesia we have to work for money!" Dewi's quick answer aptly points to what many mothers see as some of the benefits of life in Hong Kong compared with Indonesia; in that sense, they are grateful beneficiaries of humanitarian aid. But Dewi's answer also glibly covers up the unfairness that many of the mothers also perceive: the diapers they cannot get from NGOs (or from their own stingy partners), the paradox of having to work to buy diapers and other goods but the risks that working poses, and the catch-22 of pursuing legal claims but not being permitted to work while doing so. Thus, asylum/torture claims become a means to accessing their rights.

Dewi's answer also omits the subtle and complex reasons why many migrant workers, and especially single mothers, do not want to return home. Had I phrased the question differently and asked, "Why don't you and other mothers want to go home?" she might have highlighted not only the attractions of Hong Kong but also the many drawbacks of "home," something that women are often loath to think about. The next chapter turns to the special precarity of home as encountered by single mothers, who are often viewed as "failed migrants."

8   The Migratory Cycle of Atonement

Indonesians have a deep sense of shame about children born
out of wedlock. According to Islam we should not have premarital sex. Men shouldn't either, but they are not blamed
for it, only women are. Women who have babies [in Hong
Kong] are looked down on, and thought immoral. They will
form their own groups and meet with women in similar situations. Filipinos may not have such condemnation of it. In
Indonesia, it [premarital sex] happens too, but no one
knows about it, because if someone is pregnant, they will
often marry, and men there can have more than one wife.

— Angel, an Indonesian domestic worker and activist, in 2011

GOING HOME

Throughout my research, many mothers, NGO staff, and social workers
echoed the same advice: migrant mothers who want to keep their children
(as opposed to the few who give them for adoption) must talk to their own
parents, let the news sink in, let the anger wear off, let acceptance set in,
and then go home and do their best to raise their children. At one
PathFinders discussion group, the speaker, a Chinese woman pastor, promoted several income-generating ideas that she said had worked in
Indonesia and that she encouraged the mothers to consider for their
future subsistence. This included things like making prawn crackers, raising fish in small plastic ponds, growing fruit trees, and planting vegetables
on urban rooftops. Some women seemed genuinely interested in these
ideas, but others mumbled or whispered that "many people already sell
that in my place," implying that it would not work for them.

During the question-and-answer session, the pastor asked the women for other income-generating ideas. Riana said, "Be a migrant worker." The speaker, having spent the past hour arguing for what they could do *at home*, was evidently displeased with the answer. She had stressed things women could do to earn money or for subsistence while their babies sleep or are at school. Implicit in her presentation was that, when women return, they should—or should want to—stay at home with their children. To her, migration was a problem, not a solution. Riana's response clearly bothered her, but it resonated with much of what I heard from women who were about to go home and from several who had already left (with whom I had stayed in touch). Most of them said that, if there was someone to take care of their children, they would return to work abroad when their children were a little older.

Asked about their future plans, women like Rose, who still hoped or expected to stay in Hong Kong, said things like, "I don't even want to think about it" or "It is too bad to think about." Others were resigned to going home and expected that it might bring some relief from the pressures of Hong Kong. Indah was unusual in her desire to leave Hong Kong because of her isolation and fear of arrest and imprisonment for overstaying; she occasionally fantasized about a future in Nepal with her husband and in-laws, but, if she expressed hope at all, it was more often about returning to her mother's spacious home and warm welcome in Central Java. When Mia's torture claim ended and she knew she would leave soon, she doubled her efforts to save money. Eka was uncharacteristically depressed and in a panic. Despite having shipped three large boxes home, two weighing over seventy kilos and filled with ISS food supplies she had accumulated over the previous few months, including sugar, rice, oil, milk powder, and baby formula, she sent me a series of frantic text messages: "My head aches." "How can I go home with no money no presents?" "How can I support five people?"

Despite the mixed messages of longing and anxiety, I had somehow imagined that those who were finally returning home to their parents would be okay and that returning home would be a relief and a happy ending of sorts. In retrospect, my naivete surprises me, especially since I had written more than a decade earlier about the deep ambivalence of going home for domestic workers (Constable 1999). Yet I listened more easily to mothers' optimism as though it was more significant than their expressions of worry and concern. Given that I knew how long and hard they fought to stay in Hong Kong, why was I so eager to share the fantasy of a welcome return into familial open arms? Once mothers and children return home, life is often very different from the imagined happy family reunion at the airport. What may begin with a warm welcome can turn to cool and angry accusations once the reality of having two or three more mouths to feed sets in, and the mother's savings, if she has any, run out, or her partner's remittances, if he sends any, stop.

MELODRAMAS OF MOBILITY

In September 2012, I went with two friends to visit mothers and babies we knew in Central and East Java. One of my travel companions was Tina, a former domestic worker who had married a local Hong Kong resident, and the other had worked at two NGOs for migrant mothers. The visit was eye-opening. As the following stories show, returning home is not an easy or logical solution, nor does it provide the anticipated closure or happy ending to this book that I had naively imagined. Instead, they illustrate some of the intense and emotional "melodramas of mobility," to borrow a phrase from Nancy Abelmann (2003).

Leaving Sarah Again

During our whirlwind week-long visit, we had planned to visit seven mother's homes, including Tina's. Joy was a very kind-hearted woman in her late twenties and a friend of several women I knew. Three years earlier, she had had a baby in Hong Kong with a Nepalese man. The relationship ended and, tragically, Joy was diagnosed with an advanced and aggressive form of cancer that required many months of hospitalization, intensive treatment, and separation from her baby. During that time, Joy and her daughter, Sarah, earned a place in the heart of many of the other Indonesian mothers and NGO staff. After her treatment, when Joy was in remission, she returned with Sarah to Indonesia. We had planned to see them both, but, when we got to her town in East Java, we learned that Joy was already at a training camp, preparing to go to work in Singapore, and she was not allowed to leave the facility. Instead, she suggested by phone that we visit three-year-old Sarah, who was living with a middle-aged pastor and his wife nearby. During the visit, Sarah would not play with Tina's daughter or with Mia's daughter Annie, whom she had known in Hong Kong. She clung anxiously to her foster parents and to the small bag of gifts we had brought. The couple, who had a spacious house that doubled as a small church, had agreed to take care of Sarah because, as they explained, Joy had no family to help her, she was Christian and a member of their congregation, and their own children had all grown up and left. When we asked if they had adopted Sarah, they said no, because they wanted to give Joy the chance to have Sarah back one day if she could. Although the couple said they would look after Sarah regardless of whether Joy sent money, Joy felt she had little choice but to work abroad. If she stayed, she had no way to support Sarah. Meanwhile, she knew that Sarah was in good hands, forever if necessary.

New Parents for André

Maya, who had been a close friend of Tina's in Hong Kong, had a four-year-old son named André. André's father was a Chinese married man many years Maya's senior. He and Maya met when she was working in the building where he lived. Early in their relationship, he promised to leave his wife, but it became clear later on that he never would. When Maya got pregnant and her visa was about to expire, he helped her and André go to Macau, where he could visit regularly. A year later, Maya was caught by Macau immigration and deported without André. "Blacklisted" in Macau, Maya obtained a new passport with a new name so that she could return there to get André. Meanwhile, friends took care of André, and his father sometimes visited him. When she returned to Macau, Maya's name no longer matched the name on André's birth certificate, so she could not take him home. With the help of two NGOs, a lawyer, and the Indonesian Consulate in Hong Kong, Maya proved her maternity with a DNA test, was granted clemency, and returned with André to Indonesia. She never heard from André's father again; his number was changed, and she could not reach him.

Luckily for Maya, her parents were eager to have her back, and they embraced their grandson. Through a close contact, Maya's parents obtained hospital certification that André was locally born and they were his parents. At additional cost, they also planned to get legal certification to add him to their family card, which would erase his "illegitimacy" and entitle him to free public education. Although some neighbors were aware that Maya was André's mother, they were accepting, and the story and the paperwork would serve their purpose. Shortly before our visit, Maya had left André with her parents and went to work in Jakarta for a month, but the low salary (under US$50 per month) could not compensate for the stress that an active four-year-old placed on her parents, so they all agreed that it was better, for the time being, for Maya to stay and take care of him until he settled down a bit. Meanwhile, Maya's sister who worked in Taiwan sent remittances, and her brother and sister-in-law worked locally, contributing to the family's income and allowing them to install a tile floor, which lent the rural house an air of prosperity. In the end, Maya and André seemed to have managed fairly well. The local birth certificate would save them many problems. Their various sources of income meant they would have food and shelter and that their presence would not place an undue hardship on the family. Eventually, Maya planned to leave André with her parents, go abroad, and remit her earnings again. She hoped one day to meet a man with "serious intentions" but worried that her reputation would make that dream impossible.

Mia and Annie's Return

Mia and Annie (chapter 7) were in a much more difficult situation than Maya and André. Mia's parents were kind and had welcomed them at first, but their financial situation was bad, and they were not pleased that she had converted to Christianity in Hong Kong. Her parents were older than Maya's, and Mia's mother, who earned money selling vegetables in the market, was in poor health. The middle child of many siblings, Mia had young sisters still in school, and the family had no land and little income. The money Mia had saved in Hong Kong was quickly spent. She had hoped to sell cooked food but thus far had only accompanied her mother to sell vegetables during the early morning hours, before Annie woke up.

They had been home a few months, but strong-willed Annie was unwilling to let Mia out of her sight and was fiercely combative toward other children. Mia faced a problem getting papers for Annie. Birth certificates obtained from the Indonesian Consulate in Hong Kong were not accepted by local leaders, who insisted on having local birth and marriage certificates to register a child officially as part of the household. Given that Annie's father was African and she did not look Javanese, it would have been difficult to claim that she belonged to Mia's parents or other relatives. Moreover, Mia's family lacked money for new documents. Mia's mother warned her, for the sake of her reputation (and that of her sisters), not to go out alone and to tell nosy neighbors and local gossips that she was married in Hong Kong and that her husband will come "when he can." This story did not help, and Mia said that she tried to ignore "all the gossip" and "neighbors who say bad things" about Annie. She told herself, "They don't mean anything." Meanwhile, Mia prayed for strength to be a good mother and hoped that one day Annie would adapt well enough that she could go abroad and earn money again. Last I heard, Mia had a falling out with her parents, and she and Annie had gone to live with her grandmother.

Shame and Success

In one region of Central Java, we visited two mothers. One was Megawati, who I had met with Caitrin at the shelter where they were staying during their maternity leave in 2011 (chapter 6). The other was Megawati's friend Anti, who lived about fifteen minutes away by motorcycle, and whom I got to know before she returned home with her daughter in 2011. Despite the fact that both Megawati and Anti were "single mothers," their situations were remarkably different. Megawati was married, but her husband stayed around only long enough to meet his new son and then "ran away," possibly to work in Malaysia. Megawati had not heard from him in almost a year. Despite her husband's abandonment, for which women are normally blamed, Megawati maintained good relations with her family and neighbors; they knew that she was officially married, that the baby was undoubtedly her husband's, and that he had a bad reputation, but Megawati's hard work, resourcefulness, and entrepreneurial skills earned her their respect. With her savings from Hong Kong, supplemented by a loan from her sister who worked abroad, Megawati had started a mushroom farm. Of all the women I knew, she was the only one who had developed a successful and relatively unique income-generating plan. She woke early and worked hard with her toddler strapped to her chest. She had set up thousands of containers in which to grow mushrooms that she sold to restaurants with upscale clientele in the nearby town. Far from being a burden to her family, she was a source of support. The earliest remittances that she initially sent to her husband were apparently "wasted" (he bought a motorcycle and other things that he later lost gambling). Remittances that she had sent to her mother were, by contrast, used to build a small cement house, to buy goats and chickens, and to invest in a small patch of farmland. Although the mushroom farm was not yet at the point where it could generate as much money as Megawati wanted, she reinvested her profits and slowly expanded it. Still, she hoped to go abroad again for "just two years" when the baby was old enough for her to leave, so as to double the size of the mushroom farm and then come home for good. Her mother agreed to take care of the children, on condition that Megawati officially divorce her husband. By 2013, she was working in Singapore.

Before I left for Indonesia, I had been warned by Dewi that Anti's "house is so ugly, it will make you cry." In fact, it was not the poorest house I saw, but it had a dirt floor, as opposed to Megawati's cement one and Maya's tile one, and, instead of newer concrete walls, the walls of Anti's house were made of thin pieces of wood with gaps in between. The roof was thatched, and above her bed was a large plastic sheet to catch the rain during the wet season. The house was spacious but had few of the improvements of those nearby. The mood was also different. Although Anti welcomed us warmly, her smile looked strained. When I had met her almost a year earlier, she was preparing to go home with her nine-month-old. Her Pakistani husband cried and begged her to stay, but she thought it best to leave while her baby was young, and she supported his plan to later join her there. Before she left Hong Kong, Anti learned she was pregnant, and she took medicine to induce miscarriage. She had bled and assumed the pregnancy ended, but, when she returned home, she was still pregnant, and shortly before our visit she gave birth. Her husband, whom she had married in a Muslim ceremony, sent some money but not enough to change her circumstances. Her relatives came in and out of the room to say hello and take a look at us while Anti spoke to us in English about her difficulties. Although she had bought land with her earlier remittances, her grandmother used it and would not let her have it. She told her relatives and neighbors that her husband was coming, but they constantly asked, "When?" and she repeatedly explained how difficult it was for him to leave work and get papers to come to Indonesia. When I asked if she thought he would come, she said his parents were pressuring him to marry in Pakistan. Meanwhile, his asylum claim was rejected, and she expected he would have to return to Pakistan first anyway. Her older child, who had her father's eyes but could otherwise pass as Javanese, seemed to play well with her cousins and neighbors. For that reason, Anti was glad she returned when she did. But when I asked how she was doing, she answered vaguely, "I am in this situation." Anti did not know at that time (or pretended not to) that her husband was about to marry a Chinese woman in Hong Kong. He had begged Dewi not to tell Anti and insisted he still loves her and was "doing this for them"—presumably so as to keep working in Hong Kong and to send them money. When I asked Anti if she wanted me to give her husband photos of her and the children, she first declined, but the next day she asked me to give Dewi a few photographs for him.

Poverty and Isolation

Visiting Indah, Tika, and baby Nina (chapter 1) was the most difficult part of the trip. Earlier in 2012, we had cried tears of joy and thought that the worst of Indah's nightmare was over. Her court date had come up, she appeared in court on the charge of overstaying for more than six years, and the sympathetic judge—who was swayed by her desire to leave Hong Kong, the hardships she had experienced there, and the need for Tika to go to school as soon as possible—gave her a suspended sentence rather than several months in prison and forcing Tika to go to a welfare institution. We breathed many sighs of relief, and Indah headed home as she had long hoped to do.

Indah's parents' house was much smaller, darker, and more dilapidated than Anti's. It was far from the lovely haven she had described and that I had pictured in my mind. Surrounded by a littered, dried-up stream and tobacco fields, with trays of drying tobacco leaves in flat woven trays along the roads, the area looked much poorer than others we had visited. Indah's family had sold their last piece of land, and they were on bad terms with their neighbors. At the tender age of six, Tika, who was no longer as healthy as she had been in Hong Kong, was hit and teased by a neighbor boy, whose mother did nothing to stop him as he taunted her repeatedly, chanting "You have no father" while other children said that she "speaks TV language" (English, which they could not understand). The family's poverty was visible. Their social isolation was also evident. At all the other homes we visited, curious neighbors and friendly relatives had stopped by to say hello or to feed their curiosity, but no one came to Indah's house. The neighbors stared and murmured to themselves as Tika and I walked hand in hand down the dusty lane.

Late in 2012, while I was first drafting this chapter, I called Indah on Skype. She had clearly been crying. "What's wrong?" I asked. "It's awful," she said. "They don't want me. I can't live here [her parents' house] any-more." Her parents, in their utter poverty, after the initial welcome and happy reunion, resented having three more mouths to feed and the appar-ent shame that Indah's presence brought them. Her mother fought with the neighbor whose son taunted Tika and who also said Indah was a bad woman. She shouted at Indah, and the children cried. Indah's brother repeatedly called her "trash" (conveniently forgetting how her earlier remit-tances—now long gone—had helped cover his wedding costs and his sub-sequent divorce). Indah's brother's verbal thrashing finally led her to pack her bag. When I asked where she would go, with Nina still small and Tika having just finished her first day of school, her voice choked again and she explained that her only choice was to stay with a distant male "cousin." Staying with him while her family cooled off, or while she sought a better option, could sully her reputation even more, as her mother had warned her to stay away from him, but Indah had no other options short of sleeping on the street.

The same day I talked to Indah, I heard from Eka, who had been back in Indonesia with her two-year-old for less than a month. The Eka I knew was tough and resilient, angrily brushing off any insults that came her way. But, as we were chatting online, she wrote, "Things not so good. I have been crying and crying all morning cuz it so hard here."

Eka's two-year-old had been fighting with her older children, and Eka's mother was angry and complaining. "She wants me to leave again cuz she says it is too sad and hard to have me here. . . . But where to find money?" The question of "where to find money" is a constant refrain amid the sense that they bring shame and embarrassment and also financial hardship to their families by returning home penniless and with a child. Several months later, Eka was exploring the possibility of going to work in Macau but still agonized over who might care for her child.

TAKING RESPONSIBILITY

The main objective of migrating for work is to invest in the family and lessen its burdens; it is initially a hopeful and optimistic move to live a better life. Although women like Indah and Eka try to convince themselves that it is also "better" or inevitable to leave Hong Kong and go home, and they are encouraged by NGOs, immigration officers, and social workers to "take responsibility" for their children and go home, those who have returned often regret it as yet another example of cruel optimism. It is much harder to support oneself and child, find a job, earn money, enroll children in school or secure their health, education, and citizenship, and be accepted "back home" than it is in Hong Kong. The imagined scenario of warm and supportive family members (as opposed to Hong Kong life that lacks family support) can quickly evaporate. Eka and Mia constantly struggled to find a relative who would take them in and someone who might help with childcare so they could work. Eka, Mia, and Indah were resolved to "be strong" for their children but expressed little hope of how their situations might ever improve except with another stint of labor migration. The other option—one that a few of the younger women seemed hopeful about but those who had been married before were highly skeptical and mistrustful of—was getting married.

Ara and Ina's plans (chapter 3) to live together as "two mothers" and to care for Angela at Ina's place did not last a month. Within a few weeks, Ara left with Angela to join her family, and a few months later both Ara and Ina announced their engagements and posted wedding photos on

Facebook. When I talked to Tina about Ara's and Ina's marriages, she said it was not so surprising in Ina's case: she was a tomboy in Hong Kong but "became a pretty girl" when she went back; moreover, she was not a single mother. Ara's marriage, given her single motherhood, was more of a surprise and a challenge to explain. Several Indonesian friends claimed that Indonesian men will not respect or marry a woman with a child out of wedlock. One Indonesian friend said she does not trust such men. Another said that some men will marry anyone if they think she will go abroad to work and send him money. Both women worried about what would happen to Angela. In 2013, Ara and her husband had a new baby, and Ara told me that "Angela is living far way from us" with a relative, so she does not see her very often.

Hope (chapter 2), whose violent relationship with Ahmed continued for many cycles of abuse and reconciliation, was severely beaten by Ahmed again after I left in 2012. That time, Libby's papers were finally in place, and Hope and Libby left for the Philippines in a desperate hurry. When I spoke with Hope after that, she was "resting and relaxing" at home, but Libby was afraid of the male relatives and screamed when her uncles and grandfather came near her. Hope's sister encouraged her to let Libby settle in and then to come to work with her in Dubai. Still agonizing over leaving, Hope spoke of going back to Hong Kong to visit Ahmed. The day I visited Melinda in Hong Kong in 2013, Hope called her from the Hong Kong airport. She had come on a tourist visa with Libby to see Ahmed, perhaps hoping he had changed. But immigration refused her entry, and she was forced to return to the Philippines. Ahmed reportedly had a new girlfriend but was still pursuing Hope.

Melinda (chapters 2 and 3) missed Hope a lot, and her son Nicholas missed Libby. In 2013, Melinda told me that immigration officials were rounding up overstayers in her area, so her housemates had left, and she and Nicholas were bored and lonely, just waiting. A few months later, she was called for her immigration hearing. She was charged with overstaying and served a sentence (reduced for good behavior) of almost four months. However, things were looking up. She and Niko were in the process of getting divorces so they could legally marry. A lawyer assured them that Melinda would have a good chance of remaining in Hong Kong after she served her time and they got married.

When Gerry encountered Rose (chapter 7) at the first family court meeting, he claimed he had never seen her before and refused to submit a DNA sample. Rose was fit to be tied. Reassured by her lawyer, the next hearing was scheduled, by which time Gerry had submitted a DNA sample that proved he was indeed Barney's father. At almost three years old, Barney obtained a new birth certificate indicating his right of residency. Meanwhile, Gerry urged Rose not to take him to court for a maintenance settlement, offering to support Barney and to build Rose a house in Indonesia if she left Hong Kong. Rose was reluctant to leave Hong Kong and was weighing her lawyer's advice to settle the process formally in court. She wisely told Gerry, "Build the house first and then we'll see."

Lilik and Rashid's torture claims (chapters 2 and 4) were both rejected in 2013, but they had not yet been forced to leave; desperate for more time together, Lilik appealed the torture-claim decision, and, when that was rejected as well, she filed an asylum claim with the UNHCR. As of this writing, her asylum claim was about to be turned down, and she and others hoped to pursue a new sort of claim on the basis of "CIDTP" (cruel, inhuman, degrading treatment or punishment). Such a claim would require that the Immigration Department consider grounds beyond the narrow definition of "torture" in its screening process (Vision First 2013) and could potentially buy Lilik and others at least more time.

As of this writing, two mothers were in Pakistan with their husbands and children. Rumor had it that one of them was unhappy and wanted to return to Indonesia "but her husband won't let her." The other, based on my telephone conversation with her and on her friends' impressions, was very happy there. Several other mothers I knew in Hong Kong were making plans to return home because their torture or asylum claims had been rejected. Caitrin was adamant that it was her "last contract." Her baby back in the Philippines was now walking and talking; her marriage, like Megawati's, had ended. Dewi had another baby. Bethany was divorcing her husband in Java and said she planned to marry Christophe soon. Many others—like Marah and Endri—were still waiting to see what would happen next and were hoping that the process would go as slowly as possible. Marah's partner Kareem (chapters 3 and 4) was arrested for doing illegal work while on an FDH visa, which would likely dash Mohamed's hopes of ever gaining residency, but, in the meantime, Marah's asylum claim was still active, she managed to make ends meet, and Mohamed was doing well in school. At the PathFinders meeting I attended in 2013, there were dozens of new mothers and babies. Bethany, Dewi, and many others were there, too, but their older children were now in preschool.

HEARTLESS POLICIES, HEART-FILLED LIVES

Migrant worker's lives—worldwide—are shaped by a multitude of laws and policies, many of which, on the sending side, are reputedly intended to protect them and, on the receiving side, are meant to protect them and their employers. Hong Kong's laws and policies have unintended negative consequences on *all* migrant workers, not just migrant mothers and their children, though mothers and children illustrate the fault lines in a system of exploited labor most clearly. As I have argued, thousands of Hong Kong–born babies and their mothers are among the worst victims of heartless local policies such as the two-week rule, the live-in requirement, and recruitment agency charges that harm all migrant domestic workers, render them highly vulnerable to abuse, and unintentionally promote overstaying and illegal work. Excluding FDWs from right of abode, charging them for visas, and prohibiting them from working while they pursue cases against their employers, and prohibiting asylum or torture claimants from working, are tied to Hong Kong's uniquely troubled history of inequality paired with its exclusionary lifeboat mentality. More troubling is the ironic fact that Hong Kong grants migrant workers more rights than other Asian destination countries and that it is widely considered to be one of the best destinations in Asia for migrant workers. Despite its unique history, Hong Kong allows us to see the problems with "guest worker" plans more broadly.

Migrant mothers and their babies are certainly not the only casualties of guest-worker systems, but their stories are among the most poignant and troubling and might therefore be effective in illustrating the problems and bringing about change. In the spirit of public anthropology, paired with feminist-ethnographic-activism, my hope is that this study can add to the chorus of voices clamoring to persuade policy makers of the damage caused by rules and regulations that, at best, are ineffective and, at worst, create far more problems than they solve. At the root of the problem is the neoliberal assumption that migrant workers are like charity cases. According to humanitarian work-as-aid reasoning, they should be grateful to have jobs—even if it is for jobs that locals do not want, under conditions locals would not accept, and for far less than locals are paid. I agree with Geraldine Pratt (2012) that domestic workers should ideally be treated like all other "skilled" foreign workers who earn a competitive wage and have routes to becoming residents and citizens. In Hong Kong at present, this is a pipe dream. Until it becomes reality, smaller, critical changes need to be made, such as abolishing the two-week rule, the live-in requirement, and the system of agency fees and loans.

In migrants' home countries, more research is needed to better understand the problems faced by children who are born abroad and brought back to their mother's home countries. Based on the women and children I knew, the problems continue despite supposed protections. According to the Refugee Review Tribunal, the "children of unmarried mothers" in Indonesia are labeled "illegitimate and experience social discrimination" (2010, 1). Although "the legal requirement for women to have a marriage certificate in order to obtain birth certificates for their children is no longer in force," still "in most cases, 'normal' birth certificates will not be issued in the absence of a marriage certificate. The birth certificates of children born to unmarried mothers state either 'born out of wedlock' or 'illegitimate', both of which have a social stigma attached" (3). Even though the "absence of a marriage certificate" is officially no longer a problem for children born locally, my preliminary observations and the reports from mothers suggest it still poses a significant problem for Javanese return migrants and their babies.

The above examples of single mothers whose children were born abroad and who returned to East or Central Java suggest that they face dismal prospects of legally securing locally acceptable birth certificates. Although these women obtained Indonesian birth certificates for their children from the Indonesian Consulate in Hong Kong, local officials were unwilling to accept them. For their children to receive the benefits of citizens, mothers had to get new birth certificates, and they were told they needed marriage certificates to do so, which required that they utilize further creative tactics (De Certeau 1984) to legitimize their children through clever fictions and manipulations, all of which required money—which most did not have. Without these papers, children cannot enroll in school or avail themselves of other public benefits.

THE MIGRATORY CYCLE OF ATONEMENT

As I was told and came to understand more fully after my visit to Indonesia in 2012, there are many reasons why mothers prefer to remain in Hong Kong. It is widely experienced by most foreign domestic workers as a desirable location that is wealthy, beautiful, modern, cosmopolitan, and clean, and it is a place where migrant workers can potentially earn more money than they would at home. If all goes well, in Hong Kong they can take on new and modern identities as wage earners, consumers, and investors in their families' futures. It is a place where women experience new freedom and independence, new gendered and sexual roles away from the surveillance they would experience at home. However, if all does not go well, for a variety of reasons, the situation is very different.

For women who face poor work situations, who are underpaid, or whose contracts are terminated before they can pay back their employment agency costs, their experience in Hong Kong can turn into an escalating cycle of mounting debt and exploitation, and, rather than helping the situation at home, they make it worse. For migrant workers who become mothers in Hong Kong, especially those from Indonesia and to a lesser degree those from the Philippines, the stakes are even higher than for other women migrant workers. Whereas most migrant workers can usually return and continue some semblance of their former lives at home, regardless of how successful they were at earning money, those who become single mothers abroad face deep stigma when they return home. Remaining abroad allows them to escape—at least temporarily—the shame, dishonor, disgrace, and discrimination that await them. Remaining in Hong Kong as long as possible allows children freedom from being teased or shunned as out of wedlock, illegitimate, or biracial. As I have illustrated with their stories, returning to Indonesia or the Philippines without a husband, regardless of whether the woman was married in a religious or civil ceremony in Hong Kong, appears as "single motherhood," which, especially in Java, blurs into the category of "bad girls" and "prostitutes." Having sufficient money, or having a partner who sends money, can be a major extenuating factor. Especially when paired with poverty, however, mothers who return with their foreign-born children can be socially stigmatized, shunned, or even excommunicated.

As described in chapter 7, mothers make good use of asylum/torture claims and overstaying as tactics to provide them with valuable time in Hong Kong. There, in contrast to Java, pregnant women and single mothers can manage and survive on their own. They are still considered "bad women" and relegated to the lower rungs of society in Hong Kong— indeed, some people, including employers, NGO caseworkers, and other workers, express extremely condescending views of FDWs who get pregnant—but part of Hong Kong's modernity includes its anonymity, privacy, and a sense that women can ignore or curse back at anyone who insults them on the street. Women in Hong Kong devise ways to insulate themselves from critical employers, rude remarks from strangers, disapproving looks from fellow migrant workers, or condescending attitudes of caseworkers. In Hong Kong, they can define themselves—despite criticism— as good mothers who can at least support their children. But in Indonesia, disparagement comes from all sides; the forces of shame remain strong and difficult to escape. The only thing to do, as Mia explained, is to stay at home. Or as Lilik—the only Indonesian mother I knew with a college degree and a profession before going to Hong Kong—planned, she would go and live in a different town, spare her family the gossip, and get a job as a teacher. As long as Rashid, or maybe his older, well-educated, Hong Kong resident cousin, came to visit her family to demonstrate the sincerity of their marriage, and as long as she has a job and money to support her son, she could manage.

Given the situation upon return, it is no wonder that so many migrant mothers plan to reenter the migratory cycle. As Claudia Liebelt (2010) describes of Filipino migrant workers in Israel, some practice a circular pattern of repeated migration to the same destination country and home again, whereas others migrate "on and on" looking for ever-better destinations in terms of pay and living and working conditions. Many of the migrant mothers I knew planned to migrate "on and on," but as "single mothers" their goals and motivations may differ somewhat from other migrants. Not only can leaving again potentially resolve their financial problems, converting them from "failed migrants" to economically successful ones, but it can also spare their parents, siblings, and children the stigma of having a bad or shameful daughter, sister, or mother. By reentering what I call the migratory cycle of atonement, women hope to prove to themselves and to others that they are of value and to compensate for earlier migratory failures or disappointments through their remittances.

With their dreams of a better life, money is the lure that initially draws women into global migration and exposes them to its potentially corrupting or liberating transgressions. It is also the means through which such gendered transgressions can be remedied, forgiven and absolved, or mediated. This self-perpetuating global capitalist cycle of inequality, like that of guest workers in many parts of the world, has the power to produce and reinforce differences between privileged citizens and marginal others, to quash hopes and dreams, and to produce ever more precarious lives.

Notes

CHAPTER 1

1. According to the PathFinders 2011 Annual Report (based on Hong Kong Immigration Department data and the 2010 Hong Kong Annual Digest of Statistics), there are approximately 6,000 "migrant pregnant women, mothers and children in Hong Kong" (2012, 8). In early 2013, PathFinders estimated there are over 3,000 pregnancies each year (personal communication, Apr. 2013).

2. The DREAM Act would have granted youth whose undocumented parents brought them to the United States as children, who were "of good moral character," and who had graduated from U.S. high schools a route to permanent residency on condition they served two years in the military or received four years of higher education. In January 2011, conservative U.S. lawmakers proposed legislation opposing the Constitution's Fourteenth Amendment guaranteeing birthright citizenship. They argued that children of undocumented immigrants, so-called "anchor babies," should be excluded.

3. UNICEF Israel called the decision to deport 400 children a "blatant violation" of the International Convention on the Rights of the Child (Haaretz.com, Aug. 1, 2010), and Prime Minister Benjamin Netanyahu described it as a balance between "humanitarian and Zionist" considerations (Haaretz.com, July 25, 2010).

4. The song "Locus World," which expressed hostility toward mainlanders, went viral in 2012. See http://www.youtube.com/watch?v = ueNr7mfFZu8&

feature = player_embedded and http://www.chinasmack.com/2012/stories/
hong-kongers-sing-locust-world-harassing-mainland-tourists.html (accessed
Apr. 3, 2012).

5. According to Schedule 1, paragraph 2, of the Immigration Ordinance (CAP
115), a permanent resident with right of abode in Hong Kong includes the
following:

   a. A Chinese citizen born in Hong Kong before or after the establishment of the
   HKSAR.

   b. A Chinese citizen who has ordinarily resided in Hong Kong for a continuous
   period of not less than 7 years before or after the establishment of the HKSAR.

   c. A person of Chinese nationality born outside Hong Kong before or after the
   establishment of the HKSAR to a parent who, at the time of birth of that person,
   was a Chinese citizen falling within category (a) or (b).

   d. A person not of Chinese nationality who has entered Hong Kong with a valid
   travel document, has ordinarily resided in Hong Kong for a continuous period of
   not less than 7 years and has taken Hong Kong as his or her place of permanent
   residence before or after the establishment of the HKSAR.

   e. A person under 21 years of age born in Hong Kong to a parent who is a
   permanent resident of the HKSAR in category (d) before or after the
   establishment of the HKSAR if at the time of his or her birth, or at any
   later time before he or she attains 21 years of age, one parent has the right
   of abode in Hong Kong.

   f. A person other than those residents in categories (a) to (e), who, before the
   establishment of the HKSAR, had the right of abode in Hong Kong only.

http://www.gov.hk/en/residents/immigration/idcard/roa/faqroa.htm#/q1
(accessed Apr. 24, 2012).

6. As Pnina Werbner and Nina Yuval-Davis have argued (1999, 4), citizenship
must be seen as *more than* "the formal relationship between an individual and
the state"; it should also be seen as a relationship that is "inflected by identity,
social positioning, cultural assumptions, institutional practices, and a sense of
belonging."

CHAPTER 2

1. Hui Yan Yu wrote: "Constable's work on employer-employee household relationships portrays employers as 'demanding,' 'unreasonable' and 'evil', while
employees are shown to be 'subordinated,' 'ill-treated' and 'victims under global
capitalism' (1997). It is not my intention to argue against the main discourse;
nonetheless, there are other perspectives to discuss rather than just the exploitation of foreign domestic helpers. The relationships between foreign domestic
helpers and their employers are not necessarily hostile. In fact, 'normal' relations
are very common" (2011, 3).

2. The term "partial truths" was used by James Clifford in the introduction to *Writing Culture* (1986).

3. The term "overstayers" is used in Hong Kong to describe those who arrive with a visa but who remain after it expires. The terms "undocumented" or "illegal immigrant" are problematic because they conflate those who never had visas with those whose visas have expired (De Genova 2002). These terms are also misnomers when applied to those who hold "recognizance papers," which are given to individuals who surrender to Hong Kong immigration or who file torture or asylum claims.

4. Divorce is permitted in Indonesia but not in the Philippines (see chapter 3).

5. Curiously, in two of three cases in which I was supposedly reputed to be the mother-in-law, two in which the mothers had returned to Indonesia, the children's fathers were not white.

6. Toward the end of my research, when women were heading home with their children and after I visited several mothers and their children in Indonesia, I altered my approach and did give some gifts of money. I also donated funds specifically for mothers' and children's medical needs through one NGO.

7. I offered PathFinders assistance in small ways: I wrote small pieces for their outreach and website, summarized client files and complicated bureaucratic materials, contributed to their photographic and video records, arranged chairs at meetings, folded and distributed clothes, kept records of attendees, and reimbursed women's travel expenses. I introduced them to pro bono doctors, and, for a few Saturdays in 2011, I opened the office for women with newborns who had no other place to meet. I presented my research findings to PathFinders' directors and advisory board, and led two focus groups for PathFinders to solicit input from mothers.

8. Using a similar approach that combines ethnography and policy, Sara Friedman (2010a, 2010b) argues in the case of mainland wives of Taiwan husbands that couples often plead their cases and attempt to realize their goals and desires by working through or confronting existing policies and procedures—sometimes successfully, often not—in an attempt to find justice and also to realize their vision of family. This vision may include engaging with complex bureaucratic procedures.

CHAPTER 3

1. The exchange rate, as of mid-2013, is roughly US$1 to HK$7.8; thus, the agency fee of HK$21,000 is around US$2,700.

2. Abolishing the two-week rule has been a goal of activists since the 1980s. Short of that, extending the time period and allowing women to work while they pursue their cases would help. See Wee and Sim (2005) and Constable (2007,

145–48) for further discussion of problems with the two-week rule, and see Sim and Wee (2010) for its connection to undocumented workers in Macau.

3. Given the minimum allowable wage of HK$30 (US$3.85) per hour (as of May 2013), someone who works six days a week, ten hours a day, would earn roughly US$925 per month. Maximum work hours are not specified in the FDH contract, but most workers report working much more than sixty hours a week. FDWs receive room and board in addition to pay. In September 2012, the minimum monthly wage for new FDH contracts was raised to HK$3,920 (US$500) per month, less than US$10 above the 1996 monthly wage of HK$3,860.

4. See the newspaper *Sing Tao*, July 7, 2012, at http://www.singtao.com /breakingnews/20120707a183810.asp (accessed Oct. 25, 2012).

5. See the *South China Morning Post*, July 12, 2012 at http://joannachiu. wordpress.com/2012/07/12/helpers-demand-right-to-live-away-from-employ-ers (accessed Oct. 25, 2012).

6. See http://news.tvb.com/local/51bee6c56db28cc62f000003 (accessed June 20, 2013).

7. To "throw away" a baby is a common euphemism for abortion.

8. This includes women I talked with informally about various research-related topics, sometimes at social events, but from whom I did not systematically collect all of the basic demographic information in interviews.

9. Immigration Department figures on marriage do not indicate occupation, but since all but 6,000 of the 153,000 Filipinos in Hong Kong in December 2011 were FDWs, we might expect that a significant number of these marriages involve current or former FDWs. Relatively few marriages involving Filipinas were registered with the Philippine Consulate, and, of those registered, only a small number voluntarily identified their occupation as HSWs (household service workers, the Philippine government term). Babies registered with the Philippine Consulate between 2008 and 2011 averaged 443 per year, of whom 112 of their mothers identified themselves as HSWs (personal communication, Apr. 23, 2012).

10. In 2013, a new agency plan to import 200 Bangladeshi domestic workers was approved. The first eleven arrived in May 2013, but within a month nine had already been terminated. See http://news.hkheadline.com/dailynews/content_ hk/2013/06/03/240353.asp (accessed June 7, 2013).

11. Wang (2011) draws from the Hong Kong Census and Statistics Department's 2006 by-census. (In Hong Kong, a major census is conducted every ten years; the smaller by-census is conducted between the censuses.)

12. Some sources report twenty-one as the minimum age for those working abroad for an individual employer (e.g., domestic workers), but most Indonesian women reported eighteen as the minimum required age. Silvey (2006) writes of a migrant worker who was sixteen when she went to work but claimed she was eighteen. This was common among the women I knew.

13. Surveys found that between 28 and 59 percent of Indonesian FDWs had worked in another country before Hong Kong (ATKI 2005; AMC et al. 2007).

14. A 1991 survey lists the average age of Filipina FDWs as thirty-three and Indonesians as twenty-seven (AMC 2001). More recent surveys of Indonesian FDWs say that over a third are twenty-four or younger (AMC et al. 2007; ATKI 2005).

15. In one case, this created a problem when the woman whose papers were used went to work in Hong Kong as well. Both women (who were neighbors) were regularly questioned by immigration officials when they entered Hong Kong, but both feigned complete ignorance.

16. When I told Indonesian women I would use pseudonyms in my writing, some suggested I use their "real names" because no one in Hong Kong would know them by that name. I have not done so.

17. Another survey lists 52 percent of Indonesians as not yet married, 43 percent as married, 3 percent as divorced, and 2 percent as widowed (AMC et al. 2007; see also ATKI 2005).

18. See Hong Kong Judiciary, "How to Apply for Divorce," available at http://www.judiciary.gov.hk/en/crt_services/pphlt/html/divorce.htm (accessed Nov. 10, 2012).

CHAPTER 4

1. See http://www.scmp.com/article/641644/fyi-what-happened-hong-kongs-vietnamese-refugee-community (accessed Dec. 1, 2012).

2. Although China is a signatory to the 1951 Geneva Convention or Protocol Relating to the Status of Refugees, Hong Kong is not bound by it. The United Nations High Commissioner for Refugees (UNHCR) suboffice in Hong Kong processes asylum claims and third-country resettlement for refugees.

3. Some renew their visas or exit to China or Macau to do so, sometimes every two weeks or more often. Given the time, possible expense, and risk that the visa will not be renewed, some nonresidents simply overstay and work as long as they can.

4. For an interview with Kylie Uebergang, co-founder and director of Path-Finders, about sexual abuse of FDWs by employers, listen to "Kwok Talk" Radio 3 RTHK at http://programme.rthk.org.hk/channel/radio/programme.php?name = %2Fkwok_talk&d = 2013–01–25&p = 5160&e = 205547&m = episode (accessed June 10, 2013).

5. An El Shaddai church group I visited in 2009 had several such couples. In 2012, I spoke to members of a Filipino drivers' association, many of whose members were married to other domestic workers.

6. This was later reversed on appeal. See chapter 6.

7. A variation of this that I encountered among women was a preference for angry, jealous partners (who care) as opposed to partners who showed no interest.

8. They also criticized a woman I knew who had appeared in a television documentary called "Lives in Limbo." The woman was one of several former FDWs depicted in the program who got pregnant and whose boyfriend had left Hong Kong. Rather than criticize him for leaving her, George criticized the woman because "she didn't even know his full name!" According to George, she hardly knew him but had allowed him to sleep with her, so she had no one to blame but herself.

CHAPTER 5

1. One Indonesian woman's sister had been raped in Central Java and became pregnant as a result. The "resolution" was to force the man to marry her. The marriage, not surprisingly, did not last long.

2. I do not have permission to quote from these websites, so I am summarizing or paraphrasing.

3. Among poor and rural married women in Indonesia who do not use contraception, reasons include "opposition to family planning by the respondent or her spouse, religious prohibitions and lack of knowledge about contraceptive methods" (Schoemaker 2005, 109) and attitudinal factors such as "desire for more children, opposition to family planning and concerns about the health effects of contraceptive methods" (112).

4. See http://www.famplan.org.hk/fpahk/en/template1.asp?style = template1.asp&content = sexual/what.asp (accessed May 2, 2011).

5. I write "give for adoption," not "give up for adoption," because it better conveys the women's sense that they are giving a gift rather than surrendering a burden.

CHAPTER 6

1. According to the Immigration Department, there were approximately 1,850 registered marriages of Filipino women and 980 of Indonesian women between 2007 and 2011. In 2007 the number was 180 and 70, respectively, and by 2010 it had risen to 460 and 270 (S. Lai, personal communication, Mar. 12, 2012). A majority of these women were probably former FDWs, given that the highest numbers of Filipinos and Indonesians in Hong Kong are FDWs, but this is not certain.

2. As discussed below, the meaning of "ordinary residence" has been debated in court. Children deemed to be "ordinarily resident" in Hong Kong who obtained right of abode appear to fit several criteria. They had visas allowing them to stay

as residents (not visitors); Hong Kong was their home and place of residence; and they spoke the local language (Cantonese) and attended local schools.

3. As noted in chapter 1, I draw from Agamben's distinction (1998) between bare existence and good life, the latter of which is made possible by the role of the state-maintained distinction between noncitizen women household workers and citizens whose good life depends on the exclusion of others.

CHAPTER 7

1. Many women are aware that the sentence for overstaying for less than two years is normally two months' suspended sentence (no custodial time). This may be incentive to remain for up to two years if one overstays. The sentence is more, and not likely suspended, if one is caught doing illegal work while overstaying.

2. Since Hong Kong does not accept refugees permanently, they await third-country resettlement.

3. See http://www.unhcr.org/3b66c2aa10.html (accessed Oct. 21, 2012).

4. See http://www.hrweb.org/legal/cat.html (accessed May 2, 2011).

5. The Immigration Department notes, "In 2008, a number of large-scale litigation cases were instituted by legally-aided torture claimants. There were judicial review applications challenging, inter alia, the Administration's policy of not providing torture claimants with legal representation during the torture claim screening process, not allowing the presence of legal representation in the process of torture claim interview, etc. On December 5, 2008, the Court of First Instance (CFI) in its judgment which was not in the Administration's favour held, inter alia, that the then policies/screening process for torture claim were unlawful and did not meet the high standards of fairness required. The screening of torture claims had been suspended for devising enhanced procedures by the Administration. On December 24, 2009, the screening of torture claims was resumed under an enhanced screening mechanism, following an agreement reached between the Administration and the Duty Lawyer Service on the administrative arrangements of a pilot scheme of providing publicly-funded legal assistance to torture claimants" (http://www.immd.gov.hk/a_report_09-10/eng/ch4/#b3, accessed Oct. 23, 2012).

6. Judgment, June 8, 2004, Court of Final Appeal of the Hong Kong SAR, Final Appeal No. 16 of 2003 (Civil) (On appeal from CACV No. 211 OF 2002) between Secretary for Security and Sakthevel Prabakar. See http://legalref.judiciary.gov.hk/lrs/common/search/search_result_detail_frame.jsp?DIS = 40511&QS = %24%28torture%7Cclaim%29&TP = JU (accessed Oct. 21, 2012).

7. "During the year . . . there were judicial review applications challenging, inter alia, the Administration's policy of not granting extension of stay to torture claimants and not allowing the screened-in torture claimants to work in Hong

Kong. The ruling of the court upholds the Government's policy of not granting extension of stay to torture claimants and not allowing screened-in torture claimants and mandated refugees to take up employment generally. Furthermore, the new Section 38AA of the Immigration Ordinance, which came into effect on November 14, 2009, provides that it is an offence for any illegal immigrants or any persons under a removal order or a deportation order to take any paid or unpaid employment, or to establish or join in any business" (Immigration Department 2011).

8. One journalist estimated, perhaps tongue in cheek, that given the current rate of reviewing torture claims it would take thirty-one years to process all the claimants (see Tsang 2011).

9. The Immigration Department Year-end Reports note that a high percentage of torture claims were submitted after the person was arrested, under removal or deportations orders, or rejected by the UNHCR.

10. According to April and others, a variety of nationalities of women were housed together, but mainland Chinese women were housed separately.

11. A few days later, I brought "boy clothes" from PathFinders for April's baby, which Melinda delivered to her.

12. See http://www.isshk.org/e/customize/migrants_assistance.asp (accessed June 21, 2013).

13. For a 2013 report about complaints against the ISS, see http://visionfirstnow.org/2013/06/21/tvb-exposes-iss-suspicious-contracts/ (accessed June 21, 2013). In Sept. 2013, complaints against the inadequate housing of asylum seekers mounted. See http://www.scmp.com/news/hong-kong/article/1305929/un-concern-plight-hong-kong-asylum-seekers-living-squalor?page=all and http://www.scmp.com/news/hong-kong/article/1315388/government-admits-putting-asylum-seekers-homes-not-fit-live. The stream of vehement criticism of the ISS led the head of the Council for Social Service to call for more competitive bidding for service provision. See http://www.scmp.com/news/hong-kong/article/1330532/outgoing-social-services-chief-urges-break-asylum-welfare-contract (accessed Oct. 25, 2013).

14. If a refugee is arrested for illegal work, it can potentially cause a country to refuse him resettlement.

15. In one paternity case I followed, the mother reported that her child's father, a Pakistani Muslim, told the judge that he would need to consult with his imam in the United Arab Emirates before agreeing to a DNA test, and the judge reportedly replied, "Did you check with your imam before you fucked her as well?"

16. In 2013, however, I was told this was probably no longer the case: there were rumors of a mother who was given the choice of taking her H.K. resident child home with her or leaving him at the Po Leung Kuk welfare institution.

References

Abelmann, Nancy. 2003. *The Melodrama of Mobility: Women, Talk and Class in Contemporary South Korea*. Honolulu: University of Hawaii Press.

Abu-Lughod, Lila. 1990. Can There Be a Feminist Ethnography? *Women and Performance: A Journal of Feminist Theory* 5 (1): 7–27.

Agamben, Giorgio. 1998. Homo Sacer: Sovereign Power and Bare Life. Translated by Daniel Heller-Roazen. Stanford: Stanford University Press.

AMC (Asian Migrant Centre). 2001. *Baseline Research on Gender and Racial Discrimination towards Filipino, Indonesian, and Thai Domestic Helpers in Hong Kong*. Hong Kong: AMC, ADWU, Forum of Filipino Reintegration and Savings Groups, IMWU, Thai Women's Association.

AMC (Asian Migrant Centre), IMWU (Indonesian Migrant Workers Union), and KOTKIHO (The Hong Kong Coalition of Indonesian Migrant Workers Organization). 2007. *Underpayment II. The Continuing Systematic Extortion of Indonesian Domestic Workers in Hong Kong: An In Depth Study of Indonesian Labor Migration in Hong Kong*. Hong Kong: AMC.

Appadurai, Arjun. 2006. *Fear of Small Numbers: An Essay on the Geography of Anger*. Durham: Duke University Press.

Arendt, Hannah. 1958. *The Human Condition*. Chicago: University of Chicago Press.

ATKI (Association of Indonesian Migrant Workers in Hong Kong). 2005. *Second Survey of the Conditions of Indonesian Migrant Workers in Hong Kong*. Hong Kong: ATKI.

Benhabib, Seyla, and Judith Resnick. 2009. Introduction: Citizenship and Migration Theory Engendered. In *Migrations and Mobilities: Citizenship, Borders and Gender*, edited by S. Benhabib and J. Resnick, 1–44. New York: NYU Press.

Benitez, Mary Ann. 2006a. Filipino Maid's Children Win Residency South China Morning Post. Feb. 22.

———. 2006b. Why All the Fuss, Asks New Resident? South China Morning Post Feb 20.

Berlant, Laurent. 2011. *Cruel Optimism*. Durham: Duke University Press.

Bernstein, Elizabeth. 2007. *Temporarily Yours: Intimacy, Authenticity, and the Commerce of Sex*. Chicago: University of Chicago Press.

Bhabha, Jacqueline. 2009. The 'Mere Fortuity of Birth'? Children, Mothers, Borders, and the Meaning of Citizenship. In *Migrations and Mobilities: Citizenship, Borders and Gender*, edited by S. Benhabib and J. Resnick, 187–227. New York: NYU Press.

Biehl, João. 2005. *Vita: Life in a Zone of Social Abandonment*. Berkeley: University of California Press.

Blackburn, Susan. 2004. *Women and the State in Modern Indonesia*. Cambridge, Engl.: Cambridge University Press.

Bosniak, Linda. 2001. Denationalizing Citizenship. In *Citizenship Today: Global Perspectives and Practices*, edited by T. Alexander Aleinkoff and Douglas Klusmeyer, 237–52. Washington, D.C.: Carnegie Endowment for International Peace, 237–52.

———. 2009. Citizenship, Noncitizenship, and the Transnationalization of Domestic Work. In *Migrations and Mobilities: Citizenship, Borders and Gender*, edited by S. Benhabib and J. Resnick, 127–56. New York: NYU Press.

Bourgois, Philippe, and Jeffrey Schonberg. 2009. *Righteous Dopefiend*. Berkeley: University of California Press.

Bowring, P. 2011. Asia's Baby Shortage. *Asia Sentinel*, Sept. 20. http://www.asiasentinel.com (accessed Feb. 20, 2012).

Butler, Judith. 2004. *Precarious Life: The Power of Mourning and Violence*. New York: Verso Press.

Butler, Judith, and Gayatri Chakravorty Spivak. 2007. *Who Sings the Nation State?* London: Seagull Books.

Castles, Stephen. 1986. The Guest-Worker in Western Europe: An Obituary. *International Migration Review* 20 (4): 761–78.

Cheung, Andrew, CJHC. 2012. CACV 204/2011 in the High Court of the Hong Kong Special Administrative Region Court of Appeal, Civil Appeal No. 204 of 2011 (on appeal from HCAL 124/2010) Between Vallejos Evangeline Banao Also Known as Vallejos Evangeline B and Commissioner of Registration. http://legalref.judiciary.gov.hk/lrs/common/ju/judgment.jsp (accessed Mar. 29, 2012).

Clifford, James. 1986. Introduction: Partial Truths. In *Writing Culture*, edited by James Clifford and George Marcus, 1–26. Berkeley: University of California Press.

Constable, Nicole. 1996. Jealousy, Chastity and Abuse: Chinese Maids and Foreign Helpers in Hong Kong. *Modern China* 22 (4): 448–79.

———. 1997. Sexuality and Discipline among Filipina Domestic Workers in Hong Kong. *American Ethnologist* 24 (3): 539–58.

———. 1999. At Home, But Not at Home: Filipina Narratives of Ambivalent Returns. *Cultural Anthropologist* 14 (2): 203–28.

———. 2000. Dolls, T-Bird, and Ideal Workers: The Negotiation of Filipino Identity in Hong Kong. In *Home and Hegemony: Domestic Service and Identity Politics in South and Southeast Asia*, edited by K. Adams and S. Dickey, 221–47. Ann Arbor: University of Michigan Press.

———. 2003. A Transnational Perspective on Divorce and Marriage: Filipina Wives and Workers' Identities. *Global Studies in Culture and Power* 10 (2): 163–80.

———. 2007. *Maid to Order in Hong Kong: Stories of Migrant Workers*. Ithaca, N.Y.: Cornell University Press.

———. 2009. Migrant Workers and the Many States of Protest in Hong Kong. *Critical Asian Studies* 41 (1): 143–64.

———. 2010. Telling Tales of Migrant Workers in Hong Kong: Transformations of Faith, Life Scripts, and Activism. *Asia Pacific Journal of Anthropology* 11 (3): 311–27.

———. Forthcoming *a*. Migrant Workers, Hong Kong Law, and the Art of Temporary Family Formation. *Oñati Socio-Legal Series* (online journal).

———. Forthcoming *b*. Temporary Shelter in the Shadows: Migrant Mothers and Torture Claims in Hong Kong. In *Encountering the State: Intimate Labor Migrations across Asia*, edited by Pardis Mahdavi and Sara Friedman (under review).

Cortes, Patricia, and Jessica Pan. 2009. Outsourcing Household Production: Foreign Domestic Helpers and Native Labor Supply in Hong Kong. Unpublished paper, University of Chicago, Booth School of Business.

De Certeau, Michel. 1984. *The Practice of Everyday Life*. Translated by Stephen F. Rendall. Berkeley: University of California Press.

De Genova, N. 2002. Migrant "Illegality" and Deportability in Everyday Life. *Annual Review of Anthropology* 31: 419–47.

Desjarlais, Robert. 2003. *Sensory Biographies: Lives and Deaths among Nepal's Yolmo Buddhists*. Berkeley: University of California Press.

Fassin, Didier. 2012. *Humanitarian Reason: A Moral History of the Present*. Berkeley: University of California Press.

French, Caroline. 1986a. Filipina Domestic Workers in Hong Kong. Ph.D. diss., University of Surrey.

———. 1986b. The Filipina in Hong Kong: A Preliminary Survey. Occasional Paper #11. Centre for Hong Kong Studies, Chinese University of Hong Kong.

Friedman, Sara L. 2010a. Determining "Truth" at the Border: Immigration Interviews, Chinese Marital Migrants, and Taiwan's Sovereignty Dilemmas. *Citizenship Studies* 14 (2): 167–83.

———. 2010b. Marital Immigration and Graduated Citizenship: Post-Naturalization Restrictions on Mainland Chinese Spouses in Taiwan. *Pacific Affairs* 83 (1): 73–93.

Frost, Stephen. 2004. Building Hong Kong: Nepalese Labour in the Construction Sector. *Journal of Contemporary Asia* 34 (3): 364–76.

Geertz, Clifford. 1973. *The Interpretation of Cultures*. New York: Basic Books.

Guevarra, Anna R. 2006. Managing "Vulnerabilities" and "Empowering" Migrant Filipina Workers: The Philippines' Overseas Employment Program. *Social Identities* 12 (5): 523–41.

Guttmacher Institute. 2008. Abortion in Indonesia. *In Brief 2008* (Series 2). New York: Guttmacher Institute.

———. 2010a. Facts on Barriers to Contraceptive Use in the Philippines. *In Brief 2010* (May). New York: Guttmacher Institute.

———. 2010b. *Indonesia: Summary of Available Indicators. Contraception*. New York: Guttmacher Institute.

———. 2010c. *Philippines: Summary of Available Indicators. Contraception*. New York: Guttmacher Institute.

Hawwa, Sithi. 2000a. From Cross to Crescent: The Religious Conversion of Filipina Domestic Helpers in Hong Kong. *Islam and Christian–Muslim Relations* 11 (3): 347–67.

———. 2000b. From Cross to Crescent: The Religious Conversion of Filipina Domestic Helpers in Hong Kong. Master's thesis, Hong Kong University of Science and Technology.

HCAL20. 2006. Maura Juliet A. Raquiza v. The Department of Immigration 2006-July-11. http://legalref.judiciary.gov.hk/lrs/common/search/search_result_detail_frame.jsp?DIS = 53222&QS = %2B&TP = JU (accessed Oct. 5, 2012).

HCAL28. 2011. Comilang Milagros Tecson and others v. Commissioner of Registration and others, 2012-June-15. http://legalref.judiciary.gov.hk/lrs/common/search/search_result_detail_frame.jsp?DIS = 82223&QS = %2B&TP = JU (accessed Oct. 5, 2012).

Immigration Department. 2008. Immigration Department Year-End Briefing. http://www.immd.gov.hk/ehtml/20090119.htm (accessed Oct. 23, 2012).

———. 2009. Immigration Department Year-End Briefing. http://www.immd.gov.hk/ehtml/20100125.htm (accessed Oct. 23, 2012).

———. 2010. Immigration Department Year-End Briefing. http://www.immd.gov.hk/ehtml/20110113.htm (accessed Oct. 23, 2012).

———. 2011. Immigration Department Year-End Briefing. http://www.immd. gov.hk/ehtml/20120120.htm (accessed Oct. 23, 2012).

Immigration Ordinance. 2012 [1997]. CAP 115. http://www.legislation.gov.hk/ eng/home.htm. (accessed Oct. 5, 2012).

Johnson, Mark, and Pnina Werbner. 2010. Introduction: Diasporic Encounters, Sacred Journeys: Ritual, Normativity and the Religious Imagination among International Asian Migrant Women. In a special issue, edited by Mark Johnson and Pnina Werbner, of *Asia Pacific Journal of Anthropology* 11 (3–4): 205–18.

Juarez, Fatima, Josefina Cabigon, Susheela Singh, and Rubina Hussain. 2005. The Incidence of Induced Abortion in the Philippines: Current Level and Recent Trends. *International Family Planning Perspectives* 31 (3): 140–49.

Julve, S. D. 2007. Domestic Helpers Not Entitled to Right of Abode, Says CA. *The Sun*, mid-Aug. http://www.sunweb.com.hk/Story.asp?hdnStoryCode = 4957& (accessed Apr. 10, 2012).

Killias, Olivia. 2010. "Illegal" Migration as Resistance: Legality, Morality and Coercion in Indonesian Domestic Worker Migration to Malaysia. *Asian Journal of Social Science* 38: 897–914.

Knowles, Caroline, and Douglas Harper. 2009. *Hong Kong: Migrant Lives, Landscapes, and Journeys*. Chicago: University of Chicago Press.

Labour Department. 2012. Practical Guide for the Employment of Domestic Helpers. http://www.labour.gov.hk/eng/public/wcp/FDHguide.pdf (accessed Nov. 17, 2012).

Lan, Pei-Chia. 2006. *Global Cinderellas: Migrant Domestics and Newly Rich Employers in Taiwan*. Durham: Duke University Press.

Lee, Maggy. 2007. Women's Imprisonment as a Mechanism of Migration Control in Hong Kong. *British Journal of Criminology* 47: 847–60.

Lee, Peggy W. Y., and Carole Petersen. 2006. Forced Labour and Debt Bondage: A Study of Indonesian and Filipina Migrant Domestic Workers. Occasional Paper #16, Centre for Comparative and Public Law, University of Hong Kong. http://www.law.hku.hk/ccpl/pub/Documents/16-LeePetersen.pdf.

Liebelt, Claudia. 2010. On Sentimental Orientalists, Christian Zionists, and Working Class Cosmopolitans: Filipina Domestic Worker's Journeys to Israel and Beyond. In *Migrant Workers in Asia: Distant Divides and Intimate Connections*, edited by N. Constable, 13–26. New York: Routledge Press.

Lindquist, Johan. 2009. Petugas Lapangan, Field Agent. In *Figures of Indonesian Modernity*, edited by Joshua Barker and Johan Lindquist, 55–57. *Indonesia* 87 (Apr.).

———. 2010. Labour Recruitment, Circuits of Capital and Gendered Mobility: Reconceptualizing the Indonesian Migration Industry. *Pacific Affairs* 83 (1): 115.

Lo, Alex. 2012. An Injustice to Our Most Oppressed Expats. *South China Morning Post*, Mar. 30. http://www.scmp.com/portal/site/SCMP (accessed Mar. 30, 2012).

Luibheid, Eithne. 2004a. Childbearing Against the State? Asylum Seeker Women in the Irish Republic. *Women's Studies International Forum* 27: 335–49.

———. 2004b. Heteronormativity and Immigration Scholarship: A Call for Change. *GLQ: A Journal of Lesbian and Gay Studies* 10 (2): 227–35.

Marshall, T. H. 1998. Citizenship and Social Class. In *The Citizenship Debates: A Reader*, edited by G. Shafir, 93–112. Minneapolis: University of Minnesota Press.

Mathews, Gordon. 2011. *Ghetto at the Center of the World: Chungking Mansions Hong Kong*. Chicago: University of Chicago Press.

Mission for Migrant Workers. 2012. *Mission for Migrant Workers Data and Statistics 2011*. Hong Kong: FMW Ltd, St. Johns's Cathedral.

Moy, P. 2012. Filipino Mother Challenges Refusal to Extend Her Stay. *South China Morning Post*, May 9. http://archive.scmp.com/showarticles.php (accessed Aug. 28, 2012).

Newendorp, Nicole. 2008. *Uneasy Reunions: Immigration, Citizenship, and Family Life in Post-1997 Hong Kong*. Stanford: Stanford University Press.

Ngo, J. 2012. HK's One Child Problem. *South China Morning Post*, Apr. 10. http://www.scmp.com/portal/site/SCMP (accessed July 15, 2012).

O'Connor, Paul. 2012. *Islam and Hong Kong: Muslims and Everyday Life in China's World City*. Hong Kong: Hong Kong University Press.

Ong, Aihwa. 2009. A Bio-Cartography: Maids, Neo-Slavery, and NGOs. In *Migrations and Mobilities: Citizenship, Borders and Gender*, edited by S. Benhabib and J. Resnick, 157–84. New York: NYU Press.

Ornellas, M. 2012. Hong Kong–Mainland China Couples' Struggles for Reproductive Rights: Initial Findings and Implications. Paper presented at Chinese University of Hong Kong, Friday Seminar Series, Jan. 20.

Oswin, N. 2010. The Modern Model Family at Home in Singapore: A Queer Geography. *Transactions of the Institute of British Geographers* 35: 256–68.

———. 2012. The Queer Time of Creative Urbanism: Family, Futurity and Global City Singapore. *Environment and Planning* A44: 1624–40.

Palmer, Wayne. 2010. Costly Inducements: Pocket Money Given to Intending Migrant Domestic Workers Comes at a Price . *Inside Indonesia* 100 (Apr.–June). http://www.insideindonesia.org/feature-editions/costly-inducements.

Parent and Child Ordinance. 1997. CAP 429. http://www.legislation.gov.hk/eng/home.htm (accessed Oct. 25, 2013).

Parreñas, Rhacel. 2001. *Servants of Globalization: Women, Migration, and Domestic Work*. Stanford: Stanford University Press.

————. 2005. *Children of Global Migration: Transnational Families and Gendered Woes*. Stanford: Stanford University Press.

PathFinders. 2012. PathFinders 2011 Annual Report. Tai Kok Tsui, Kowloon, Hong Kong: PathFinders.

Pessar, P. 1999. Engendering Migration Studies. *American Behavioral Scientist* 42: 153–84.

Pratt, Geraldine. 2012. *Families Apart: Migrant Mothers and the Conflicts of Labor and Love*. Minneapolis: University of Minnesota Press.

Puar, Jasbir. 2012. Precarity Talk: A Virtual Roundtable with Lauren Berlant, Judith Butler, Bojana Cvejić, Isabell Lorey, Jasbir Puar, and Ana Vujanović. *TDR: The Drama Review* 56 (4): 163–77.

Rafael, Vincente. 2000. *White Love and Other Events in Filipino History*. Durham: Duke University Press.

Refugee Review Tribunal, Australian Government. 2010. Country Advice Indonesia. IDN37051. Women-Single Mothers-Children-Female Headed Households. http://www.refworld.org/docid/4f4b82cc2.html (accessed June 20, 2013).

Robinson, Kathryn. 2000. Gender, Islam, and Nationality: Indonesian Domestic Servants in the Middle East. In *Home and Hegemony: Domestic Service and Identity Politics in South and Southeast Asia*, edited by K. Adams and S. Dickey, 249–82. Ann Arbor: University of Michigan Press.

Rodriguez, Robyn Magalit. 2010. *Migrants for Export: How the Philippine State Brokers Labor to the World*. Minneapolis: University of Minnesota Press.

Rosaldo, Renato. 1994. Cultural Citizenship and Educational Democracy. *Cultural Anthropology* 9 (3): 402–11.

Sayres, Nicole J. 2007. *An Analysis of the Situation of Filipino Domestic Workers*. Manila, Philippines: International Labour Organization.

Schoemaker, Juan. 2005. Contraceptive Use Among the Poor in Indonesia. *International Family Planning Perspectives* 31 (3): 106–14.

Scott, James L. 1985. *Weapons of the Weak: Everyday Forms of Peasant Resistance*. New Haven: Yale University Press.

————. 1998. *Seeing Like a State: How Certain Schemes to Improve the Human Condition Have Failed*. New Haven: Yale University Press.

Shipper, Apichai. 2010. Introduction: Politics of Citizenship and Transnational Gendered Migration in East and Southeast Asia. In a special issue of *Pacific Affairs* 83 (1): 11–29.

Silvey, Rachel. 2004. Transnational Domestication: Indonesian Domestic Workers in Saudi Arabia. *Political Geography* 23: 245–64.

————. 2006. Consuming the Transnational Family: Indonesian Migrant Domestic Workers to Saudi Arabia. *Global Networks* 6 (1): 23–40.

————. 2007. Unequal Borders: Indonesian Transnational Migrants at Immigration Control. *Geopolitics*, 12: 265–79.

————. 2009. TKW (Tenaga Kerja Wanita), the Overseas Female Labor Migrant. In *Figures of Indonesian Modernity*, edited by Joshua Barker and Johan Lindquist, 53–55. *Indonesia* 87 (Apr.).

Sim, Amy. 2009. The Sexual Economy of Desire: Girlfriends, Boyfriends and Babies among Indonesian Women Migrants in Hong Kong. http://www. wemc.com.hk/web/rf/Sim_Sexual_Economy_of_Desire.pdf (accessed Nov. 20, 2011).

Sim, Amy, and Vivienne Wee. 2010. Undocumented Indonesian Workers in Macau: The Human Outcome of Colluding Interests. In *Migrant Workers in Asia*, edited by N. Constable, 145–63. New York: Routledge.

South Asian Asylum Seekers Withdraw Torture Claims in Hong Kong. 2010. *Earth Times*, Jan. 5. http://www.earthtimes.org/articles/news/302135,south-asian-asylum-seekers-withdraw-torture-claims-in-hong-kong.html (accessed Feb. 5, 2011). See also http://news.monstersandcritics.com/asiapacific/news/article_1523288.php/South-Asian-asylum-seekers-with-draw-torture-claims-in-Hong-Kong (accesssed Nov. 10, 2012).

Soysal, Yasemin. 1994. *The Limits of Citizenship: Migrants and Post-national Membership in Europe*. Chicago: University of Chicago Press.

Stacey, Judith. 1988. Can There Be a Feminist Ethnography? *Women's Studies International Forum* 11 (1): 21–27.

Suzuki, Nobue. 2010. Outlawed Children: Japanese Filipino Children, Legal Defiance, and Ambivalent Citizenships. *Pacific Affairs* 83 (1): 31–50.

Tam, Siumi Maria. 2010. Dealing with Double Marginalization: Three Generations of Nepalese Women in Hong Kong. *Asian Journal of Women's Studies* 16 (2): 32–51.

Thompson, E. P. 1975. *Whigs and Hunters: The Origin of the Black Act*. New York: Penguin Books.

Torrevillas, D. M. 1996. Violence against Filipina OCWs: The Flor Contemplacion and Sara Balabagan Cases. In *Filipino Women Migrant Workers: At the Crossroads and Beyond Beijing*, edited by R. P. Beltran and G. F. Rodriguez, 46–68. Quezon City, Philippines: Giraffe Books.

Tsang, Phyllis. 2011. Cases Pending as Torture Claimants Prove Slow to Screen. Updated on Jan. 14, 2011. http://visionfirstnow.org/2011/01/14/6700-cases-pending-as-torture-claimants-prove-slow-to-screen (posted on Vision First website, accessed Feb. 5, 2011).

Ullah, A. K. M. Ahsan. 2010. Premarital Pregnancies among Migrant Workers: The Case of Domestic Helpers in Hong Kong. *Asian Journal of Asian Studies* 16 (1): 62–90.

————. 2013. Bangladeshi migrant workers in Hong Kong: Adaptation strategies in an ethnically distant destination. *International Migration* 51 (2): 165–80.

Van Walsum, Sarah K. 2009. Transnational Mothering, National Immigration Policy, and European Law: The Experience of the Netherlands. In *Migra-*

tions and Mobilities: Citizenship, Borders and Gender, edited by S. Benhabib and J. Resnick, 228–51. New York: NYU Press.

Vision First. 2013. Immigration Department's Refusal to Entertain CIDTP Claims. http://visionfirstnow.org/2013/06/10/immigration-departments-refusal-to-entertain-cidtp-claims/ (accessed Nov. 5, 2013).

Visweswaran, Kamala. 1994. *Fictions of Feminist Ethnography*. Minneapolis: University of Minnesota Press.

Wang, Hongbo. 2011. The Use of Foreign Domestic Helpers in Hong Kong: A Discrete Analysis. Presentation for International Conference on Social Inequality and Mobility in Chinese Societies: Towards a Comparative Study, Dec. 17.

Watson, Rubie S. 2010. The Anatomy of Fertility Decline: Unmarried, No Children in Hong Kong. *Harvard China Review* 6 (1): 31–43.

Wee, Vivienne, and Amy Sim. 2005. Hong Kong as a Destination for Migrant Domestic Workers. In *Asian Women as Transnational Domestic Workers*, edited by S. Huang, B. Yeoh, and N. Rahman, 175–209. Singapore: Marshall Cavendish Academic.

Weiss, Anita M. 1991. South Asian Muslims in Hong Kong: Creation of "Local Boy" Identity. *Modern Asian Studies* 25 (3): 417–53.

Werbner, Pnina, and Nira Yuval-Davis. 1999. Introduction: Women and the New Discourse of Citizenship. In *Women, Citizenship, and Difference*, edited by N. Yuval-Davis and P. Werbner, 1–38. New York: Zed Books.

White, Barbara-Sue. 1994. *Turbans and Traders: Hong Kong's Indian Communities*. Hong Kong: Oxford University Press.

Willen, Sarah S. 2007a. Toward a Critical Phenomenology of "Illegality": State Power, Criminalization, and Abjectivity among Undocumented Migrant Workers in Tel Aviv, Israel. *International Migration* 45 (3): 8–38.

———. 2007b. *Transnational Migration to Israel in Global Comparative Context*. New York: Lexington Books.

Yu, Hui Yan. 2011. Imagination of Self and the Other: Inter-ethnic Attitudes between Filipino Domestic Helpers and Their Employers after the Manila Hostage Crisis. *Hong Kong Anthropologist* 5: 1–24.

Zelizer, Viviana. 2005. *The Purchase of Intimacy*. Princeton, N.J.: Princeton University Press.

Index

Abelmann, Nancy, 218

abortion: euphemism for, 236n7; illegal, 77, 152–53; regulations, experiences, and costs, 67–68, 114, 135–42; women's views of, 22, 31, 33

Abu, 159

abuse: by employers, 62, 63, 72; by recruitment agencies, 60, 62. *See also* domestic abuse

addiction, 105–6

adoption: decisions regarding, 30, 114, 128, 145–46; numbers and practices, 148–52; option of, 22, 31, 33, 68, 123

Africans, 17, 92; demographics and experiences of, 90, 91, 96, 107–10, 112; migrants in Hong Kong, 8, 27, 30, 43, 76, 97; views of sex and gender, 89, 116, 126, 134–35

Agamben, Giorgio, 12. *See also* "bare life"; "good life"

agencies, *see* recruitment

age requirements, 73–75, 89

Ahmed, 45–55, 91, 102, 107, 226

Ali, 108

Amal, 123, 125, 170–72, 173, 178

Americas, 90. *See also individual countries*

Analie, 128

anchor babies, 2, 233n2

André, 219–20

Angel, 216

Angela, 58, 66–69, 88, 108, 128, 225–26

Annie, 39, 40, 204–7, 208, 219, 220–21

Anti, 221, 222

April, 34, 184, 193–97, 214, 240n10

Ara, 88, 108, 139, 202, 214; story of, 66–69, 128, 225–26; as example of overstaying and being arrested, 58, 185, 186, 192

Arendt, Hannah, 12, 64

Arida, 136

arrests, 68, 69. *See also* prisons

Asia, *see individual areas, countries*

Asian Migrant Centre (AMC), 70

Association of Indonesian Migrant Workers (ATKI), 70

asylum claims: definition, regulation, and numbers of, 187–93; "political" vs. "economic," 16–17, 107, 109, 190; reasons to file, 29, 156, 185–86; stories of, 193–200; subsistence during pending claim, 200–204

asylum seekers: in history of Hong Kong, 91; and marriage, 207–11; men, in this study, 43, 96, 115; nationalities of, 4, 8, 30, 43, 93, 107–9; paternity and, 11, 90, 141–42,

migration: age restrictions, 73–75, 89; international policies, 2–3; Philippine and
Indonesian laws, 56–59; privilege vs. precarity, 157, 186; reasons for, 9–10, 197–98.
See also FDWs; guest workers
migratory cycle of atonement, xiii, 9–10, 22,
216–32
Mindanao, 46, 82
miscarriage, 84, 114, 152–53
Misoprostol, *see* Cytotek
Mission for Migrant Workers, 60, 70
Mo, 208, 210
Mohamed, 85, 86, 87, 91, 168, 227–28
money: sending home, *see* remittances
money-making, *see* subsistence
Mongkok, 137
morality: and contraceptives, 131–34; men's
views of women's, 77, 117–19; and premarital sex, 216; standards for women, 9–10,
17, 56–58, 126–28, 230–31
mothers, *see* gender roles; maternity; single
mothers; women
Mother's Choice (home for children up for
adoption), 148–49, 150
MTR, *see* Mass-Transit Railway
Muslims, *see* Islam

Nellie, 80, 88, 90, 113
Nepalese, 4, 8, 59, 96, 101, 104–6
Netanyahu, Benjamin, 233n3
Netherlands, 96, 114, 181
Netty, 36–37
New Conditions of Stay, *see* two-week rule
New Order regime (Indonesia), 71
New Territories, 4, 98, 114, 122, 201
NGOs (nongovernmental organizations):
complaints about, 201; view on fathers,
14; as granters/deniers of aid, 35, 36;
helping migrants, 19–20, 28, 31, 32, 37,
63, 72; helping with travel documents,
54; and humanitarian aid, 16–20; and
paternity claims, 114; and recruitment
practices, 60, 61–62; and state-sanctioned
migration, 56–57
Nicholas, 44, 45, 226
Niger, 8, 96
Nigeria, 8, 96, 118
nikah ceremonies (Muslim religious blessing), 81, 85–86, 88, 103, 109, 127
Niko, 86, 88, 113, 185; story of, 44, 45, 54,
226
Nina, 4, 6, 7, 15, 223–24
Nisha, 199, 202, 207
Nora, 155, 163–64, 181

North America, 8

"one country, two systems," 91
Ong, Aihwa, 65
"ordinary residence," 175, 176, 181, 238n2
"out of wedlock" children: law regarding, 30;
in Indonesia, 81, 216, 229–30; in Philippines, 150–51; precarity for mothers of,
156; religious attitudes toward, 80
overstayers: definition of, 235n3; and torture
or asylum claims, 29, 191; men as, 96,
98–99; precarity of, 6, 13, 22, 92, 156,
239n1; reasons for becoming, xiii, 59, 63,
184–86, 228; stories of, 47, 66–69, 111–12;
strategies for subsistence, 204. *See also*
FDWs; subsistence

Pakistan: British colonial history, 101; marriage practices, 93, 160–61; migrant
fathers from, 8, 76, 96, 101–5
Pakistanis: Ahmed's story, 46–47, 48, 49;
Hakim's story, 92–95; Rashid's story,
99–101
Palmer, Wayne, 61–62
papers, *see* recognizance papers
Parreñas, Rhacel, 77
passports, 53, 54, 55, 61, 74
paternity: claims, 114, 149, 211–14, 227,
240n15; fathers' reluctance to acknowledge, 46, 113
PathFinders (charity organization), 5; and
adoption, 68, 148, 150; author's work
with, 35, 70, 235n7; and donated clothing, 38, 40; helping women navigate
social services, 37; meetings, 28–29, 32,
41–42, 89, 216; and paternity claims, 111
PEKKA (Women Headed Household
Empowerment), 79
permanent residency, *see* right of abode
petugas lapangan (PL; field agents), 61, 74
Philippines: and abortion, 135; and adoption,
150; attitudes toward Chinese, 112; and
contraceptives, 131, 132; demographics
and history of migrant workers from, 7, 8,
17–18, 59, 70–82, 96; marriage and
divorce in, 30, 80, 86; policies regarding
migration, xi, 57, 89; and recruitment
agencies, 60–61; religion in, 102; returning home to, 230–31; views of women in,
56–57, 88; wages of workers in, 64
Philippine Consulate, 43, 54, 55, 80
Philippine Women Center of British Columbia, 23
Po Leung Kuk, 240n16